סדר תפלות ישראל

The Union Prayerbook

for

JEWISH WORSHIP

NEWLY REVISED EDITION

EDITED AND PUBLISHED BY

THE CENTRAL CONFERENCE OF AMERICAN RABBIS

PART II

NEW YORK

1962

TABLE OF CONTENTS

Services for the New Year

EVENING SERVICE

MORNING SERVICE

THOUGHTS ON ROSH HASHONAH

In the seventh month, on the first day of the month, shall be a solemn rest unto you, a memorial proclaimed with the blast of horns, a holy convocation.

—Leviticus 23: 24

This day is holy unto our Lord; be ye not grieved; for the joy of the Lord is your strength.

—Nehemiah 8: 10

The blowing of the Shofar on Rosh Hashanah is an ordinance of Scripture but it has also a deeper meaning. It says to us: Awake, ye slumberers, from your slumber, and rouse yourselves from your deep sleep. Search your deeds and turn ye in repentance. Remember your Creator, ye who forget truth because of the vanity of the hour; who go astray all through the year in pursuit of trifles which can neither profit nor save. Look to your souls and mend your ways and your deeds. Let every one of you forsake his wicked path and his evil purpose.

—Maimonides, Hilkot Teshubah iii: 4

The House of Israel intones its prayers and praises:
O God, we beseech Thee, heal now its infirmities.
May the year and its ills end now together.
Be strong and rejoice for oppression shall cease,
Hope in the Rock, who keepeth His covenant.
May the year and its blessings begin now together.

—Abraham Hazzan, Ahot Ketanah

Evening Service for the
New Year

Choir

(Psalm cxxi)

I lift mine eyes unto the hills; whence cometh my help? My help cometh from the Lord, who made heaven and earth. He will not suffer thy foot to stumble; thy guardian doth not slumber. Behold, the guardian of Israel, He slumbereth not, and He sleepeth not. The Lord is thy guardian; the Lord is thy shade at thy right hand. The sun shall not smite thee by day, nor the moon by night. The Lord shall preserve thee from all evil; He will preserve thy soul. The Lord will watch over thy going out, and thy coming in, from this time forth and for evermore.

אֶשָּׂא עֵינַי אֶל הֶהָרִים.
מֵאַיִן יָבֹא עֶזְרִי: עֶזְרִי
מֵעִם יְיָ. עֹשֵׂה שָׁמַיִם
וָאָרֶץ: אַל־יִתֵּן לַמּוֹט
רַגְלֶךָ. אַל־יָנוּם שֹׁמְרֶךָ:
הִנֵּה לֹא־יָנוּם וְלֹא יִישָׁן.
שׁוֹמֵר יִשְׂרָאֵל: יְיָ שֹׁמְרֶךָ.
יְיָ צִלְּךָ עַל יַד יְמִינֶךָ:
יוֹמָם הַשֶּׁמֶשׁ לֹא יַכֶּכָּה.
וְיָרֵחַ בַּלָּיְלָה: יְיָ יִשְׁמָרְךָ
מִכָּל־רָע. יִשְׁמֹר אֶת־
נַפְשֶׁךָ: יְיָ יִשְׁמָר צֵאתְךָ
וּבוֹאֶךָ. מֵעַתָּה וְעַד
עוֹלָם׃

7

Reader

Heavenly Father! In the twilight of the vanishing year, we lift up our hearts to Thee to thank Thee for all Thy mercies in the past, and to implore Thy guidance and Thy blessing for the future. Thy providence has watched over us and Thy lovingkindness has sustained us. In affliction Thou hast strengthened us; in sorrow Thou hast comforted us. Thou hast brightened our lives with the happiness of home and the joys of friendship. Thou hast blessed us with the satisfaction that comes from performing our daily duties and serving our fellowmen.

As we thank Thee for the joys of life, so we praise Thee for its sorrows. Many burdens have been laid upon us; many tears have furrowed our cheeks; many tender ties have been broken. With a father's love dost Thou discipline us, that we may learn to understand life's holy purpose.

With deep humility we approach Thee, O our God, at this sacred hour. May we listen reverently to its solemn admonition. Give us the will to serve Thee with singleness of heart, so that, as we grow older in years, we may grow stronger in wisdom, broader in charity and more steadfast in faith.

Hidden from our sight are the events of the future. But we trust in Thee and fear not. Open unto us in mercy the portals of the new year, and grant us life and health, contentment and peace.

Choir: Amen.

Responsive Reading

Reader

Lord, Thou hast been our dwelling place in all generations.

Congregation

*Before the mountains were brought forth, or ever
Thou hadst formed the earth and the world.*

Even from everlasting to everlasting, Thou art God.

*Thou turnest man to contrition; and sayest, return
ye children of men.*

For a thousand years in Thy sight are but as yesterday
when it is past, and as a watch in the night.

*Thou carriest them away as with a flood, they are as
a sleep.*

In the morning they are like grass which groweth up.

*In the morning it flourisheth and groweth up, in the
evening it is cut down, and withereth.*

The days of our years are threescore years and ten, or
even by reason of strength fourscore years;

*Yet is their pride but travail and vanity; for it is
speedily gone, and we fly away.*

So teach us to number our days that we may get us a
heart of wisdom.

*O satisfy us in the morning with Thy mercy, that
we may rejoice and be glad all our days.*

Make us glad according to the days wherein Thou hast
afflicted us, according to the years wherein we
have seen evil.

*Let Thy work appear unto Thy servants, and Thy
glory upon their children.*

Let the graciousness of the Lord our God be upon us.

*Establish Thou also upon us the work of our hands;
yea, the work of our hands establish Thou it.*

(Congregation rises)

Reader

Praise ye the Lord, to whom all praise is due.

Choir and Congregation

Praised be the Lord to whom all praise is due forever and ever.

(Congregation is seated)

Reader

Praised be Thou, O Lord our God, ruler of the world, by whose law the shadows of evening fall and the gates of morn are opened. In wisdom Thou hast established the changes of times and seasons and ordered the ways of the stars in their heavenly courses.

Thou didst lay the foundations of the earth and the heavens are the work of Thy hands. They may perish but Thou shalt endure; Thy years shall have no end. Creator of heaven and earth, O living God, rule Thou over us forever. Praised be Thou, O Lord, for the day and its work and for the night and its rest.

Congregation and Reader

Infinite as is Thy power, even so is Thy love. Thou didst manifest it through Israel, Thy people. By laws and commandments, by statutes and ordinances hast Thou led us in the way of righteousness and brought us to the light of truth. Happy the man who knoweth Thee and delighteth greatly in Thy commandments.

(Congregation rises)

Reader

בָּרְכוּ אֶת־יְיָ הַמְבֹרָךְ:

Choir and Congregation

בָּרוּךְ יְיָ הַמְבֹרָךְ לְעוֹלָם וָעֶד:

(Congregation is seated)

Reader

בָּרוּךְ אַתָּה יְיָ אֱלֹהֵינוּ מֶלֶךְ הָעוֹלָם. אֲשֶׁר בִּדְבָרוֹ מַעֲרִיב עֲרָבִים. בְּחָכְמָה פּוֹתֵחַ שְׁעָרִים. וּבִתְבוּנָה מְשַׁנֶּה עִתִּים וּמַחֲלִיף אֶת־הַזְּמַנִּים. וּמְסַדֵּר אֶת־הַכּוֹכָבִים בְּמִשְׁמְרוֹתֵיהֶם בָּרָקִיעַ כִּרְצוֹנוֹ. בּוֹרֵא יוֹם וָלָיְלָה. יְיָ צְבָאוֹת שְׁמוֹ. אֵל חַי וְקַיָּם תָּמִיד יִמְלֹךְ עָלֵינוּ לְעוֹלָם וָעֶד. בָּרוּךְ אַתָּה יְיָ הַמַּעֲרִיב עֲרָבִים:

אַהֲבַת עוֹלָם בֵּית יִשְׂרָאֵל עַמְּךָ אָהָבְתָּ. תּוֹרָה וּמִצְוֹת חֻקִּים וּמִשְׁפָּטִים אוֹתָנוּ לִמַּדְתָּ. עַל־כֵּן יְיָ אֱלֹהֵינוּ בְּשָׁכְבֵּנוּ וּבְקוּמֵנוּ נָשִׂיחַ בְּחֻקֶּיךָ. וְנִשְׂמַח בְּדִבְרֵי תוֹרָתֶךָ וּבְמִצְוֹתֶיךָ לְעוֹלָם וָעֶד. כִּי הֵם

Happy the man whose strength is in Thee, in whose heart are Thy ways. Therefore at our lying down and our rising up, we will meditate on Thy teachings and find in Thy laws true life and length of days. O that Thy love may never depart from our hearts. Praised be Thou, O Lord, who hast revealed Thy love through Israel.

(Congregation rises)

Reader

Hear, O Israel: The Lord our God, the Lord is One. Praised be His name whose glorious kingdom is forever and ever.

(Congregation is seated)

Congregation and Reader

Thou shalt love the Lord, thy God, with all thy heart, with all thy soul, and with all thy might. And these words, which I command thee this day, shall be upon thy heart. Thou shalt teach them diligently unto thy children, and shalt speak of them when thou sittest in thy house, when thou walkest by the way, when thou liest down, and when thou risest up. Thou shalt bind them for a sign upon thy hand, and they shall be for frontlets between thine eyes. Thou shalt write them upon the doorposts of thy house and upon thy gates: That ye may remember and do all My commandments and be holy unto your God.

חַיֵּינוּ וְאֹרֶךְ יָמֵינוּ. וּבָהֶם נֶהְגֶּה יוֹמָם וָלָיְלָה.
וְאַהֲבָתְךָ אַל־תָּסִיר מִמֶּנּוּ לְעוֹלָמִים. בָּרוּךְ אַתָּה
יְיָ אוֹהֵב עַמּוֹ יִשְׂרָאֵל:

(Congregation rises)

Reader and Congregation, then Choir

שְׁמַע יִשְׂרָאֵל יְהֹוָה אֱלֹהֵינוּ יְהֹוָה אֶחָד:
בָּרוּךְ שֵׁם כְּבוֹד מַלְכוּתוֹ לְעוֹלָם וָעֶד:

(Congregation is seated)

Reader

וְאָהַבְתָּ אֵת יְיָ אֱלֹהֶיךָ בְּכָל־לְבָבְךָ וּבְכָל־נַפְשְׁךָ
וּבְכָל־מְאֹדֶךָ: וְהָיוּ הַדְּבָרִים הָאֵלֶּה אֲשֶׁר אָנֹכִי
מְצַוְּךָ הַיּוֹם עַל־לְבָבֶךָ: וְשִׁנַּנְתָּם לְבָנֶיךָ וְדִבַּרְתָּ
בָּם. בְּשִׁבְתְּךָ בְּבֵיתֶךָ וּבְלֶכְתְּךָ בַדֶּרֶךְ וּבְשָׁכְבְּךָ
וּבְקוּמֶךָ: וּקְשַׁרְתָּם לְאוֹת עַל־יָדֶךָ. וְהָיוּ לְטֹטָפֹת
בֵּין עֵינֶיךָ: וּכְתַבְתָּם עַל־מְזֻזוֹת בֵּיתֶךָ וּבִשְׁעָרֶיךָ:
לְמַעַן תִּזְכְּרוּ וַעֲשִׂיתֶם אֶת־כָּל־מִצְוֹתָי וִהְיִיתֶם
קְדֹשִׁים לֵאלֹהֵיכֶם: אֲנִי יְיָ אֱלֹהֵיכֶם:

Responsive Reading

Reader

Eternal truth it is that Thou alone art God, and there is none else.

Congregation

Thy righteousness is like the mighty mountains; Thy judgments are like the great deep;

How precious is Thy lovingkindness, O God!

The children of men take refuge in the shadow of Thy wings.

For with Thee is the fountain of life; in Thy light do we see light.

Through Thy power alone has Israel been redeemed from the hand of oppressors.

Thy mercy has sustained us in the hour of trial.

Thy love has watched over us in the night of oppression;

Thou hast kept us in life; our footsteps have not faltered.

And now that we live in a land of freedom may we continue to be faithful to Thee and Thy word.

May Thy law rule the life of all Thy children and Thy truth unite their hearts in fellowship.

O God, our refuge and our hope, we glorify Thy name now as did our fathers in ancient days.

Choir

Who is like unto Thee, O Lord, among the mighty?

Who is like unto Thee, glorious in holiness, awe inspiring, working wonders?

Responsive Reading

אֱמֶת וֶאֱמוּנָה כָּל זֹאת וְקַיָּם עָלֵינוּ. כִּי הוּא יְיָ
אֱלֹהֵינוּ וְאֵין זוּלָתוֹ. וַאֲנַחְנוּ יִשְׂרָאֵל עַמּוֹ:

הָעֹשֶׂה גְדֹלוֹת עַד־אֵין חֵקֶר. וְנִפְלָאוֹת עַד־אֵין
מִסְפָּר:

הַשָּׂם נַפְשֵׁנוּ בַּחַיִּים. וְלֹא נָתַן לַמּוֹט רַגְלֵנוּ:

צִדְקָתְךָ כְּהַרְרֵי־אֵל מִשְׁפָּטֶיךָ תְּהוֹם רַבָּה:

מַה־יָּקָר חַסְדְּךָ אֱלֹהִים וּבְנֵי אָדָם בְּצֵל כְּנָפֶיךָ
יֶחֱסָיוּן:

כִּי עִמְּךָ מְקוֹר חַיִּים. בְּאוֹרְךָ נִרְאֶה־אוֹר:

הָעֹשֶׂה לָנוּ נִסִּים בְּמִצְרָיִם. אוֹתֹת וּמוֹפְתִים
בְּאַדְמַת בְּנֵי־חָם:

וְרָאוּ בָנָיו גְּבוּרָתוֹ. שִׁבְּחוּ וְהוֹדוּ לִשְׁמוֹ.

Choir

מִי־כָמֹכָה בָּאֵלִים יְיָ. מִי כָּמֹכָה נֶאְדָּר בַּקֹּדֶשׁ
נוֹרָא תְהִלֹּת עֹשֵׂה פֶלֶא:

Reader

Thy children acknowledged Thy sovereign power, and exclaimed:

Choir

The Lord shall reign forever and ever.

Reader

As Thou hast redeemed Israel and saved him from arms stronger than his own, so mayest Thou redeem all who are oppressed and persecuted. Praised be Thou, O Lord, Redeemer of Israel.

Congregation and Reader

Cause us, O Lord our God, to lie down each night in peace, and to awaken each morning to renewed life and strength. Spread over us the tabernacle of Thy peace. Help us to order our lives by Thy counsel, and lead us in the paths of righteousness. Be Thou a shield about us, protecting us from hate and war, from pestilence and sorrow. Curb Thou also within us the inclination to do evil, and shelter us beneath the shadow of Thy wings. Guard our going out and our coming in unto life and peace from this time forth and for evermore.

Choir

Sing joyfully unto God our strength; shout unto the God of Jacob. Blow the horn at the new moon, at the return of our solemn feast. For it is a statute for Israel, an ordinance of the God of Jacob.

Reader

מַלְכוּתְךָ רָאוּ בָנֶיךָ. זֶה אֵלִי עָנוּ וְאָמְרוּ.

Choir

יְיָ יִמְלֹךְ לְעֹלָם וָעֶד:

Reader

וְנֶאֱמַר כִּי פָדָה יְהֹוָה אֶת יַעֲקֹב וּגְאָלוֹ מִיַּד חָזָק
מִמֶּנּוּ. בָּרוּךְ אַתָּה יְיָ גָּאַל יִשְׂרָאֵל:

Congregation and Reader

הַשְׁכִּיבֵנוּ יְיָ אֱלֹהֵינוּ לְשָׁלוֹם וְהַעֲמִידֵנוּ מַלְכֵּנוּ
לְחַיִּים. וּפְרוֹשׂ עָלֵינוּ סֻכַּת שְׁלוֹמֶךָ. וְתַקְּנֵנוּ בְּעֵצָה
טוֹבָה מִלְּפָנֶיךָ. וְהוֹשִׁיעֵנוּ לְמַעַן שְׁמֶךָ. וְהָגֵן בַּעֲדֵנוּ
וְהָסֵר מֵעָלֵינוּ אוֹיֵב דֶּבֶר וְחֶרֶב וְרָעָב וְיָגוֹן. וּבְצֵל
כְּנָפֶיךָ תַּסְתִּירֵנוּ. כִּי אֵל שׁוֹמְרֵנוּ וּמַצִּילֵנוּ אָתָּה. כִּי
אֵל מֶלֶךְ חַנּוּן וְרַחוּם אָתָּה. וּשְׁמוֹר צֵאתֵנוּ וּבוֹאֵנוּ
לְחַיִּים וּלְשָׁלוֹם מֵעַתָּה וְעַד עוֹלָם. בָּרוּךְ אַתָּה יְיָ
שׁוֹמֵר עַמּוֹ יִשְׂרָאֵל לָעַד:

Choir

הַרְנִינוּ לֵאלֹהִים עוּזֵּנוּ הָרִיעוּ לֵאלֹהֵי יַעֲקֹב:
תִּקְעוּ בַחֹדֶשׁ שׁוֹפָר בַּכֶּסֶה לְיוֹם חַגֵּנוּ: כִּי חֹק
לְיִשְׂרָאֵל הוּא. מִשְׁפָּט לֵאלֹהֵי יַעֲקֹב:

Reader

Praised be Thou, O Lord, God of our fathers, God of Abraham, Isaac and Jacob, great, mighty, and exalted. Thou bestowest lovingkindness upon all Thy children. Thou rememberest the devotion of the fathers. In Thy love, Thou bringest redemption to their descendants for the sake of Thy name.

Remember us unto life, O King, who delightest in life, and inscribe us in the book of life, for Thy sake, O God of life. Thou art our King and Helper, our Savior and Protector. Praised be Thou, O Lord, Shield of Abraham.

Eternal is Thy power, O Lord, Thou art mighty to save. In lovingkindness Thou sustainest the living; in the multitude of Thy mercies, Thou preservest all. Thou upholdest the falling and healest the sick; freest the captives and keepest faith with Thy children in death as in life. Who is like unto Thee, Almighty God, Author of life and death, Source of Salvation?

Who is like unto Thee, O merciful Father, who rememberest Thy creatures unto life? Praised be Thou, O Lord, who hast implanted within us eternal life.

Thou art holy, Thy name is holy and Thy worshipers proclaim Thy holiness.

Reader

בָּרוּךְ אַתָּה יְיָ אֱלֹהֵינוּ וֵאלֹהֵי אֲבוֹתֵינוּ. אֱלֹהֵי
אַבְרָהָם אֱלֹהֵי יִצְחָק וֵאלֹהֵי יַעֲקֹב. הָאֵל הַגָּדוֹל
הַגִּבּוֹר וְהַנּוֹרָא. אֵל עֶלְיוֹן. גּוֹמֵל חֲסָדִים טוֹבִים.
וְקֹנֵה הַכֹּל וְזוֹכֵר חַסְדֵי אָבוֹת. וּמֵבִיא גְאֻלָּה לִבְנֵי
בְנֵיהֶם. לְמַעַן שְׁמוֹ בְּאַהֲבָה:

זָכְרֵנוּ לַחַיִּים. מֶלֶךְ חָפֵץ בַּחַיִּים. וְכָתְבֵנוּ בְּסֵפֶר
הַחַיִּים. לְמַעַנְךָ אֱלֹהִים חַיִּים:

מֶלֶךְ עוֹזֵר וּמוֹשִׁיעַ וּמָגֵן. בָּרוּךְ אַתָּה יְיָ מָגֵן
אַבְרָהָם:

אַתָּה גִבּוֹר לְעוֹלָם אֲדֹנָי. רַב לְהוֹשִׁיעַ. מְכַלְכֵּל
חַיִּים בְּחֶסֶד. מְחַיֵּה הַכֹּל בְּרַחֲמִים רַבִּים. סוֹמֵךְ
נוֹפְלִים וְרוֹפֵא חוֹלִים וּמַתִּיר אֲסוּרִים. וּמְקַיֵּם
אֱמוּנָתוֹ לִישֵׁנֵי עָפָר. מִי כָמוֹךָ בַּעַל גְּבוּרוֹת. וּמִי
דוֹמֶה־לָּךְ. מֶלֶךְ מֵמִית וּמְחַיֶּה. וּמַצְמִיחַ יְשׁוּעָה:

מִי כָמוֹךָ אַב הָרַחֲמִים. זוֹכֵר יְצוּרָיו לַחַיִּים
בְּרַחֲמִים: בָּרוּךְ אַתָּה יְיָ נֹטֵעַ בְּתוֹכֵנוּ חַיֵּי עוֹלָם:

אַתָּה קָדוֹשׁ וְשִׁמְךָ קָדוֹשׁ וּקְדוֹשִׁים בְּכָל־יוֹם
יְהַלְלוּךָ סֶּלָה.

Reader

O Lord, our God, let Thy presence be manifest to us in all Thy works, that reverence for Thee may fill the hearts of all Thy creatures. May all the children of men come before Thee in humility and unite to do Thy will with perfect heart. May all acknowledge that Thine are power, dominion, and majesty, and that Thy name is exalted above all.

Grant honor, O Lord, to them that revere Thee, inspire with courage those who wait for Thee, and fulfill the hope of all who trust in Thy name. Hasten the day that will bring gladness to all who dwell on earth and victory of the spirit to those who bear witness to Thy unity. Then shall the just see and exult, the righteous be glad, and the pious sing for joy. Then shall iniquity be made dumb, and wickedness vanish like smoke; for the dominion of arrogance shall have passed away from the earth.

Thou alone, O Lord, shalt reign over all Thy works, as it is written in Thy holy word: The Lord shall reign forever, thy God, O Zion, from generation to generation. Hallelujah.

Holy art Thou, awe-inspiring is Thy name, there is no God but Thee. The Lord of hosts is exalted through justice, and the holy God is sanctified through righteousness. Praised be Thou, O Lord, King of holiness.

Reader

וּבְכֵן תֵּן פַּחְדְּךָ יְיָ אֱלֹהֵינוּ עַל כָּל־מַעֲשֶׂיךָ
וְאֵימָתְךָ עַל כָּל־מַה־שֶּׁבָּרָאתָ. וְיִירָאוּךָ כָּל־הַמַּעֲשִׂים
וְיִשְׁתַּחֲווּ לְפָנֶיךָ כָּל־הַבְּרוּאִים. וְיֵעָשׂוּ כֻלָּם אֲגֻדָּה
אַחַת לַעֲשׂוֹת רְצוֹנְךָ בְּלֵבָב שָׁלֵם. כְּמוֹ שֶׁיָּדַעְנוּ יְיָ
אֱלֹהֵינוּ שֶׁהַשִּׁלְטוֹן לְפָנֶיךָ עֹז בְּיָדְךָ וּגְבוּרָה בִּימִינֶךָ
וְשִׁמְךָ נוֹרָא עַל־כָּל־מַה־שֶּׁבָּרָאתָ:

וּבְכֵן תֵּן כָּבוֹד יְיָ לְעַמֶּךָ תְּהִלָּה לִירֵאֶיךָ וְתִקְוָה
לְדוֹרְשֶׁיךָ וּפִתְחוֹן פֶּה לַמְיַחֲלִים לָךְ. שִׂמְחָה לְכָל־
יֹשְׁבֵי תֵבֵל אַרְצֶךָ וּצְמִיחַת קֶרֶן לִמְיַחֲדֵי שְׁמֶךָ.
בִּמְהֵרָה בְיָמֵינוּ:

וּבְכֵן צַדִּיקִים יִרְאוּ וְיִשְׂמָחוּ וִישָׁרִים יַעֲלֹזוּ
וַחֲסִידִים בְּרִנָּה יָגִילוּ וְעוֹלָתָה תִּקְפָּץ־פִּיהָ. וְכָל־
הָרִשְׁעָה כֻּלָּהּ כֶּעָשָׁן תִּכְלֶה. כִּי תַעֲבִיר מֶמְשֶׁלֶת
זָדוֹן מִן־הָאָרֶץ:

וְתִמְלוֹךְ אַתָּה יְיָ לְבַדֶּךָ עַל כָּל־מַעֲשֶׂיךָ. כַּכָּתוּב
בְּדִבְרֵי קָדְשֶׁךָ יִמְלֹךְ יְיָ לְעוֹלָם אֱלֹהַיִךְ צִיּוֹן לְדֹר
וָדֹר הַלְלוּיָהּ:

קָדוֹשׁ אַתָּה וְנוֹרָא שְׁמֶךָ. וְאֵין אֱלוֹהַּ מִבַּלְעָדֶיךָ.
כַּכָּתוּב. וַיִּגְבַּהּ יְיָ צְבָאוֹת בַּמִּשְׁפָּט. וְהָאֵל הַקָּדוֹשׁ
נִקְדַּשׁ בִּצְדָקָה. בָּרוּךְ אַתָּה יְיָ הַמֶּלֶךְ הַקָּדוֹשׁ:

Reader

We render thanks unto Thee that Thou hast called us to Thy service and entrusted us with Thy commandments. In love Thou hast given us this Day of Remembrance that we may consecrate ourselves unto Thee and unto Thy law of righteousness.

Almighty God and Father, in this solemn hour we would draw nigh unto Thee. Help us to build our lives on the abiding foundations of Thy law that we may attain peace of mind and steadfastness of purpose. Open our eyes to the nobility of life and its sacred opportunities for service.

O Thou who dealest graciously with the children of men, give us the grace to show forbearance unto those who offend against us. When the wrongs and injustices of men sadden our hearts, may we seek shelter in the knowledge of Thy truth and find joy in the fulfillment of Thy will. May no trial, however severe, embitter our souls and shake our trust in Thee. When beset by trouble and sorrow, our fathers put on the armor of faith and fortitude. May we too find strength to meet adversity with quiet courage and unshaken trust. Weeping may tarry for the night, but joy cometh in the morning. Help us to understand that injustice and hate will not forever afflict the sons of men; that righteousness and mercy will triumph in the end.

Reader and Congregation

Our God, and God of our fathers, may Thy kingdom come speedily, that worship of Thy name and obedience to Thy law may unite all men in brotherhood and

Reader

אַתָּה בְחַרְתָּנוּ מִכָּל־הָעַמִּים. קִדַּשְׁתָּנוּ בְּמִצְוֹתֶיךָ.
וְקֵרַבְתָּנוּ לַעֲבוֹדָתֶךָ. וְשִׁמְךָ הַגָּדוֹל וְהַקָּדוֹשׁ עָלֵינוּ
קָרָאתָ. וַתִּתֶּן־לָנוּ יְיָ אֱלֹהֵינוּ בְּאַהֲבָה אֶת־יוֹם הַזִּכָּרוֹן
הַזֶּה. יוֹם תְּרוּעָה מִקְרָא קֹדֶשׁ זֵכֶר לִיצִיאַת מִצְרָיִם.
קַדְּשֵׁנוּ בְּמִצְוֹתֶיךָ וְתֵן חֶלְקֵנוּ בְּתוֹרָתֶךָ. שַׂבְּעֵנוּ
מִטּוּבֶךָ וְשַׂמְּחֵנוּ בִּישׁוּעָתֶךָ וְטַהֵר לִבֵּנוּ לְעָבְדְּךָ
בֶּאֱמֶת. כִּי אַתָּה אֱלֹהִים אֱמֶת וּדְבָרְךָ אֱמֶת וְקַיָּם
לָעַד. בָּרוּךְ אַתָּה יְיָ מֶלֶךְ עַל כָּל הָאָרֶץ מְקַדֵּשׁ
(הַשַּׁבָּת וְ) יִשְׂרָאֵל וְיוֹם הַזִּכָּרוֹן:

Reader and Congregation

אֱלֹהֵינוּ וֵאלֹהֵי אֲבוֹתֵינוּ מְלוֹךְ עַל כָּל־הָעוֹלָם
כֻּלּוֹ בִּכְבוֹדֶךָ. וְהִנָּשֵׂא עַל כָּל־הָאָרֶץ בִּיקָרֶךָ.
וְהוֹפַע בַּהֲדַר גְּאוֹן עֻזֶּךָ עַל כָּל יוֹשְׁבֵי תֵבֵל אַרְצֶךָ.
וְיֵדַע כָּל־פָּעוּל כִּי אַתָּה פְעַלְתּוֹ וְיָבִין כָּל־יְצוּר
כִּי אַתָּה יְצַרְתּוֹ וְיֹאמַר כֹּל אֲשֶׁר נְשָׁמָה בְאַפּוֹ יְיָ
אֱלֹהֵי יִשְׂרָאֵל מֶלֶךְ וּמַלְכוּתוֹ בַּכֹּל מָשָׁלָה:

peace; that every creature may know that Thou art its Creator, and every living being exclaim: The Lord, the God of Israel, ruleth and His dominion endureth forever.

Sanctify us by Thy commandments and bring us near unto Thy service, that we may be worthy to proclaim Thy truth unto all mankind. Satisfy us with Thy goodness, and gladden us with Thy salvation. Purify our hearts that we may serve Thee in truth. For Thou, O God, art Truth, and Thy word endureth forever. Praised be Thou, O Lord, who sanctifiest (the Sabbath) Israel and the Day of Remembrance.

Reader

Look with favor, O Lord, upon us, and may our service be acceptable unto Thee. Praised be Thou, O Lord, whom alone we serve in reverence.

Congregation and Reader

We gratefully acknowledge, O Lord our God, that Thou art our support and salvation. Thee alone do we worship, and unto Thee do we give grateful praise. We thank Thee, O God, for Thy favor unto this, our land, and for the blessings of liberty and the ideals of righteousness which our nation cherishes. Protect and prosper it, and let the New Year bring security and abundance to all. Praised be Thou, O Lord, from whom all goodness comes and to whom all thanks are due.

רְצֵה יְיָ אֱלֹהֵינוּ בְּעַמְּךָ יִשְׂרָאֵל. וּתְפִלָּתָם
בְּאַהֲבָה תְקַבֵּל. וּתְהִי לְרָצוֹן תָּמִיד עֲבוֹדַת יִשְׂרָאֵל
עַמֶּךָ. בָּרוּךְ אַתָּה יְיָ שֶׁאוֹתְךָ לְבַדְּךָ בְּיִרְאָה נַעֲבוֹד:

מוֹדִים אֲנַחְנוּ לָךְ. שָׁאַתָּה הוּא יְיָ אֱלֹהֵינוּ וֵאלֹהֵי
אֲבוֹתֵינוּ לְעוֹלָם וָעֶד. צוּר חַיֵּינוּ מָגֵן יִשְׁעֵנוּ אַתָּה
הוּא לְדוֹר וָדוֹר. נוֹדֶה לְךָ וּנְסַפֵּר תְּהִלָּתֶךָ. עַל־
חַיֵּינוּ הַמְּסוּרִים בְּיָדֶךָ. וְעַל־נִשְׁמוֹתֵינוּ הַפְּקוּדוֹת
לָךְ. וְעַל נִסֶּיךָ שֶׁבְּכָל־יוֹם עִמָּנוּ. וְעַל נִפְלְאוֹתֶיךָ
שֶׁבְּכָל־עֵת. עֶרֶב וָבֹקֶר וְצָהֳרָיִם. הַטּוֹב כִּי־לֹא
כָלוּ רַחֲמֶיךָ. וְהַמְרַחֵם כִּי־לֹא תַמּוּ חֲסָדֶיךָ. מֵעוֹלָם
קִוִּינוּ לָךְ:

וְעַל־כֻּלָּם יִתְבָּרַךְ וְיִתְרוֹמַם שִׁמְךָ מַלְכֵּנוּ תָּמִיד
לְעוֹלָם וָעֶד:

וּכְתוֹב לְחַיִּים טוֹבִים כָּל בְּנֵי בְרִיתֶךָ:

Congregation and Reader

וְכֹל הַחַיִּים יוֹדוּךָ סֶּלָה וִיהַלְלוּ אֶת־שִׁמְךָ בֶּאֱמֶת
הָאֵל יְשׁוּעָתֵנוּ וְעֶזְרָתֵנוּ סֶלָה. בָּרוּךְ אַתָּה יְיָ הַטּוֹב
שִׁמְךָ וּלְךָ נָאֶה לְהוֹדוֹת:

Reader

Grant us peace, Thy most precious gift, O Thou
eternal source of peace, and enable Israel to be its
messenger unto the peoples of the earth. Bless our
country that it may ever be a stronghold of peace, and
its advocate in the council of nations. May contentment reign within its borders, health and happiness
within its homes. Strengthen the bonds of friendship
and fellowship among all the inhabitants of our land.
Plant virtue in every soul, and may the love of Thy
name hallow every home and every heart. Inscribe us
in the book of life, and grant unto us a year of prosperity and joy. Praised be Thou, O Lord, Giver of
peace.

Choir: Amen.

שָׁלוֹם רָב עַל יִשְׂרָאֵל עַמְּךָ תָּשִׂים לְעוֹלָם. כִּי
אַתָּה הוּא מֶלֶךְ אָדוֹן לְכָל הַשָּׁלוֹם. וְטוֹב בְּעֵינֶיךָ
לְבָרֵךְ אֶת עַמְּךָ יִשְׂרָאֵל בְּכָל עֵת וּבְכָל שָׁעָה
בִּשְׁלוֹמֶךָ:

בְּסֵפֶר חַיִּים בְּרָכָה וְשָׁלוֹם וּפַרְנָסָה טוֹבָה נִזָּכֵר
וְנִכָּתֵב לְפָנֶיךָ אֲנַחְנוּ וְכָל־עַמְּךָ בֵּית יִשְׂרָאֵל לְחַיִּים
טוֹבִים וּלְשָׁלוֹם. בָּרוּךְ אַתָּה יְיָ עוֹשֶׂה הַשָּׁלוֹם:

Silent Prayer
(or such other prayer as the heart may prompt)

Unto Thee, O Lord my God, do I open my heart at this time of the turn of the year. As I review my conduct during the months that are passed, I am deeply conscious of my shortcomings. Often righteousness called to me in vain and I yielded to selfishness, anger and pride. I acknowledge my failings and I repent of them. I pray for Thy forgiveness and for the forgiveness of those whom I have wronged and hurt. Whatever life has brought me during the year now ended, grant that it may become unto me a source of strength and wisdom. O that the year now begun may be for me a new year indeed; new in consecration of purpose and in renewal of earnestness and sincerity; steadfast in rejecting all that is unworthy of me and of my heritage. Grant me strength of will to live as Thou wouldst have me live. Incline Thine ear unto me; be gracious unto me, O Lord. Lead me and guide me for my times are in Thy hand. Amen.

Choir

May the words of my mouth and the meditation of my heart be acceptable to Thee, O Lord, my Rock and my Redeemer. Amen.

יִהְיוּ לְרָצוֹן אִמְרֵי פִי וְהֶגְיוֹן לִבִּי לְפָנֶיךָ יְיָ צוּרִי
וְגֹאֲלִי:

(Congregation rises)

Reader, then Congregation

Our Father, our King, hear our prayer.

Our Father, our King, we have sinned before Thee.

Our Father, our King, have mercy upon us and upon our children.

Our Father, our King, keep far from our country pestilence, war and famine.

Our Father, our King, cause all hate and oppression to vanish from the earth.

Our Father, our King, inscribe us for blessing in the book of life.

Our Father, our King, grant unto us a year of happiness.

(Congregation is seated)

SERMON

HYMN

(Congregation rises)

אָבִינוּ מַלְכֵּנוּ שְׁמַע קוֹלֵנוּ:

אָבִינוּ מַלְכֵּנוּ חָטָאנוּ לְפָנֶיךָ:

אָבִינוּ מַלְכֵּנוּ חֲמוֹל עָלֵינוּ וְעַל־עוֹלָלֵינוּ וְטַפֵּנוּ:

אָבִינוּ מַלְכֵּנוּ כַּלֵּה דֶּבֶר וְחֶרֶב וְרָעָב מֵעָלֵינוּ:

אָבִינוּ מַלְכֵּנוּ כַּלֵּה כָל־צַר וּמַשְׂטִין מֵעָלֵינוּ:

אָבִינוּ מַלְכֵּנוּ כָתְבֵנוּ בְּסֵפֶר חַיִּים טוֹבִים:

אָבִינוּ מַלְכֵּנוּ חַדֵּשׁ עָלֵינוּ שָׁנָה טוֹבָה:

(Congregation is seated)

SERMON

HYMN

ADORATION

(Congregation rises)

Congregation and Reader

Let us adore the ever-living God, and render praise unto Him who spread out the heavens and established the earth, whose glory is revealed in the heavens above and whose greatness is manifest throughout the world. He is our God; there is none else.

We bow the head in reverence, and worship the King of kings, the Holy One, praised be He.

Choir and Congregation

וַאֲנַחְנוּ כֹּרְעִים וּמִשְׁתַּחֲוִים וּמוֹדִים לִפְנֵי מֶלֶךְ
מַלְכֵי הַמְּלָכִים הַקָּדוֹשׁ בָּרוּךְ הוּא:

(Congregation is seated)

Reader

May the time not be distant, O God, when Thy name shall be worshiped in all the earth, when unbelief shall disappear and error be no more. Fervently we pray that the day may come when all men shall invoke Thy name, when corruption and evil shall give way to purity and goodness, when superstition shall no longer enslave the mind nor idolatry blind the eye, when all who dwell on earth shall know that to Thee alone every knee must bend and every tongue give homage.

O may all, created in Thine image, recognize that they are brethren, so that, one in spirit and one in fellowship, they may be forever united before Thee. Then shall Thy kingdom be established on earth and the word of Thine ancient seer be fulfilled: The Lord will reign forever and ever.

Congregation (or Choir)

On that day the Lord shall be One and His name shall be One.

בַּיּוֹם הַהוּא יִהְיֶה יְיָ אֶחָד וּשְׁמוֹ אֶחָד:

Reader

A year has gone; a new year has come. In the sight of God, a thousand years are but as yesterday when it is past. Our life is but a fleeting gleam between two eternities. Yet though generations come and go, the word of our God stands forever. Only the dust returns to the earth, the spirit returns to God who gave it. Our dear ones have passed through the gateway of the grave into the endless peace of life eternal. All of us must inevitably tread the same path, though we know not when the hour may come. May we so live that when this hour comes, it shall find us prepared. We look unto Thee with hope, O God, firmly believing that what Thou doest is for the best. With abiding trust in Thy wisdom, we bow in submission to Thy supreme will and in devout resignation, we give praise and glory unto Thy name.

(Mourners rise)

Reader

Extolled and hallowed be the name of God throughout the world which He has created according to His will. And may He speedily establish His kingdom of righteousness on earth. Amen.

Congregation

Praised be His glorious name unto all eternity.

Reader

Praised and glorified be the name of the Holy One, though He be above all the praises which we can utter. Our guide is He in life and our redeemer through all eternity.

Congregation

Our help cometh from Him, the creator of heaven and earth.

Reader

The departed whom we now remember have entered into the peace of life eternal. They still live on earth in the acts of goodness they performed and in the hearts of those who cherish their memory. May the beauty of their life abide among us as a loving benediction.

Congregation: Amen.

Reader

May the Father of peace send peace to all who mourn, and comfort all the bereaved among us.

Congregation: Amen.

(Mourners are seated)

(Mourners rise)

Reader

יִתְגַּדַּל וְיִתְקַדַּשׁ שְׁמֵהּ רַבָּא. בְּעָלְמָא דִי בְרָא
כִרְעוּתֵהּ. וְיַמְלִיךְ מַלְכוּתֵהּ. בְּחַיֵּיכוֹן וּבְיוֹמֵיכוֹן
וּבְחַיֵּי דְכָל בֵּית יִשְׂרָאֵל. בַּעֲגָלָא וּבִזְמַן קָרִיב.
וְאִמְרוּ אָמֵן:

Congregation

יְהֵא שְׁמֵהּ רַבָּא מְבָרַךְ לְעָלַם וּלְעָלְמֵי עָלְמַיָּא:

Reader

יִתְבָּרַךְ וְיִשְׁתַּבַּח וְיִתְפָּאַר וְיִתְרוֹמַם וְיִתְנַשֵּׂא
וְיִתְהַדָּר וְיִתְעַלֶּה וְיִתְהַלָּל שְׁמֵהּ דְּקוּדְשָׁא. בְּרִיךְ
הוּא. לְעֵלָּא מִן כָּל בִּרְכָתָא וְשִׁירָתָא. תֻּשְׁבְּחָתָא
וְנֶחֱמָתָא. דַּאֲמִירָן בְּעָלְמָא. וְאִמְרוּ אָמֵן:

עַל יִשְׂרָאֵל וְעַל צַדִּיקַיָּא. וְעַל־כָּל־מַן דְּאִתְפְּטַר
מִן־עָלְמָא הָדֵין כִּרְעוּתֵהּ דֶּאֱלָהָא. יְהֵא לְהוֹן
שְׁלָמָא רַבָּא וְחִנָּא וְחִסְדָּא מִן־קֳדָם מָרֵא שְׁמַיָּא
וְאַרְעָא. וְאִמְרוּ אָמֵן:

יְהֵא שְׁלָמָא רַבָּא מִן־שְׁמַיָּא וְחַיִּים. עָלֵינוּ וְעַל־
כָּל־יִשְׂרָאֵל. וְאִמְרוּ אָמֵן:

עֹשֶׂה שָׁלוֹם בִּמְרוֹמָיו. הוּא יַעֲשֶׂה שָׁלוֹם עָלֵינוּ
וְעַל־כָּל־יִשְׂרָאֵל. וְאִמְרוּ אָמֵן:

(Mourners are seated)

CLOSING HYMN

The Lord of all, who reigned supreme
Ere first creation's form was framed;
When all was finished by His will
His name Almighty was proclaimed.

When this, our world, shall be no more,
In majesty He still shall reign,
Who was, who is, who will for aye
In endless glory still remain.

Alone is He, beyond compare,
Without division or ally,
Without initial date or end,
Omnipotent He rules on high.

He is my God, my Savior He,
To whom I turn in sorrow's hour—
My banner proud, my refuge sure,
Who hears and answers with His power.

Then in His hand myself I lay,
And trusting, sleep, and wake with cheer;
My soul and body are His care;
The Lord doth guard, I have no fear.

BENEDICTION

CLOSING HYMN

אֲדוֹן עוֹלָם אֲשֶׁר מָלַךְ. בְּטֶרֶם כָּל־יְצִיר נִבְרָא ׃

לְעֵת נַעֲשָׂה בְחֶפְצוֹ כֹּל. אֲזַי מֶלֶךְ שְׁמוֹ נִקְרָא ׃

וְאַחֲרֵי כִּכְלוֹת הַכֹּל. לְבַדּוֹ יִמְלֹךְ נוֹרָא ׃

וְהוּא הָיָה וְהוּא הֹוֶה. וְהוּא יִהְיֶה בְּתִפְאָרָה ׃

וְהוּא אֶחָד וְאֵין שֵׁנִי. לְהַמְשִׁיל לוֹ לְהַחְבִּירָה ׃

בְּלִי רֵאשִׁית בְּלִי תַכְלִית. וְלוֹ הָעֹז וְהַמִּשְׂרָה ׃

וְהוּא אֵלִי וְחַי גֹּאֲלִי. וְצוּר חֶבְלִי בְּעֵת צָרָה ׃

וְהוּא נִסִּי וּמָנוֹס לִי. מְנָת כּוֹסִי בְּיוֹם אֶקְרָא ׃

בְּיָדוֹ אַפְקִיד רוּחִי. בְּעֵת אִישַׁן וְאָעִירָה ׃

וְעִם רוּחִי גְּוִיָּתִי. יְיָ לִי וְלֹא אִירָא ׃

BENEDICTION

SANCTIFICATION FOR THE NEW YEAR
KIDDUSH

On Sabbath Eve:

We praise Thee, O God, and thank Thee for all the blessings of the week that is gone; for life, health and strength; for home, love and friendship; for the discipline of our trials and temptations; for the happiness of our success and prosperity. Thou hast commanded us: Six days shalt thou labor and do all thy work, but the seventh day is a Sabbath unto the Lord thy God. Thou hast ennobled us, O God, by the blessings of work, and in love and grace sanctified us by the blessings of rest.

On Week Days:

Praised be Thou, O Lord our God, Ruler of the world, who hast created the fruit of the vine.

Praised be Thou, O Lord our God, King of the Universe, who has sanctified us with Thy commandments. In love hast Thou given us, O Lord our God, solemn days of joy, this season of the New Year, the time of the sounding of the Shofar. Thou hast called us to Thy service and sanctified us to proclaim Thy law among all nations. Thy word is truth and abides forever. Praised be Thou, O Lord our God, who sanctifiest the Sabbath, Israel and the New Year.

Praised be Thou, O Lord our God, Ruler of the world, who hast granted us life, sustained us and permitted us to commemorate this solemn festival.

קידוש

When the festival occurs on שבת begin here:

וַיְהִי עֶרֶב וַיְהִי בֹקֶר

יוֹם הַשִּׁשִּׁי: וַיְכֻלּוּ הַשָּׁמַיִם וְהָאָרֶץ וְכָל־צְבָאָם:
וַיְכַל אֱלֹהִים בַּיּוֹם הַשְּׁבִיעִי מְלַאכְתּוֹ אֲשֶׁר עָשָׂה
וַיִּשְׁבֹּת בַּיּוֹם הַשְּׁבִיעִי מִכָּל־מְלַאכְתּוֹ אֲשֶׁר עָשָׂה:
וַיְבָרֶךְ אֱלֹהִים אֶת־יוֹם הַשְּׁבִיעִי וַיְקַדֵּשׁ אֹתוֹ כִּי בוֹ
שָׁבַת מִכָּל־מְלַאכְתּוֹ אֲשֶׁר־בָּרָא אֱלֹהִים לַעֲשׂוֹת:

When the festival occurs on week-days, begin here:

בָּרוּךְ אַתָּה יְיָ אֱלֹהֵינוּ מֶלֶךְ הָעוֹלָם בּוֹרֵא פְּרִי
הַגָּפֶן:

בָּרוּךְ אַתָּה יְיָ אֱלֹהֵינוּ מֶלֶךְ הָעוֹלָם אֲשֶׁר בָּחַר
בָּנוּ מִכָּל־עָם וְרוֹמְמָנוּ מִכָּל־לָשׁוֹן וְקִדְּשָׁנוּ בְּמִצְוֹתָיו.
וַתִּתֶּן־לָנוּ יְיָ אֱלֹהֵינוּ בְּאַהֲבָה אֶת (יוֹם הַשַּׁבָּת הַזֶּה
וְאֶת) יוֹם הַזִּכָּרוֹן הַזֶּה יוֹם (זִכְרוֹן) תְּרוּעָה
(בְּאַהֲבָה) מִקְרָא קֹדֶשׁ זֵכֶר לִיצִיאַת מִצְרָיִם. כִּי
בָנוּ בָחַרְתָּ וְאוֹתָנוּ קִדַּשְׁתָּ מִכָּל־הָעַמִּים. וּדְבָרְךָ
אֱמֶת וְקַיָּם לָעַד. בָּרוּךְ אַתָּה יְיָ מֶלֶךְ עַל כָּל־
הָאָרֶץ מְקַדֵּשׁ (הַשַּׁבָּת וְ)יִשְׂרָאֵל וְיוֹם הַזִּכָּרוֹן:

בָּרוּךְ אַתָּה יְיָ אֱלֹהֵינוּ מֶלֶךְ הָעוֹלָם שֶׁהֶחֱיָנוּ
וְקִיְּמָנוּ וְהִגִּיעָנוּ לַזְּמַן הַזֶּה:

THE MOURNER'S KADDISH

Reader

Yis-gad-dal v'yis-kad-dash sh'meh rab-bo, b'ol-mo
di'v-ro kir'-u-seh v'yam-lich mal-chu-seh, b'cha-ye-chon
u-v'yo-me-chon u-v'cha-yeh d'chol bes yis-ro-el, ba-a-
go-lo u-viz-man ko-riv, v'im-ru O-men.

Congregation

Y'heh sh'meh rab-bo m'vo-rach, l'o-lam ul'ol'meh ol-
ma-yo:

Reader

Yis-bo-rach v'yish-tab-bach, v'yis-po-ar, v'yis-ro-mam,
v'yis-nas-seh, v'yis-had-dor, v'yis-al-leh, v'yis-hal-lol, sh'-
meh d'kud'-sho, b'rich hu. L'e-lo min kol bir-cho-so
v'shi-ro-so, tush-b'cho-so v'ne-cho-mo-so, da-a-mi-ron
b'ol-mo, v'im-ru: O-men.

Al yis-ro-el v'al tsa-de-ka-yo, v'al kol man d'isp'tar min
ol-mo ho-dain kir-ooseh de-e-lo-ho, y'hai l'hon shlo-mo
rab-bo v'chino v'chis-do min ko-dom mo-rai sh'ma-yo
v'ar-o, v'im-ru: O-men.

Y'heh sh'lo-mo rab-bo min sh'ma-yo v'cha-yim, o-le-
nu v'al kol yis-ro-el, v'imru: O-men.

O-seh sho-lom bim'-ro-mov, hu ya-a-seh sho-lom,
o-le-nu v'al kol yis-ro-el, v'imru: O-men.

Morning Service for the New Year

ANTHEM

(Psalm c)

Raise the voice of joy unto the Lord, all ye lands. Serve the Lord with gladness; come before His presence with singing. Know ye that the Eternal is God. It is He that hath made us; we are His people, and the flock of His pasture. Enter His gates with thanksgiving, and His courts with praise; be thankful unto Him and bless His name. For the Lord is good, His mercy is everlasting; and His truth endureth to all generations.

הָרִיעוּ לַיָי כָּל־הָאָרֶץ: עִבְדוּ אֶת־יְיָ בְּשִׂמְחָה. בֹּאוּ לְפָנָיו בִּרְנָנָה: דְּעוּ כִּי־יְיָ הוּא אֱלֹהִים. הוּא עָשָׂנוּ. וְלוֹ אֲנַחְנוּ. עַמּוֹ וְצֹאן מַרְעִיתוֹ: בֹּאוּ שְׁעָרָיו בְּתוֹדָה. חֲצֵרֹתָיו בִּתְהִלָּה. הוֹדוּ לוֹ בָּרְכוּ שְׁמוֹ: כִּי טוֹב יְיָ. לְעוֹלָם חַסְדּוֹ. וְעַד־דֹּר וָדֹר אֱמוּנָתוֹ:

Reader

Master of the universe, great and holy God, Thy wisdom ruleth the world, Thou dost abide forever. Thou girdest the feeble with strength and givest courage to the faint of heart. In Thy hand are our lives and our destinies. Thy Fatherly love sustains and shields us; blessings without number Thou bestowest upon us. We thank Thee for the life which Thou hast given us and for the manifold bounties with which Thou hast favored us during the past year. And now, at the beginning of the new year, we beseech Thee to grant us life and sustenance, contentment and peace.

Reader

אלהי נשמה

The soul which Thou, O God, hast given unto me came pure from Thee. Thou hast created it, Thou hast formed it, Thou hast breathed it into me; Thou hast preserved it in this body and, at the appointed time, Thou wilt take it from this earth that it may enter upon life everlasting. While the breath of life is within me, I will worship Thee, Sovereign of the world and Lord of all souls. Praised be Thou, O God, in whose hands are the souls of all the living and the spirits of all flesh.

רבון כל העולמים

Lord of all worlds, not in reliance upon our own merit do we lay our supplications before Thee, but trusting in Thine infinite mercy alone. For what are we, what is our life, what our goodness, what our power? What can we say in Thy presence? Are not all the mighty men as naught before Thee and those of great renown as though they had never been; the wisest as if without knowledge, and men of understanding as if without discernment? Many of our works are vain, and our days pass away like a shadow. Our life would be altogether vanity, were it not for the soul, which fashioned in Thine own image, gives us assurance of our higher destiny and imparts to our fleeting days an abiding value.

Help us, O God, to banish from our hearts all vainglory, pride of worldly possessions, and self-sufficient leaning upon our own reason. Fill us with the spirit of meekness and the grace of modesty that we may grow in wisdom and in reverence. May we never forget that all we have and prize is but lent to us, a trust for which we must render account to Thee. O heavenly Father, put into our hearts the love and awe of Thee, that we may consecrate our lives to Thy service and glorify Thy name in the eyes of all men.

Congregation and Reader

אתה הוא

Almighty and merciful God, who hast called our fathers to Thy service, and hast opened their eyes to behold Thy wondrous works and to proclaim Thy law unto all nations, Thou art the same today even as Thou wast at the beginning; Thou art our God in this life, and Thou art our hope and refuge in the life to come. Creator of heaven and earth, of the sea and all that is therein, Thine alone is the power in the heaven above and on the earth below, and none can say unto Thee: What doest Thou? Our heavenly Father, help us that by our lives we may sanctify Thy name before men, and testify of Thee and of Thy holy law. Praised be Thou, O Lord, who hast revealed to us Thy law of truth.

Reader

Every living soul shall praise Thee; the spirit of all flesh shall glorify Thy name. Thou art God from everlasting to everlasting and besides Thee there is no redeemer nor savior. Thou art the first and the last, the Lord of all generations. Thou rulest the world in kindness and all Thy creatures in mercy. Thou art our guardian who sleepeth not and slumbereth not. To Thee alone we give thanks. Yet, though our lips should overflow with song, and our tongues with joyous praise, we should still be unable to thank Thee even for a thousandth part of the bounties which Thou hast bestowed upon our fathers and upon us. Thou hast been our protector and our savior in every trial and peril. Thy mercy has watched over us, and Thy lovingkindness has never failed us.

Congregation and Reader

Praised be Thy holy name. Thou hast made Thine eternal law our portion, and hast given us a goodly heritage. Open our eyes to the beauty of Thy truth and help us so to exemplify it in our lives that we may win all men for Thy law of righteousness. Gather all Thy children around Thy banner of truth that Thy name may be hallowed through us in all the world and the entire human family may be blessed with truth and peace. Amen.

נִשְׁמַת כָּל־חַי תְּבָרֵךְ אֶת־שִׁמְךָ יְיָ אֱלֹהֵינוּ. וְרוּחַ
כָּל־בָּשָׂר תְּפָאֵר וּתְרוֹמֵם זִכְרְךָ מַלְכֵּנוּ תָּמִיד: מִן
הָעוֹלָם וְעַד־הָעוֹלָם אַתָּה אֵל. וּמִבַּלְעָדֶיךָ אֵין
לָנוּ מֶלֶךְ גּוֹאֵל וּמוֹשִׁיעַ פּוֹדֶה וּמַצִּיל. וּמְפַרְנֵס
וּמְרַחֵם. בְּכָל־עֵת צָרָה וְצוּקָה. אֵין לָנוּ מֶלֶךְ אֶלָּא
אָתָּה: אֱלֹהֵי הָרִאשׁוֹנִים וְהָאַחֲרוֹנִים. הַמְּנַהֵג עוֹלָמוֹ
בְּחֶסֶד וּבְרִיּוֹתָיו בְּרַחֲמִים. לַךְ לְבַדְּךָ אֲנַחְנוּ
מוֹדִים: אִלּוּ פִינוּ מָלֵא שִׁירָה כַיָּם וּלְשׁוֹנֵנוּ רִנָּה
כַּהֲמוֹן גַּלָּיו. וְשִׂפְתוֹתֵינוּ שֶׁבַח כְּמֶרְחֲבֵי רָקִיעַ. אֵין
אֲנַחְנוּ מַסְפִּיקִים לְהוֹדוֹת לְךָ יְיָ אֱלֹהֵינוּ וֵאלֹהֵי
אֲבוֹתֵינוּ. עַל־כָּל הַטּוֹבוֹת שֶׁעָשִׂיתָ עִם־אֲבוֹתֵינוּ
וְעִמָּנוּ: מִמִּצְרַיִם גְּאַלְתָּנוּ יְיָ אֱלֹהֵינוּ וּמִבֵּית עֲבָדִים
פְּדִיתָנוּ. בְּרָעָב זַנְתָּנוּ. וּבְשָׂבָע כִּלְכַּלְתָּנוּ: מֵחֶרֶב
הִצַּלְתָּנוּ וּמִדֶּבֶר מִלַּטְתָּנוּ. וּמֵחֳלָיִם רָעִים וְנֶאֱמָנִים
דִּלִּיתָנוּ: עַד־הֵנָּה עֲזָרוּנוּ רַחֲמֶיךָ. וְלֹא־עֲזָבוּנוּ
חֲסָדֶיךָ. וְאַל־תִּטְּשֵׁנוּ יְיָ אֱלֹהֵינוּ לָנֶצַח: עַל־כֵּן
נְהַלֶּלְךָ וּנְשַׁבֵּחֲךָ וּנְפָאֶרְךָ וּנְבָרֵךְ אֶת־שֵׁם קָדְשֶׁךָ:
בָּרוּךְ אַתָּה יְיָ. אֵל מֶלֶךְ גָּדוֹל בַּתִּשְׁבָּחוֹת. אֵל
הַהוֹדָאוֹת. אֲדוֹן הַנִּפְלָאוֹת. הַבּוֹחֵר בְּשִׁירֵי זִמְרָה.
מֶלֶךְ אֵל חֵי הָעוֹלָמִים:

(Congregation rises)

Reader

Praise ye the Lord to whom all praise is due.

Choir and Congregation

Praised be the Lord to whom all praise is due forever and ever.

(Congregation is seated)

Reader

Praised be Thou, O Lord our God, Ruler of the world, who in Thy mercy makest light to shine over the earth and all its inhabitants, and renewest daily the work of creation. How manifold are Thy works, O Lord! In wisdom hast Thou made them all. The heavens declare Thy glory. The earth reveals Thy creative power. Thou formest light and darkness, ordainest good out of evil, bringest harmony into nature and peace to the heart of man.

Thou didst lay the foundations of the earth and the heavens are Thy handiwork. They may perish but Thou shalt endure. Thy years shall have no end. O everliving God, Creator of heaven and earth, rule Thou over us forever. Praised be Thou, O Lord, Creator of light.

Great has been Thy love for us and Thy compassion boundless. Our fathers put their trust in Thee and Thou didst teach them the law of life. Be gracious also unto us that we may understand and fulfil the teachings of Thy word. Enlighten our eyes in Thy law

(Congregation rises)

Reader

בָּרְכוּ אֶת־יְיָ הַמְבֹרָךְ:

Choir and Congregation

בָּרוּךְ יְיָ הַמְבֹרָךְ לְעוֹלָם וָעֶד:

(Congregation is seated)

Reader

בָּרוּךְ אַתָּה יְיָ אֱלֹהֵינוּ מֶלֶךְ הָעוֹלָם. יוֹצֵר אוֹר
וּבוֹרֵא חְשֶׁךְ. עֹשֶׂה שָׁלוֹם וּבוֹרֵא אֶת־הַכֹּל:
הַמֵּאִיר לָאָרֶץ וְלַדָּרִים עָלֶיהָ בְּרַחֲמִים. וּבְטוּבוֹ
מְחַדֵּשׁ בְּכָל־יוֹם תָּמִיד מַעֲשֵׂה בְרֵאשִׁית: מָה
רַבּוּ מַעֲשֶׂיךָ יְיָ. כֻּלָּם בְּחָכְמָה עָשִׂיתָ. מָלְאָה
הָאָרֶץ קִנְיָנֶךָ: תִּתְבָּרַךְ יְיָ אֱלֹהֵינוּ עַל־שֶׁבַח מַעֲשֵׂה
יָדֶיךָ. וְעַל־מְאוֹרֵי־אוֹר שֶׁעָשִׂיתָ יְפָאֲרוּךָ סֶּלָה:
בָּרוּךְ אַתָּה יְיָ יוֹצֵר הַמְּאוֹרוֹת:
אַהֲבָה רַבָּה אֲהַבְתָּנוּ יְיָ אֱלֹהֵינוּ. חֶמְלָה גְדוֹלָה
וִיתֵרָה חָמַלְתָּ עָלֵינוּ: אָבִינוּ מַלְכֵּנוּ. בַּעֲבוּר
אֲבוֹתֵינוּ שֶׁבָּטְחוּ בְךָ וַתְּלַמְּדֵם חֻקֵּי חַיִּים. כֵּן

that we may cling unto Thy commandments. Unite our hearts to love and revere Thee. We trust in Thee and rejoice in Thy saving power, for from Thee cometh our help. Thou hast called us and drawn us nigh unto Thee to serve Thee in faithfulness.

Happy the man who knoweth Thee and delighteth greatly in Thy commandments. Happy the man whose strength is in Thee, in whose heart are Thy ways. Joyfully do we lift up our voices and proclaim Thy unity. Praised be Thou, O Lord, who in Thy love hast called Thy people Israel to serve Thee.

(Congregation rises)

Reader

Hear, O Israel: The Lord our God, the Lord is One.

Praised be His name whose glorious kingdom is forever and ever.

(Congregation is seated)

Congregation and Reader

Thou shalt love the Lord, thy God, with all thy heart, with all thy soul, and with all thy might. And these words, which I command thee this day, shall be upon thy heart. Thou shalt teach them diligently unto thy children, and shalt speak of them when thou sittest in thy house, when thou walkest by the way, when thou liest down, and when thou risest up. Thou shalt bind them for a sign upon thy hand and they shall be for frontlets between thine eyes. Thou shalt write them upon the doorposts of thy house and upon thy gates: That ye may remember and do all My commandments and be holy unto your God.

תְּחָנֵּנוּ וּתְלַמְּדֵנוּ: הָאֵר עֵינֵינוּ בְּתוֹרָתֶךָ. וְדַבֵּק לִבֵּנוּ
בְּמִצְוֹתֶיךָ. וְיַחֵד לְבָבֵנוּ לְאַהֲבָה וּלְיִרְאָה שְׁמֶךָ:
כִּי בְשֵׁם קָדְשְׁךָ בָּטָחְנוּ. נָגִילָה וְנִשְׂמְחָה בִּישׁוּעָתֶךָ.
כִּי אֵל פּוֹעֵל יְשׁוּעוֹת אָתָּה. וּבָנוּ בָחַרְתָּ וְקֵרַבְתָּנוּ
לְשִׁמְךָ הַגָּדוֹל סֶלָה בֶּאֱמֶת לְהוֹדוֹת לְךָ וּלְיַחֶדְךָ
בְּאַהֲבָה. בָּרוּךְ אַתָּה יְיָ הַבּוֹחֵר בְּעַמּוֹ יִשְׂרָאֵל
בְּאַהֲבָה:

(Congregation rises)

Reader, then Choir and Congregation

שְׁמַע יִשְׂרָאֵל יְהֹוָה אֱלֹהֵינוּ יְהֹוָה אֶחָד:
בָּרוּךְ שֵׁם כְּבוֹד מַלְכוּתוֹ לְעוֹלָם וָעֶד:

(Congregation is seated)

Reader

וְאָהַבְתָּ אֵת יְיָ אֱלֹהֶיךָ בְּכָל-לְבָבְךָ וּבְכָל-נַפְשְׁךָ
וּבְכָל-מְאֹדֶךָ: וְהָיוּ הַדְּבָרִים הָאֵלֶּה אֲשֶׁר אָנֹכִי
מְצַוְּךָ הַיּוֹם עַל-לְבָבֶךָ: וְשִׁנַּנְתָּם לְבָנֶיךָ וְדִבַּרְתָּ
בָּם. בְּשִׁבְתְּךָ בְּבֵיתֶךָ וּבְלֶכְתְּךָ בַדֶּרֶךְ וּבְשָׁכְבְּךָ
וּבְקוּמֶךָ: וּקְשַׁרְתָּם לְאוֹת עַל-יָדֶךָ. וְהָיוּ לְטֹטָפֹת
בֵּין עֵינֶיךָ: וּכְתַבְתָּם עַל-מְזֻזוֹת בֵּיתֶךָ וּבִשְׁעָרֶיךָ:
לְמַעַן תִּזְכְּרוּ וַעֲשִׂיתֶם אֶת-כָּל-מִצְוֹתָי וִהְיִיתֶם
קְדֹשִׁים לֵאלֹהֵיכֶם: אֲנִי יְיָ אֱלֹהֵיכֶם:

Responsive Reading

Reader

True and enduring is Thy word which Thou hast spoken through Thy prophets.

Congregation

Thou art the living God, Thy words bring life and light to the soul.

Thou art the strength of our life, the rock of our salvation; Thy kingdom and Thy truth abide forever.

Thou hast been the help of our fathers in time of trouble and art our refuge in all generations.

Thou art the first and the last, and besides Thee there is no redeemer nor helper.

As Thou hast saved Israel from Egyptian bondage, so mayest Thou send Thy help to all who are oppressed.

May Thy law rule in the hearts of all Thy children, and Thy truth unite them in bonds of fellowship.

May the righteous of all nations rejoice in Thy grace and triumph by Thy power.

O God, who art our refuge and our hope, we glorify Thy name now as did our fathers in ancient days:

Choir

Who is like unto Thee, O Lord? Who is like unto Thee, glorious in holiness, awe-inspiring, working wonders?

Responsive Reading

אֱמֶת. אֱלֹהֵי עוֹלָם מַלְכֵּנוּ. צוּר יַעֲקֹב מָגֵן יִשְׁעֵנוּ:

לְדוֹר וָדוֹר הוּא קַיָּם וּשְׁמוֹ קַיָּם. וּמַלְכוּתוֹ

וֶאֱמוּנָתוֹ לָעַד קַיֶּמֶת:

וּדְבָרָיו חָיִים וְקַיָּמִים. נֶאֱמָנִים וְנֶחֱמָדִים לָעַד

וּלְעוֹלְמֵי עוֹלָמִים:

עֶזְרַת אֲבוֹתֵינוּ אַתָּה הוּא מֵעוֹלָם. מָגֵן וּמוֹשִׁיעַ

לִבְנֵיהֶם אַחֲרֵיהֶם בְּכָל־דּוֹר וָדוֹר:

אַשְׁרֵי אִישׁ שֶׁיִּשְׁמַע לְמִצְוֹתֶיךָ וְתוֹרָתְךָ וּדְבָרְךָ

יָשִׂים עַל־לִבּוֹ:

אֱמֶת. שָׁאַתָּה הוּא יְיָ אֱלֹהֵינוּ. צוּר יְשׁוּעָתֵנוּ.

פּוֹדֵנוּ וּמַצִּילֵנוּ מֵעוֹלָם שְׁמֶךָ. אֵין אֱלֹהִים זוּלָתֶךָ:

אַתָּה הוּא רִאשׁוֹן וְאַתָּה הוּא אַחֲרוֹן. וּמִבַּלְעָדֶיךָ

אֵין לָנוּ מֶלֶךְ גּוֹאֵל וּמוֹשִׁיעַ:

מִמִּצְרַיִם גְּאַלְתָּנוּ יְיָ אֱלֹהֵינוּ. וּמִבֵּית עֲבָדִים

פְּדִיתָנוּ:

עַל־זֹאת שִׁבְּחוּ אֲהוּבִים וְרוֹמְמוּ אֵל:

Choir

מִי כָמֹכָה בָּאֵלִים יְיָ. מִי כָּמֹכָה נֶאְדָּר בַּקֹּדֶשׁ

נוֹרָא תְהִלֹּת עֹשֵׂה־פֶלֶא:

Reader

A new song the redeemed sang unto Thy name. They proclaimed Thy sovereignty and said:

Choir

The Lord shall reign forever and ever.

Reader

O Rock of Israel, redeem those who are oppressed and deliver those who are persecuted. Praised be Thou, our Redeemer, the Holy One of Israel.

Amen

Reader

Praised be Thou, O Lord, God of our fathers, God of Abraham, Isaac and Jacob, great, mighty, and exalted. Thou bestowest lovingkindness upon all Thy children. Thou rememberest the devotion of the fathers. In Thy love Thou bringest redemption to their descendants for the sake of Thy name.

Remember us unto life, O Sovereign who ordainest life, and inscribe us in the book of life, for Thy sake, O God of life. Thou art our King and Helper, our Savior and Protector. Praised be Thou, O Lord, Shield of Abraham.

Eternal is Thy power, O Lord, Thou art mighty to save. In lovingkindness Thou sustainest the living; in the multitude of Thy mercies Thou preservest all. Thou upholdest the falling and healest the sick; freest

Reader

שִׁירָה חֲדָשָׁה שִׁבְּחוּ גְאוּלִים לְשִׁמְךָ עַל־שְׂפַת
הַיָּם יַחַד כֻּלָּם הוֹדוּ וְהִמְלִיכוּ וְאָמְרוּ:

Choir and Congregation

יְיָ יִמְלֹךְ לְעֹלָם וָעֶד:

Reader

צוּר יִשְׂרָאֵל. קוּמָה בְּעֶזְרַת יִשְׂרָאֵל. גְּאָלֵנוּ יְיָ
צְבָאוֹת. שְׁמוֹ קְדוֹשׁ יִשְׂרָאֵל. בָּרוּךְ אַתָּה יְיָ גָּאַל
יִשְׂרָאֵל:

Choir: Amen.

Reader

בָּרוּךְ אַתָּה יְיָ אֱלֹהֵינוּ וֵאלֹהֵי אֲבוֹתֵינוּ. אֱלֹהֵי
אַבְרָהָם אֱלֹהֵי יִצְחָק וֵאלֹהֵי יַעֲקֹב. הָאֵל הַגָּדוֹל
הַגִּבּוֹר וְהַנּוֹרָא. אֵל עֶלְיוֹן. גּוֹמֵל חֲסָדִים טוֹבִים.
וְקֹנֵה הַכֹּל וְזוֹכֵר חַסְדֵי אָבוֹת. וּמֵבִיא גְאֻלָּה לִבְנֵי
בְנֵיהֶם לְמַעַן שְׁמוֹ בְּאַהֲבָה:

זָכְרֵנוּ לְחַיִּים. מֶלֶךְ חָפֵץ בַּחַיִּים. וְכָתְבֵנוּ בְּסֵפֶר
הַחַיִּים. לְמַעַנְךָ אֱלֹהִים חַיִּים:

מֶלֶךְ עוֹזֵר וּמוֹשִׁיעַ וּמָגֵן. בָּרוּךְ אַתָּה יְיָ מָגֵן
אַבְרָהָם:

the captives and keepest faith with Thy children in death as in life. Who is like unto Thee, Almighty God, Author of life and death, Source of salvation?

Who is like unto Thee, Father of mercies, who rememberest Thy children unto life eternal. Praised be Thou, O God, who hast implanted within us immortal life.

Thou art holy, Thy name is holy, and Thy worshipers proclaim Thy holiness.

SANCTIFICATION

(Congregation rises)

Congregation and Reader

We sanctify Thy name on earth, as the heavens declare Thy glory; and in the words of the prophet we say:
Holy, holy, holy is the Lord of hosts; the whole earth is full of His glory.

Reader

God our Strength, God our Lord, how excellent is Thy name in all the earth.

Congregation and Reader

Praised be the glory of God in all the world.

אַתָּה גִבּוֹר לְעוֹלָם אֲדֹנָי. רַב לְהוֹשִׁיעַ. מְכַלְכֵּל
חַיִּים בְּחֶסֶד. מְחַיֶּה הַכֹּל בְּרַחֲמִים רַבִּים. סוֹמֵךְ
נוֹפְלִים וְרוֹפֵא חוֹלִים וּמַתִּיר אֲסוּרִים. וּמְקַיֵּם
אֱמוּנָתוֹ לִישֵׁנֵי עָפָר. מִי כָמוֹךָ בַּעַל גְּבוּרוֹת. וּמִי
דּוֹמֶה לָּךְ. מֶלֶךְ מֵמִית וּמְחַיֶּה. וּמַצְמִיחַ יְשׁוּעָה:

מִי כָמוֹךָ אַב הָרַחֲמִים. זוֹכֵר יְצוּרָיו לַחַיִּים
בְּרַחֲמִים: בָּרוּךְ אַתָּה יְיָ נֹטֵעַ בְּתוֹכֵנוּ חַיֵּי עוֹלָם:

אַתָּה קָדוֹשׁ וְשִׁמְךָ קָדוֹשׁ וּקְדוֹשִׁים בְּכָל־יוֹם
יְהַלְלוּךָ סֶּלָה:

SANCTIFICATION

(Congregation rises)

נְקַדֵּשׁ אֶת־שִׁמְךָ בָּעוֹלָם. כְּשֵׁם שֶׁמַּקְדִּישִׁים אוֹתוֹ
בִּשְׁמֵי מָרוֹם. כַּכָּתוּב עַל־יַד נְבִיאֶךָ. וְקָרָא זֶה אֶל־
זֶה וְאָמַר:

Choir and Congregation

קָדוֹשׁ קָדוֹשׁ קָדוֹשׁ יְיָ צְבָאוֹת. מְלֹא כָל־הָאָרֶץ
כְּבוֹדוֹ:

Reader

אַדִּיר אַדִּירֵנוּ יְיָ אֲדוֹנֵנוּ מָה־אַדִּיר שִׁמְךָ בְּכָל־
הָאָרֶץ:

Choir and Congregation

בָּרוּךְ כְּבוֹד יְיָ מִמְּקוֹמוֹ:

Reader

Our God is one; He is our Father, He is our King, He is our Helper and in His mercy He will answer our prayers in the sight of all the living.

Congregation and Reader

The Lord will reign forever, thy God, O Zion, from generation to generation.   Hallelujah.

(Congregation is seated)

Reader

From generation to generation we declare Thy greatness and throughout all ages proclaim Thy holiness; Thy praise shall never cease from our lips.

Reader

O Lord, our God, let Thy presence be manifest to us in all Thy works, that reverence for Thee may fill the hearts of all Thy creatures. May all the children of men come before Thee in humility and unite to do Thy will with perfect heart. May all acknowledge that Thine are power, dominion, and majesty, and that Thy name is exalted above all.

Reader

אֶחָד הוּא אֱלֹהֵינוּ. הוּא אָבִינוּ. הוּא מַלְכֵּנוּ. הוּא
מוֹשִׁיעֵנוּ: וְהוּא יַשְׁמִיעֵנוּ בְּרַחֲמָיו לְעֵינֵי כָּל־חָי:

Congregation and Choir

יִמְלֹךְ יְיָ לְעוֹלָם אֱלֹהַיִךְ צִיּוֹן לְדֹר וָדֹר
הַלְלוּיָהּ:

(Congregation is seated)

Reader

לְדוֹר וָדוֹר נַגִּיד גָּדְלֶךָ. וּלְנֵצַח נְצָחִים קְדֻשָּׁתְךָ
נַקְדִּישׁ. וְשִׁבְחֲךָ אֱלֹהֵינוּ מִפִּינוּ לֹא יָמוּשׁ לְעוֹלָם
וָעֶד:

Choir: Amen.

Reader

וּבְכֵן תֵּן פַּחְדְּךָ יְיָ אֱלֹהֵינוּ עַל כָּל־מַעֲשֶׂיךָ
וְאֵימָתְךָ עַל כָּל־מַה־שֶּׁבָּרָאתָ. וְיִירָאוּךָ כָּל־הַמַּעֲשִׂים
וְיִשְׁתַּחֲווּ לְפָנֶיךָ כָּל־הַבְּרוּאִים. וְיֵעָשׂוּ כֻלָּם אֲגֻדָּה
אַחַת לַעֲשׂוֹת רְצוֹנְךָ בְּלֵבָב שָׁלֵם. כְּמוֹ שֶׁיָּדַעְנוּ יְיָ
אֱלֹהֵינוּ שֶׁהַשָּׁלְטוֹן לְפָנֶיךָ עֹז בְּיָדְךָ וּגְבוּרָה בִּימִינֶךָ
וְשִׁמְךָ נוֹרָא עַל כָּל־מַה־שֶּׁבָּרָאתָ:

Grant honor, O Lord, to them that revere Thee, inspire with courage those who wait for Thee, and fulfil the hope of all who trust in Thy name. Hasten the day that will bring gladness to all who dwell on earth and victory of the spirit to those who bear witness to Thy unity. Then shall the just see and exult, the righteous be glad, and the pious sing for joy. Then shall iniquity be made dumb, and wickedness vanish like smoke; for the dominion of arrogance shall have passed away from the earth.

Thou alone, O Lord, shalt reign over all Thy works, as it is written in Thy holy word: The Lord shall reign forever, thy God, O Zion, from generation to generation. Hallelujah.

Holy art Thou, awe-inspiring is Thy name, there is no God but Thee. The Lord of hosts is exalted through justice, and the holy God is sanctified through righteousness. Praised be Thou, O Lord, King of holiness.

We render thanks unto Thee that Thou hast called us to Thy service and entrusted us with Thy commandments. In love Thou hast given us this Day of Remembrance that we may consecrate ourselves unto Thee and unto Thy law of righteousness.

Reader

Almighty God and Father, in this solemn hour we would draw nigh unto Thee. Help us to build our lives on the abiding foundations of Thy law that we may attain peace of mind and steadfastness of purpose. Open our eyes to the nobility of life and its sacred opportunities for service.

וּבְכֵן תֵּן כָּבוֹד יְיָ לְעַמֶּךָ תְּהִלָּה לִירֵאֶיךָ וְתִקְוָה
לְדוֹרְשֶׁיךָ וּפִתְחוֹן פֶּה לַמְיַחֲלִים לָךְ. שִׂמְחָה לְכָל
יִשְׁבֵי תֵבֵל אַרְצֶךָ וּצְמִיחַת קֶרֶן לִמְיַחֲדֵי שְׁמֶךָ.
בִּמְהֵרָה בְיָמֵינוּ:

וּבְכֵן צַדִּיקִים יִרְאוּ וְיִשְׂמָחוּ וִישָׁרִים יַעֲלֹזוּ
וַחֲסִידִים בְּרִנָּה יָגִילוּ וְעוֹלָתָה תִּקְפָּץ־פִּיהָ. וְכָל־
הָרִשְׁעָה כֻּלָּהּ כֶּעָשָׁן תִּכְלֶה. כִּי תַעֲבִיר מֶמְשֶׁלֶת
זָדוֹן מִן־הָאָרֶץ:

וְתִמְלוֹךְ אַתָּה יְיָ לְבַדֶּךָ עַל־כָּל־מַעֲשֶׂיךָ. כַּכָּתוּב
בְּדִבְרֵי קָדְשֶׁךָ יִמְלֹךְ יְיָ לְעוֹלָם אֱלֹהַיִךְ צִיּוֹן לְדֹר
וָדֹר הַלְלוּיָהּ:

Reader

קָדוֹשׁ אַתָּה וְנוֹרָא שְׁמֶךָ. וְאֵין אֱלֹהַּ מִבַּלְעָדֶיךָ.
כַּכָּתוּב. וַיִּגְבַּהּ יְיָ צְבָאוֹת בַּמִּשְׁפָּט. וְהָאֵל הַקָּדוֹשׁ
נִקְדַּשׁ בִּצְדָקָה. בָּרוּךְ אַתָּה יְיָ הַמֶּלֶךְ הַקָּדוֹשׁ:

אַתָּה בְחַרְתָּנוּ מִכָּל הָעַמִּים. אָהַבְתָּ אוֹתָנוּ.
וְקִדַּשְׁתָּנוּ בְּמִצְוֹתֶיךָ. וְקֵרַבְתָּנוּ לַעֲבוֹדָתֶךָ. וְשִׁמְךָ
הַגָּדוֹל וְהַקָּדוֹשׁ עָלֵינוּ קָרָאתָ:

O Thou who dealest graciously with the children of men, give us the grace to show forbearance unto those who offend against us. When the wrongs and injustices of men sadden our hearts, may we seek shelter in the knowledge of Thy truth and find joy in the fulfillment of Thy will. May no trial, however severe, embitter our souls and shake our trust in Thee. When beset by trouble and sorrow, our fathers put on the armor of faith and fortitude. May we too find strength to meet adversity with quiet courage and unshaken trust. Weeping may tarry for the night, but joy cometh in the morning. Help us to understand that injustice and hate will not forever afflict the sons of men; that righteousness and mercy will triumph in the end.

Congregation and Reader

Our God and God of our fathers, may Thy kingdom come speedily, that worship of Thy name and obedience to Thy law may unite all men in brotherhood and peace; that every creature may know that Thou art its Creator, and every living being exclaim: The Lord, the God of Israel, ruleth and His dominion endureth forever.

Sanctify us by Thy commandments and bring us near unto Thy service, that we may be worthy to proclaim Thy truth unto all mankind. Satisfy us with Thy goodness, and gladden us with Thy salvation. Purify our hearts that we may serve Thee in truth. For Thou, O God, art Truth, and Thy word endureth forever. Praised be Thou, O Lord, who sanctifiest (the Sabbath) Israel and the Day of Remembrance.

וַתִּתֶּן־לָנוּ יְיָ אֱלֹהֵינוּ בְּאַהֲבָה אֶת־יוֹם (הַשַּׁבָּת
הַזֶּה וְאֶת יוֹם) הַזִּכָּרוֹן הַזֶּה. יוֹם (זִכְרוֹן) תְּרוּעָה
(בְּאַהֲבָה) מִקְרָא־קֹדֶשׁ זֵכֶר לִיצִיאַת מִצְרָיִם:

קַדְּשֵׁנוּ בְּמִצְוֹתֶיךָ וְתֵן חֶלְקֵנוּ בְּתוֹרָתֶךָ שַׂבְּעֵנוּ
מִטּוּבֶךָ וְשַׂמְּחֵנוּ בִּישׁוּעָתֶךָ. (וְהַנְחִילֵנוּ יְיָ אֱלֹהֵינוּ
בְּאַהֲבָה וּבְרָצוֹן שַׁבַּת קָדְשֶׁךָ וְיָנוּחוּ בָהּ יִשְׂרָאֵל
מְקַדְּשֵׁי שְׁמֶךָ) וְטַהֵר לִבֵּנוּ לְעָבְדְּךָ בֶּאֱמֶת כִּי אַתָּה
אֱלֹהִים אֱמֶת וּדְבָרְךָ (מַלְכֵּנוּ) אֱמֶת וְקַיָּם לָעַד.

אֱלֹהֵינוּ וֵאלֹהֵי אֲבוֹתֵינוּ מְלוֹךְ עַל כָּל־הָעוֹלָם
כֻּלּוֹ בִּכְבוֹדֶךָ. וְהִנָּשֵׂא עַל כָּל־הָאָרֶץ בִּיקָרֶךָ.
וְהוֹפַע בַּהֲדַר גְּאוֹן עֻזֶּךָ עַל כָּל־יוֹשְׁבֵי תֵבֵל אַרְצֶךָ.
וְיֵדַע כָּל־פָּעוּל כִּי אַתָּה פְעַלְתּוֹ וְיָבִין כָּל־יְצוּר
כִּי אַתָּה יְצַרְתּוֹ וְיֹאמַר כֹּל אֲשֶׁר נְשָׁמָה בְאַפּוֹ יְיָ
אֱלֹהֵי יִשְׂרָאֵל מֶלֶךְ וּמַלְכוּתוֹ בַּכֹּל מָשָׁלָה:
בָּרוּךְ אַתָּה יְיָ מֶלֶךְ עַל־כָּל־הָאָרֶץ מְקַדֵּשׁ (הַשַּׁבָּת
וְ)יִשְׂרָאֵל וְיוֹם הַזִּכָּרוֹן:

Reader

Look with favor, O Lord, upon us, and may our service be acceptable unto Thee. Praised be Thou, O Lord, whom alone we serve in reverence.

Congregation and Reader

We gratefully acknowledge, O Lord our God, that Thou art our support and salvation. Thee alone do we worship, and unto Thee do we give grateful praise. We thank Thee, O God, for Thy favor unto this, our land, and for the blessings of liberty and the ideals of righteousness which our nation cherishes. Protect and prosper it, and let the New Year bring security and abundance to all. Praised be Thou, O Lord, from whom all goodness comes and to whom all thanks are due.

Reader

Our God and God of our fathers, O may Thy blessing rest upon us, according to the gracious promise of Thy word, spoken through the priests of yore, ministering at Thy holy altar saying:

May the Lord bless thee and keep thee.

Choir: Amen.

May the Lord let his countenance shine upon thee and be gracious unto thee.

Choir: Amen.

May the Lord lift up His countenance upon thee and give thee peace.

Choir: Amen.

Reader

רְצֵה יְיָ אֱלֹהֵינוּ בְּעַמְּךָ יִשְׂרָאֵל. וּתְפִלָּתָם
בְּאַהֲבָה תְקַבֵּל. וּתְהִי לְרָצוֹן תָּמִיד עֲבוֹדַת יִשְׂרָאֵל
עַמֶּךָ. בָּרוּךְ אַתָּה יְיָ שֶׁאוֹתְךָ לְבַדְּךָ בְּיִרְאָה נַעֲבוֹד:

מוֹדִים אֲנַחְנוּ לָךְ. שָׁאַתָּה הוּא יְיָ אֱלֹהֵינוּ וֵאלֹהֵי
אֲבוֹתֵינוּ לְעוֹלָם וָעֶד. צוּר חַיֵּינוּ מָגֵן יִשְׁעֵנוּ אַתָּה
הוּא לְדוֹר וָדוֹר. נוֹדֶה לְךָ וּנְסַפֵּר תְּהִלָּתֶךָ. עַל
חַיֵּינוּ הַמְּסוּרִים בְּיָדֶךָ. וְעַל נִשְׁמוֹתֵינוּ הַפְּקוּדוֹת
לָךְ. וְעַל נִסֶּיךָ שֶׁבְּכָל יוֹם עִמָּנוּ. וְעַל נִפְלְאוֹתֶיךָ
שֶׁבְּכָל עֵת. עֶרֶב וָבֹקֶר וְצָהֳרָיִם. הַטּוֹב כִּי לֹא
כָלוּ רַחֲמֶיךָ. וְהַמְּרַחֵם כִּי לֹא תַמּוּ חֲסָדֶיךָ. מֵעוֹלָם
קִוִּינוּ לָךְ:

אֱלֹהֵינוּ וֵאלֹהֵי אֲבוֹתֵינוּ בָּרְכֵנוּ בַּבְּרָכָה
הַמְשֻׁלֶּשֶׁת הַכְּתוּבָה בַּתּוֹרָה:

יְבָרֶכְךָ יְיָ וְיִשְׁמְרֶךָ:

Choir: Amen.

יָאֵר יְיָ פָּנָיו אֵלֶיךָ וִיחֻנֶּךָּ:

Choir: Amen.

יִשָּׂא יְיָ פָּנָיו אֵלֶיךָ וְיָשֵׂם לְךָ שָׁלוֹם:

Choir: Amen.

Silent Devotion

O God, keep my tongue from evil and my lips from speaking guile. Be my support when grief silences my voice, and my comfort when woe bends my spirit. Plant humility in my soul, and strengthen my heart with perfect faith in Thee. Help me to be strong in trial and temptation and to be patient and forgiving when others wrong me. Guide me by the light of Thy counsel, that I may ever find strength in Thee, my Rock and my Redeemer. Amen.

Choir

May the words of my mouth and the meditations of my heart be acceptable in Thy sight, O Lord, my Rock and my Redeemer.

(Congregation rises)

Reader, then Congregation

Our Father, our King, hear our prayer.

Our Father, our King, we have sinned before Thee.

Our Father, our King, have mercy upon us and upon our children.

Our Father, our King, keep far from our country pestilence, war and famine.

Our Father, our King, cause all hate and oppression to vanish from the earth.

Our Father, our King, inscribe us for blessing in the book of life.

Our Father, our King, grant unto us a year of happiness.

(Congregation is seated)

Silent Devotion

אֱלֹהַי נְצוֹר לְשׁוֹנִי מֵרָע וּשְׂפָתַי מִדַּבֵּר מִרְמָה:
וְלִמְקַלְלַי נַפְשִׁי תִדּוֹם וְנַפְשִׁי כֶּעָפָר לַכֹּל תִּהְיֶה:
פְּתַח לִבִּי בְּתוֹרָתֶךָ וּבְמִצְוֹתֶיךָ תִּרְדּוֹף נַפְשִׁי: וְכָל
הַחוֹשְׁבִים עָלַי רָעָה מְהֵרָה הָפֵר עֲצָתָם וְקַלְקֵל
מַחֲשַׁבְתָּם. לְמַעַן יֵחָלְצוּן יְדִידֶיךָ הוֹשִׁיעָה יְמִינְךָ
וַעֲנֵנִי: יִהְיוּ לְרָצוֹן אִמְרֵי פִי וְהֶגְיוֹן לִבִּי לְפָנֶיךָ יְיָ
צוּרִי וְגוֹאֲלִי:

(Congregation rises)

Reader, then Congregation

אָבִינוּ מַלְכֵּנוּ. שְׁמַע קוֹלֵנוּ:
אָבִינוּ מַלְכֵּנוּ. חָטָאנוּ לְפָנֶיךָ:
אָבִינוּ מַלְכֵּנוּ. חֲמוֹל עָלֵינוּ וְעַל-עוֹלָלֵינוּ וְטַפֵּנוּ:
אָבִינוּ מַלְכֵּנוּ. כַּלֵּה דֶּבֶר וְחֶרֶב וְרָעָב מֵעָלֵינוּ:
אָבִינוּ מַלְכֵּנוּ. כַּלֵּה כָל-צָר וּמַשְׂטִין מֵעָלֵינוּ:
אָבִינוּ מַלְכֵּנוּ. כָּתְבֵנוּ בְּסֵפֶר חַיִּים טוֹבִים:
אָבִינוּ מַלְכֵּנוּ. חַדֵּשׁ עָלֵינוּ שָׁנָה טוֹבָה:

(Congregation is seated)

READING OF SCRIPTURE

Reader

(Micah 4: 1–4)

In the end of days it shall come to pass, that the mountain of the Lord's house shall be established as the top of the mountains, and it shall be exalted above the hills; and peoples shall flow unto it. And many nations shall go and say: Come ye, and let us go up to the mountain of the Lord, and to the house of the God of Jacob; and He will teach us of His ways, and we will walk in His paths; for out of Zion shall go forth the law, and the word of the Lord from Jerusalem. And He shall judge between many peoples, and shall decide concerning mighty nations afar off; and they shall beat their swords into plowshares, and their spears into pruning-hooks; nation shall not lift up sword against nation, neither shall they learn war any more. But they shall sit every man under his vine and under his fig-tree; and none shall make them afraid, for the mouth of the Lord of hosts hath spoken.

Choir

Lift up your heads, O ye gates, and be ye lifted up, ye everlasting doors, for the King of glory shall enter. Who is the King of glory? The Lord of hosts, He is the King of glory.	שְׂאוּ שְׁעָרִים רָאשֵׁיכֶם. וּשְׂאוּ פִּתְחֵי עוֹלָם. וְיָבֹא מֶלֶךְ הַכָּבוֹד: מִי הוּא זֶה מֶלֶךְ הַכָּבוֹד. יְיָ צְבָאוֹת. הוּא מֶלֶךְ הַכָּבוֹד סֶלָה:

(Congregation rises)
Reader, then Choir

The Lord, the Lord God, is merciful and gracious, long-suffering and abundant in goodness and ever-true; keeping mercy for thousands, forgiving iniquity, transgression and sin.

יְהוָֹה יְהוָֹה אֵל רַחוּם
וְחַנּוּן אֶרֶךְ אַפַּיִם וְרַב־
חֶסֶד וֶאֱמֶת. נוֹצֵר חֶסֶד
לָאֲלָפִים. נ שֵׂא עָוֹן וָפֶשַׁע
וְחַטָּאָה:

TAKING THE SCROLL FROM THE ARK

Reader

Let us declare the greatness of our God and render honor unto the Torah.

הָבוּ גֹדֶל לֵאלֹהֵינוּ
וּתְנוּ כָבוֹד לַתּוֹרָה.

Congregation and Choir

Praised be He who in His holiness has given the Torah unto Israel.

בָּרוּךְ שֶׁנָּתַן תּוֹרָה
לְעַמּוֹ יִשְׂרָאֵל בִּקְדֻשָּׁתוֹ:

Reader

O house of Jacob, let us walk in the light of the Lord.

בֵּית יַעֲקֹב לְכוּ וְנֵלְכָה
בְּאוֹר יְהוָֹה:

Congregation and Reader, then Choir

Hear, O Israel: The Lord, our God, the Lord is One.

שְׁמַע יִשְׂרָאֵל יְהוָֹה
אֱלֹהֵינוּ יְהוָֹה אֶחָד:

(Congregation is seated)

Choir

Thine, O Lord, is the greatness, and the power, the glory, and the victory, and the majesty; for all that is in the heaven and in the earth is Thine; Thine is the kingdom, O Lord, and Thou art exalted as head above all.

Reader

(Before reading from the Torah)

Praise ye the Lord to whom all praise is due.

Praised be the Lord to whom all praise is due forever and ever.

Praised be Thou, O Lord our God, Ruler of the world, who hast called us from among all peoples and hast given us Thy law. Praised be Thou, O Lord, Giver of the Law.

(Genesis, Chap. xxii)

And it came to pass after these things, that God did prove Abraham, and said unto him, Abraham; and he said, Behold, here am I. And He said, Take now thy son, thine only son Isaac, whom thou lovest, and get thee into the land of Moriah, and offer him there for a burnt-offering upon one of the mountains which I will tell thee of. And Abraham rose up early in the morning, saddled his ass, and took two of his young men with him, and Isaac, his son; and he cleaved the wood for a burnt-offering, and rose up, and went unto

Choir

לְךָ יְיָ הַגְּדֻלָּה וְהַגְּבוּרָה. וְהַתִּפְאֶרֶת וְהַגֵּצַח וְהַהוֹד
כִּי־כֹל בַּשָּׁמַיִם וּבָאָרֶץ. לְךָ יְיָ הַמַּמְלָכָה וְהַמִּתְנַשֵּׂא
לְכֹל לְרֹאשׁ:

Reader

(Before reading the Torah)

בָּרְכוּ אֶת־יְיָ הַמְבֹרָךְ:

בָּרוּךְ יְיָ הַמְבֹרָךְ לְעוֹלָם וָעֶד:

בָּרוּךְ אַתָּה יְיָ אֱלֹהֵינוּ מֶלֶךְ הָעוֹלָם. אֲשֶׁר בָּחַר־
בָּנוּ מִכָּל־הָעַמִּים וְנָתַן לָנוּ אֶת־תּוֹרָתוֹ. בָּרוּךְ
אַתָּה יְיָ נוֹתֵן הַתּוֹרָה:

(בראשית כב)

וַיְהִי אַחַר הַדְּבָרִים הָאֵלֶּה וְהָאֱלֹהִים נִסָּה אֶת־
אַבְרָהָם וַיֹּאמֶר אֵלָיו אַבְרָהָם וַיֹּאמֶר הִנֵּנִי: וַיֹּאמֶר
קַח־נָא אֶת־בִּנְךָ אֶת־יְחִידְךָ אֲשֶׁר־אָהַבְתָּ אֶת־
יִצְחָק וְלֶךְ־לְךָ אֶל־אֶרֶץ הַמֹּרִיָּה וְהַעֲלֵהוּ שָׁם
לְעֹלָה עַל אַחַד הֶהָרִים אֲשֶׁר אֹמַר אֵלֶיךָ: וַיַּשְׁכֵּם
אַבְרָהָם בַּבֹּקֶר וַיַּחֲבֹשׁ אֶת־חֲמֹרוֹ וַיִּקַּח אֶת־שְׁנֵי
נְעָרָיו אִתּוֹ וְאֵת יִצְחָק בְּנוֹ וַיְבַקַּע עֲצֵי עֹלָה וַיָּקָם

the place of which God had told him. On the third day, Abraham lifted up his eyes, and saw the place afar off. And Abraham said unto his young men, Abide ye here with the ass, and I and the lad will go yonder, and we will worship, and come back to you. And Abraham took the wood of the burnt-offering, and laid it upon Isaac, his son; and he took the fire in his hand, and the knife, and they went both of them together. And Isaac spoke unto Abraham, his father, and said, My father; and he said, Here am I, my son. And he said, Behold the fire and the wood; but where is the lamb for a burnt-offering? And Abraham said, God will provide himself a lamb for a burnt-offering, my son: so they went both of them together. And they came to the place which God had told him of; and Abraham built an altar there, and laid the wood in order, and bound Isaac his son, and placed him upon the altar, upon the wood. And Abraham stretched forth his hand, and took the knife to slay his son. And the angel of the Lord called unto him out of heaven, and said, Abraham, Abraham; and he said, Here am I. And he said, Lay not thy hand upon the lad, neither do thou any thing unto him; for now I know that thou fearest God, seeing thou hast not

וַיֵּלֶךְ אֶל־הַמָּקוֹם אֲשֶׁר־אָמַר־לוֹ הָאֱלֹהִים: בַּיּוֹם
הַשְּׁלִישִׁי וַיִּשָּׂא אַבְרָהָם אֶת־עֵינָיו וַיַּרְא אֶת־הַמָּקוֹם
מֵרָחֹק: וַיֹּאמֶר אַבְרָהָם אֶל־נְעָרָיו שְׁבוּ־לָכֶם פֹּה
עִם־הַחֲמוֹר וַאֲנִי וְהַנַּעַר נֵלְכָה עַד־כֹּה וְנִשְׁתַּחֲוֶה
וְנָשׁוּבָה אֲלֵיכֶם: וַיִּקַּח אַבְרָהָם אֶת־עֲצֵי הָעֹלָה
וַיָּשֶׂם עַל־יִצְחָק בְּנוֹ וַיִּקַּח בְּיָדוֹ אֶת־הָאֵשׁ וְאֶת־
הַמַּאֲכֶלֶת וַיֵּלְכוּ שְׁנֵיהֶם יַחְדָּו: וַיֹּאמֶר יִצְחָק אֶל־
אַבְרָהָם אָבִיו וַיֹּאמֶר אָבִי וַיֹּאמֶר הִנֶּנִּי בְנִי. וַיֹּאמֶר
הִנֵּה הָאֵשׁ וְהָעֵצִים וְאַיֵּה הַשֶּׂה לְעֹלָה: וַיֹּאמֶר
אַבְרָהָם אֱלֹהִים יִרְאֶה־לּוֹ הַשֶּׂה לְעֹלָה בְּנִי וַיֵּלְכוּ
שְׁנֵיהֶם יַחְדָּו: וַיָּבֹאוּ אֶל־הַמָּקוֹם אֲשֶׁר אָמַר־לוֹ
הָאֱלֹהִים וַיִּבֶן שָׁם אַבְרָהָם אֶת־הַמִּזְבֵּחַ וַיַּעֲרֹךְ אֶת־
הָעֵצִים וַיַּעֲקֹד אֶת־יִצְחָק בְּנוֹ וַיָּשֶׂם אֹתוֹ עַל־
הַמִּזְבֵּחַ מִמַּעַל לָעֵצִים: וַיִּשְׁלַח אַבְרָהָם אֶת־יָדוֹ
וַיִּקַּח אֶת־הַמַּאֲכֶלֶת לִשְׁחֹט אֶת־בְּנוֹ: וַיִּקְרָא אֵלָיו
מַלְאַךְ יְהֹוָה מִן־הַשָּׁמַיִם וַיֹּאמֶר אַבְרָהָם אַבְרָהָם
וַיֹּאמֶר הִנֵּנִי: וַיֹּאמֶר אַל־תִּשְׁלַח יָדְךָ אֶל־הַנַּעַר וְאַל־
תַּעַשׂ לוֹ מְאוּמָה כִּי עַתָּה יָדַעְתִּי כִּי־יְרֵא אֱלֹהִים

withheld thy son, thine only son, from me. And Abraham lifted up his eyes, and looked, and behold, behind him, a ram caught in a thicket by his horns; and Abraham went out and took the ram, and offered him up for a burnt-offering, in the stead of his son. And Abraham called the name of the place: Adonai jireh; as it is said to this day, In the mount where the Lord is seen. And the angel of the Lord called unto Abraham out of heaven a second time, and said, By Myself have I sworn, saith the Lord, because thou hast done this thing, and hast not withheld thy son, thine only son, that I will greatly bless thee, and exceedingly multiply thy seed, as the stars of heaven, and as the sand which is upon the sea-shore; and thy seed shall possess the gates of their enemies; and in thy seed shall all the nations of the earth be blessed; because thou hast obeyed My voice. So Abraham returned to his young men, and they rose up, and went together to Beer-sheba: and Abraham dwelt at Beer-sheba.

אַתָּה וְלֹא חָשַׂכְתָּ אֶת־בִּנְךָ אֶת־יְחִידְךָ מִמֶּנִּי: וַיִּשָּׂא
אַבְרָהָם אֶת־עֵינָיו וַיַּרְא וְהִנֵּה־אַיִל אַחַר נֶאֱחַז
בַּסְּבַךְ בְּקַרְנָיו וַיֵּלֶךְ אַבְרָהָם וַיִּקַּח אֶת־הָאַיִל
וַיַּעֲלֵהוּ לְעֹלָה תַּחַת בְּנוֹ: וַיִּקְרָא אַבְרָהָם שֵׁם־
הַמָּקוֹם הַהוּא יְהוָה יִרְאֶה אֲשֶׁר יֵאָמֵר הַיּוֹם בְּהַר
יְהוָה יֵרָאֶה: וַיִּקְרָא מַלְאַךְ יְהוָה אֶל אַבְרָהָם שֵׁנִית
מִן־הַשָּׁמָיִם: וַיֹּאמֶר בִּי נִשְׁבַּעְתִּי נְאֻם־יְהוָה כִּי יַעַן
אֲשֶׁר עָשִׂיתָ אֶת־הַדָּבָר הַזֶּה וְלֹא חָשַׂכְתָּ אֶת־בִּנְךָ
אֶת־יְחִידֶךָ: כִּי־בָרֵךְ אֲבָרֶכְךָ וְהַרְבָּה אַרְבֶּה אֶת־
זַרְעֲךָ כְּכוֹכְבֵי הַשָּׁמַיִם וְכַחוֹל אֲשֶׁר עַל־שְׂפַת הַיָּם
וְיִרַשׁ זַרְעֲךָ אֵת שַׁעַר אֹיְבָיו: וְהִתְבָּרֲכוּ בְזַרְעֲךָ כֹּל
גּוֹיֵי הָאָרֶץ עֵקֶב אֲשֶׁר שָׁמַעְתָּ בְּקֹלִי: וַיָּשָׁב אַבְרָהָם
אֶל־נְעָרָיו וַיָּקֻמוּ וַיֵּלְכוּ יַחְדָּו אֶל־בְּאֵר שָׁבַע וַיֵּשֶׁב
אַבְרָהָם בִּבְאֵר שָׁבַע:

(After reading from the Torah)

Praised be Thou, O Lord our God, Ruler of the world, who hast given us the law of truth and has implanted within us everlasting life. Praised be Thou, O Lord, Giver of the Law.

(Before reading the Haftarah)

Praised be the Lord our God, for the law of truth and righteousness which He has revealed unto Israel, for the words of the prophets filled with His spirit and for the teachings of the sages whom He raised up aforetime and in these days.

(Reading of the Haftarah)

(After reading from the Torah)

בָּרוּךְ אַתָּה יְיָ אֱלֹהֵינוּ מֶלֶךְ הָעוֹלָם. אֲשֶׁר נָתַן

לָנוּ תּוֹרַת אֱמֶת וְחַיֵּי עוֹלָם נָטַע בְּתוֹכֵנוּ.

בָּרוּךְ אַתָּה יְיָ נוֹתֵן הַתּוֹרָה:

(Before reading from the Haftarah)

בָּרוּךְ אַתָּה יְיָ אֱלֹהֵינוּ מֶלֶךְ הָעוֹלָם אֲשֶׁר בָּחַר

בִּנְבִיאִים טוֹבִים וְרָצָה בְדִבְרֵיהֶם הַנֶּאֱמָרִים בֶּאֱמֶת.

בָּרוּךְ אַתָּה יְיָ הַבּוֹחֵר בַּתּוֹרָה וּבְמֹשֶׁה עַבְדּוֹ

וּבְיִשְׂרָאֵל עַמּוֹ וּבִנְבִיאֵי הָאֱמֶת וָצֶדֶק:

THE HAFTARAH

(I Samuel, Chapter ii, 1–11)

And Hannah prayed and said, My heart rejoiceth in the Lord, mine horn is exalted in the Lord; my mouth is enlarged over mine enemies; because I rejoice in Thy salvation. There is none holy as the Lord: for there is none beside Thee; neither is there any rock like our God. Talk not exceeding proudly; let not arrogance come out of your mouth: for the Lord is a God of knowledge, and by Him actions are weighed. The bows of the mighty men are broken, and they that stumbled are girded with strength. They that were full have hired out themselves for bread; and they that were hungry ceased to want. The Lord ordereth death and giveth life; He bringeth down to the grave, and bringeth up again. The Lord maketh poor, and maketh rich; He bringeth low and lifteth up. He raiseth up the poor out of the dust, and lifteth up the beggar from his low estate, to set them among princes, and to make them inherit the throne of glory. For the pillars of the earth are the Lord's, and He hath set the world upon them. He will keep the feet of the righteous and the wicked shall be silent in darkness; for not by strength shall man prevail. The Lord shall judge the ends of the earth; and He shall give strength unto His king, and exalt the horn of His anointed.

ANOTHER HAFTARAH

(Nehemiah, Chapter viii)

And all the people gathered themselves together as one man into the street that was before the water-gate: and they spake unto Ezra, the scribe, to bring the book of the law of Moses, which the Lord had commanded to Israel. And Ezra, the priest, brought the law before the congregation, both men and women, and all that could hear with understanding, upon the first day of the month of Tishri. And Ezra, the scribe, stood upon a pulpit of wood, which they had made for the purpose. And Ezra opened the book in the sight of all the people; (for he was above all the people) and when he opened it, all the people stood up. And Ezra blessed the Lord, the great God. And all the people answered: Amen, Amen, with lifting up their hands; and they bowed their heads and worshiped the Lord with their faces to the ground. Also Jeshua and the Levites caused the people to understand the law; and the people stood in their place. So they read in the book of the law of God distinctly, and gave the sense, and caused them to understand the reading. And Nehemiah, the cupbearer, and Ezra, the priest, the scribe, and the Levites that taught the people, said unto all the people, This day is holy unto the Lord your God; mourn not, nor weep. For all the people wept when they heard the words of the law. Then he said unto them, Go your way, eat the fat and drink the sweet, and send portions unto them for whom nothing is

prepared: for this day is holy unto our Lord: neither
be ye sorry; for the joy of the Lord is your strength.
So the Levites stilled all the people, saying, Hold your
peace, for the day is holy; neither be ye grieved. And
all the people went their way to eat, and to drink, and
to send portions, and to make great mirth, because
they had understood the words that were declared unto
them.

(After reading the Haftarah)

For the Torah, for the privilege of worship, for the
prophets, and for this day of Memorial, given us for
honor and for glory, let us thank and bless the Lord
our God.

בָּרוּךְ אַתָּה יְיָ אֱלֹהֵינוּ מֶלֶךְ הָעוֹלָם צוּר כָּל־
הָעוֹלָמִים צַדִּיק בְּכָל־הַדּוֹרוֹת הָאֵל הַנֶּאֱמָן הָאוֹמֵר
וְעוֹשֶׂה הַמְדַבֵּר וּמְקַיֵּם שֶׁכָּל־דְּבָרָיו אֱמֶת וָצֶדֶק: ׀
עַל־הַתּוֹרָה וְעַל־הָעֲבוֹדָה וְעַל־הַנְּבִיאִים וְעַל
יוֹם הַזִּכָּרוֹן הַזֶּה שֶׁנָּתַתָּ לָּנוּ יְיָ אֱלֹהֵינוּ אֲנַחְנוּ מוֹדִים
לָךְ וּמְבָרְכִים אוֹתָךְ. יִתְבָּרַךְ שִׁמְךָ בְּפִי כָּל־חַי
תָּמִיד לְעוֹלָם וָעֶד. בָּרוּךְ אַתָּה יְיָ מְקַדֵּשׁ (הַשַּׁבָּת
וְ)יִשְׂרָאֵל וְיוֹם הַזִּכָּרוֹן:

SHOFAR SERVICE

Reader

The stirring sound of the Shofar proclaimed the covenant at Mount Sinai which bound Israel to God as a kingdom of priests and a holy people. Ever since that distant day, the voice of the Shofar has resounded through the habitations of Israel awakening high allegiance to God and His commandments. At the new moon, on joyous festivals as well as on solemn days of fasting and repentance, and in the Jubilee year when liberty was proclaimed throughout the land, our fathers hearkened to the tones of the ram's horn and recalled their obligation to serve the Lord with all their heart and with all their strength. Thus do we, their children, prepare to hearken now to the solemn sound of the Shofar. May it summon us to struggle against the forces of evil within our hearts and in the world. Let it arouse within us the will to righteousness and strengthen our trust in God's justice and love. May it direct our thoughts to the day when the Shofar will sound for the redemption of all mankind.

Congregation and Reader, then Choir

Happy is the people that know the joyful sound; they walk, O Lord, in the light of Thy countenance.

מלכיות

Responsive Reading

Reader

Come, let us bow down and bend the knee; let us kneel
before the Lord our Maker.

Congregation

*O worship the Lord in the beauty of holiness; trem-
ble before Him all the earth.*

Righteousness and justice are the roundation of His
throne; mercy and truth go before Him.

*Thy kingdom is a kingdom for all ages; and Thy
dominion endureth throughout all generations.*

The Lord shall be king over all the earth; in that day
shall the Lord be One and His name One.

*The Lord reigneth, let the earth rejoice; let the multi-
tude of the isles be glad.*

With trumpets and sound of the horn, shout ye before the King, the Lord.

Reader

Almighty God, who can fathom the greatness of Thy
power! What are our works gauged by Thine, O Lord,
who hast meted out the heaven with a span, compre-
hended the dust of the earth in a measure and weighed
the mountains in scales and the hills in a balance?
What are our years compared with Thine, O Lord, who
abidest, though all else perish, and who art ever the
same, though all things change? Thou didst lay the
foundations of the earth. Thou didst command the
sea: Thus far shalt thou come but no further, and here
shall thy proud waves be stayed. When the morning
stars sang together, and the heavenly hosts shouted for

joy, then Thy creative word bade the light to break
through the darkness, and life to issue forth from the
heavens above and the earth beneath.   And as Thou
hast fashioned all things from the beginning, so wilt
Thou sustain and rule them even unto the end.   Thou
are the King of eternity, the immovable rock amidst the
ebb and flow of the ages.   Thy throne is established forever.

Let this truth shine forth triumphantly, that all men
may acknowledge Thee as their King and render homage to Thy holy name, for Thine is the kingdom and
Thy dominion endureth for ever.

Praised art Thou, O
Lord our God, King of
the world, who hast sanc-
tified us by Thy com-
mandments, and com-
manded us to hearken to
the sound of the Shofar.

בָּרוּךְ אַתָּה יְיָ אֱלֹהֵינוּ
מֶלֶךְ הָעוֹלָם אֲשֶׁר קִדְּשָׁנוּ
בְּמִצְוֹתָיו וְצִוָּנוּ לִשְׁמוֹעַ
קוֹל שׁוֹפָר:

Praised art Thou, O
Lord our God, King of
the world, who hast
granted us life, sustained
us, and permitted us to
commemorate this sol-
emn festival.

בָּרוּךְ אַתָּה יְיָ אֱלֹהֵינוּ
מֶלֶךְ הָעוֹלָם שֶׁהֶחֱיָנוּ
וְקִיְּמָנוּ וְהִגִּיעָנוּ לַזְּמַן הַזֶּה:

תְּקִיעָה: שְׁבָרִים: תְּרוּעָה: תְּקִיעָה

(The Shofar is sounded)

Choir

The Lord reigneth, He is clothed with majesty; the
Lord is girded with strength.   Thy throne is established
of old.   Thou art from everlasting to everlasting.

זכרונות

Responsive Reading

Reader

The Lord is our Judge; the Lord is our Lawgiver; the Lord is our King; He will save us.

Congregation

He hath remembered His covenant forever, the word which He commanded to a thousand generations.

He hath made a memorial for His wonderful works; the Lord is gracious and full of compassion.

The Lord is good to all; His tender mercies are over all His works.

The Lord is a God of knowledge; and by Him actions are weighed.

He fashioneth the hearts of all, He considereth all their doings.

As a father hath compassion upon his children, so hath the Lord compassion on them that revere Him.

For He knoweth our frame; He remembereth that we are dust.

Reader

Thou, O Lord, knowest all the works of the past; before Thee all secrets are revealed. Naught is hidden from Thine eyes; there is no forgetfulness before the throne of Thy glory. Thou knowest the events of all times, the generations that were and those that shall be. All our deeds are remembered before Thee. Whether in chastisement or in mercy, Thou directest the destinies of men and nations according to Thy wisdom and justice. Happy the man who forgets Thee not, who finds his strength in Thee, for he who seeks Thee will not stumble, and he who trusts in Thee will not be put to shame.

Remember us in mercy, O Lord, as we enter upon the new year. Judge us in Thy loving kindness and direct our destinies in mercy. As Thou dost remember us in goodness, so may we be mindful of our need for Thee and of our obligation to serve Thee. Kindle within us the faith that Thou art ever near us, so that our souls may be aflame with zeal for Thy law. Let us never forget, O God, that we are bound to Thee by an ancient covenant, and that only through fidelity to this pledge can we be worthy to stand in Thy presence. Grant us the courage, the wisdom and the patience to bring the message of Thy power and Thy love to all Thy children, that every soul may praise Thee, O Thou who rememberest the covenant.

(The Shofar is sounded)

תקיעה: שברים: תקיעה

Choir

For the mountains shall depart, and the hills be removed; but My kindness shall not depart from thee, neither shall My covenant of peace be removed, saith the Lord that hath compassion upon thee.

שופרות

Responsive Reading

Reader
Shout unto the Lord, all the earth; break forth and
sing for joy, yea, sing praises.

Congregation
With trumpets and the sound of the Shofar, shout
ye before the King, the Lord.

Exalted is God amidst joyous shouting, the Lord amidst
the sound of the Shofar.

Sing praises unto God, sing praises; sing praises unto
our King, sing praises.

Blow the Shofar at the new moon, at the full moon for
our feast day.

For it is a statute unto Israel, an ordinance of the
God of Jacob.

Praise Him according to His abundant greatness, praise
Him with the blast of the Shofar.

All ye inhabitants of the world and ye dwellers on
the earth, when an ensign is lifted upon the
mountains, see ye; and when the Shofar is
blown, hear ye.

Reader

O Lord our God, we are reminded now of that great moment when Israel stood at Sinai, and heard the call of the Shofar. Then didst Thou covenant with our fathers that they should become a kingdom of priests and a holy people. Then didst Thou send Israel forth to proclaim those laws by which man shall live and not die.

The echo of that ever-memorable event resounds in the hearts of the men and women of Israel to this very day. We know that this covenant was made not only with our fathers at Sinai, but also with us who stand before Thee this day and with all who are not here this day, even with all the generations that are yet to be. Truly, we live by the power and spirit of that ancient covenant, the remembrance of which comes to us each year when we hear anew the solemn tones of the Shofar. May they rouse us from indolence, from indifference, from selfish ease and summon us to serve under Thy banner of truth and love, of justice and peace.

Fortify our hearts that we may labor willingly and, if need be, suffer cheerfully for the triumph of Thy word. Sustain us with hope that we may confidently await the day when knowledge of Thee shall reach the uttermost parts of the world. O hasten the blessed time when all dwellers on earth shall hearken unto the sound

of the Shofar, and shall worship as one brotherhood **at**
Thy holy mountain.

(The Shofar is sounded)

תקיעה: תרועה: תקיעה גדולה:

Choir

All ye dwellers on earth, when the Shofar is sounded,
hark ye, and when the great trumpet is blown, come **ye**
and worship the Lord at the holy mountain. **The**
Lord of hosts shall be a shield unto you.

PRAYER

Thou, who art the source of all blessings, be with **this congregation** and with all its members, their families and their households; prosper them in their various callings and occupations, help them in their needs, and guide them in their difficulties. Hear Thou the prayers of all who worship here this morning, comfort the sorrowing and cheer the silent sufferers. Bless those who guide and who serve this congregation, and those who contribute to its strength. Reward with the joy of goodness the charitable and the merciful who aid the poor, care for the sick, teach the ignorant, and extend a helping hand to those who have lost their way in the world.

Fervently we invoke Thy blessing upon our country and our nation. Guard them, O God, from calamity and injury; suffer not their adversaries to triumph over them, but let the glories of a just, righteous and God-fearing people increase from age to age. Enlighten with Thy wisdom and sustain with Thy power those whom the people have set in authority, the President, his counselors, and advisers, the judges, law-givers and executives, and all who are entrusted with our safety and with the guardianship of our rights and our liberties. May peace and good-will obtain among all the inhabitants of our land; may religion spread its blessings among us and exalt our nation in righteousness. **Amen.**

RETURNING THE SCROLL TO THE ARK

(Congregation rises)

Reader

O magnify the Lord with me and let us exalt His name together.

גַּדְּלוּ לַיְיָ אִתִּי. וּנְרוֹמְמָה שְׁמוֹ יַחְדָּו:

Choir

His glory is in the earth and in the heavens. He is the strength of all His servants, the praise of them that truly love Him, the hope of Israel, the people He brought nigh to Himself. Hallelujah.

הוֹדוֹ עַל־אֶרֶץ וְשָׁמָיִם: וַיָּרֶם קֶרֶן לְעַמּוֹ תְּהִלָּה לְכָל־חֲסִידָיו לִבְנֵי יִשְׂרָאֵל עַם קְרֹבוֹ הַלְלוּיָהּ:

Reader

The law of the Lord is perfect, restoring the soul; the testimony of the Lord is sure, making wise the simple. The precepts of the Lord are right, rejoicing the heart; the judgments of the

תּוֹרַת יְיָ תְּמִימָה. מְשִׁיבַת נָפֶשׁ. עֵדוּת יְיָ נֶאֱמָנָה. מַחְכִּימַת פֶּתִי: פִּקּוּדֵי יְיָ יְשָׁרִים. מְשַׂמְּחֵי לֵב. מִשְׁפְּטֵי יְיָ אֱמֶת.

Lord are true; they are righteous altogether. Behold, a good doctrine has been given unto you; forsake it not.

צָדְקוּ יַחְדָּו: כִּי לֶקַח טוֹב נָתַתִּי לָכֶם תּוֹרָתִי אַל־תַּעֲזֹבוּ:

(Congregation is seated)

Choir

It is a tree of life to them that hold fast to it, and its supporters are happy. Its ways are ways of pleasantness, and all its paths are peace.

עֵץ חַיִּים הִיא לַמַּחֲזִיקִים בָּהּ וְתוֹמְכֶיהָ מְאֻשָּׁר: דְּרָכֶיהָ דַרְכֵי־נֹעַם וְכָל־נְתִיבוֹתֶיהָ שָׁלוֹם:

Turn Thou us unto Thee, O Lord, and we shall be restored; renew our days as of old.

הֲשִׁיבֵנוּ יְיָ אֵלֶיךָ וְנָשׁוּבָה חַדֵּשׁ יָמֵינוּ כְּקֶדֶם:

HYMN

SERMON

HYMN

ADORATION

(Congregation rises)

Congregation and Reader

Let us adore the ever-living God, and render praise unto Him who spread out the heavens and established the earth, whose glory is revealed in the heavens above and whose greatness is manifest throughout the world. He is our God; there is none else.

We bow the head in reverence, and worship the King of kings, the Holy One, praised be He.

Choir and Congregation

וַאֲנַחְנוּ כֹּרְעִים וּמִשְׁתַּחֲוִים וּמוֹדִים לִפְנֵי מֶלֶךְ
מַלְכֵי הַמְּלָכִים הַקָּדוֹשׁ בָּרוּךְ הוּא:

(Congregation is seated)

Reader

May the time not be distant, O God, when Thy name shall be worshiped in all the earth, when unbelief shall disappear and error be no more. We fervently pray that the day may come when all men shall invoke Thy name, when corruption and evil shall give way to purity and goodness, when superstition shall no longer enslave the mind, nor idolatry blind the eye, when all who dwell on earth shall know that to Thee alone every knee must bend and every tongue give homage. O may all, created in Thine image, recognize that they are brethren, so that, one in spirit and one in fellowship, they may be forever united before Thee. Then shall Thy kingdom be established on earth and the word of Thine ancient seer be fulfilled: The Lord will reign forever and ever.

Congregation (or Choir)

On that day the Lord shall be One and His name shall be One.

בַּיּוֹם הַהוּא יִהְיֶה יְיָ אֶחָד וּשְׁמוֹ אֶחָד:

Reader

Thou, O Lord, dost give us dear ones and make them the strength of our life, the light of our eyes. They depart from us and leave us bereaved on a lonely way but Thou are the living fountain whence our healing flows. Unto Thee the stricken look for comfort and the sorrow-laden for consolation. On this solemn day of the New Year, we see life as through windows that open on eternity. We see that love abides, the soul abides, as Thou, O God, dost abide forever. We see that our years are more than grass that withers, more than flowers that fade. They weave a pattern of life that is timeless and unite us with a world that is from end to end the abode of Thy love and the vesture of Thy glory. In life and in death we cannot go where Thou art not, and where Thou art, all is well. Sustained by this assurance we praise Thy name, Almighty God:

(Mourners rise)

Reader

Extolled and hallowed be the name of God throughout the world which He has created according to His will. And may He speedily establish His kingdom of righteousness on earth. Amen.

Congregation

Praised be His glorious name unto all eternity.

Reader

Praised and glorified be the name of the Holy One, though He be above all the praises which we can utter. Our guide is He in life and our redeemer through all eternity.

Congregation

Our help cometh from Him, the creator of heaven and earth.

Reader

The departed whom we now remember have entered into the peace of life eternal. They still live on earth in the acts of goodness they performed and in the hearts of those who cherish their memory. May the beauty of their life abide among us as a loving benediction.

Congregation: Amen.

Reader

May the Father of peace send peace to all who mourn, and comfort all the bereaved among us.

Congregation: Amen.

(Mourners are seated)

(Mourners rise)

Reader

יִתְגַּדַּל וְיִתְקַדַּשׁ שְׁמֵהּ רַבָּא. בְּעָלְמָא דִּי־בְרָא
כִרְעוּתֵהּ. וְיַמְלִיךְ מַלְכוּתֵהּ. בְּחַיֵּיכוֹן וּבְיוֹמֵיכוֹן
וּבְחַיֵּי דְכָל בֵּית יִשְׂרָאֵל. בַּעֲגָלָא וּבִזְמַן קָרִיב.
וְאִמְרוּ אָמֵן:

Congregation

יְהֵא שְׁמֵהּ רַבָּא מְבָרַךְ לְעָלַם וּלְעָלְמֵי עָלְמַיָּא:

Reader

יִתְבָּרַךְ וְיִשְׁתַּבַּח וְיִתְפָּאַר וְיִתְרוֹמַם וְיִתְנַשֵּׂא
וְיִתְהַדָּר וְיִתְעַלֶּה וְיִתְהַלָּל שְׁמֵהּ דְּקוּדְשָׁא. בְּרִיךְ
הוּא. לְעֵלָּא מִן כָּל בִּרְכָתָא וְשִׁירָתָא. תֻּשְׁבְּחָתָא
וְנֶחָמָתָא. דַּאֲמִירָן בְּעָלְמָא. וְאִמְרוּ אָמֵן:

עַל יִשְׂרָאֵל וְעַל צַדִּיקַיָּא. וְעַל־כָּל־מַן דְּאִתְפְּטַר
מִן עָלְמָא הָדֵין כִּרְעוּתֵהּ דֶּאֱלָהָא. יְהֵא לְהוֹן
שְׁלָמָא רַבָּא וְחִנָּא וְחִסְדָּא מִן־קֳדָם מָרֵא שְׁמַיָּא
וְאַרְעָא. וְאִמְרוּ אָמֵן:

יְהֵא שְׁלָמָא רַבָּא מִן־שְׁמַיָּא וְחַיִּים. עָלֵינוּ וְעַל־
כָּל־יִשְׂרָאֵל. וְאִמְרוּ אָמֵן:

עֹשֶׂה שָׁלוֹם בִּמְרוֹמָיו. הוּא יַעֲשֶׂה שָׁלוֹם עָלֵינוּ
וְעַל־כָּל־יִשְׂרָאֵל. וְאִמְרוּ אָמֵן:

(Mourners are seated)

HYMN

All the world shall come to serve Thee,
And bless Thy glorious name,
And Thy righteousness triumphant
The islands shall acclaim.
Yea, the peoples shall go seeking,
Who knew Thee not before,
And the ends of earth shall praise Thee,
And tell Thy greatness o'er.

They shall build for Thee their altars,
Their idols over-thrown,
And their graven gods shall shame them
As they turn to Thee alone.
They shall worship Thee at sunrise
And feel Thy kingdom's might
And impart Thy understanding,
To those astray in night.

With the coming of Thy kingdom
The hills will shout with song,
And the islands laugh exultant,
That they to God belong.
And through all Thy congregations,
So loud Thy praise shall ring,
That the utmost peoples, hearing,
Shall hail Thee crowned King.

BENEDICTION

HYMN

וְיֶאֱתָיוּ כֹל לְעָבְדֶּךָ. וִיבָרְכוּ שֵׁם כְּבוֹדֶךָ.
וְיַגִּידוּ בָאִיִּים צִדְקֶךָ. וְיִדְרְשׁוּךָ עַמִּים לֹא יְדָעוּךָ.
וִיהַלְלוּךָ כָּל־אַפְסֵי אָרֶץ. וְיֹאמְרוּ תָמִיד יִגְדַּל יְיָ.
וְיִזְנְחוּ אֶת עֲצַבֵּיהֶם. וְיַחְפְּרוּ עִם פְּסִילֵיהֶם. וְיַטּוּ
שְׁכֶם אֶחָד לְעָבְדֶּךָ. וְיִירָאוּךָ עִם שֶׁמֶשׁ מְבַקְשֵׁי
פָנֶיךָ. וְיַכִּירוּ כֹּחַ מַלְכוּתֶךָ. וִילַמְּדוּ תוֹעִים בִּינָה.
וִימַלְלוּ אֶת־גְּבוּרָתֶךָ. וִינַשְּׂאוּךָ מִתְנַשֵּׂא לְכֹל
לְרֹאשׁ. וִיסַלְּדוּ בְחִילָה פָנֶיךָ. וִיעַטְּרוּךָ נֵזֶר
תִּפְאָרָה. וְיִפְצְחוּ הָרִים רִנָּה. וְיִצְהֲלוּ אִיִּים
בְּמָלְכֶךָ. וִיקַבְּלוּ עֹל מַלְכוּתְךָ עֲלֵיהֶם. וִירוֹמְמוּךָ
בִּקְהַל עָם. וְיִשְׁמְעוּ רְחוֹקִים וְיָבֹאוּ. וְיִתְּנוּ לְךָ
כֶּתֶר מְלוּכָה:

BENEDICTION

SELECTIONS FROM THE BIBLE AND LATER JEWISH LITERATURE

(To be read on Day of Atonement as time will permit)

From the Bible

I

(Isaiah i, 1–20)

The vision of Isaiah, the son of Amoz, which he saw concerning Judah and Jerusalem, in the days of Uzziah, Jotham, Ahaz, and Hezekiah, kings of Judah. Hear, O heavens, and give ear, O earth, for the Lord hath spoken; children I have reared, and brought up, and they have rebelled against Me. The ox knoweth his owner, and the ass his master's crib; but Israel doth not know, My people doth not consider. Ah sinful nation, a people laden with iniquity, a seed of evil-doers, children that deal corruptly; they have forsaken the Lord, they have contemned the Holy One of Israel, they are turned away backward. On what part will ye be yet stricken, seeing ye stray away more and more? The whole head is sick, and the whole heart faint; from the sole of the foot even unto the head there is no soundness in it; but wounds, and bruises, and festering sores: they have not been pressed, neither bound up, neither mollified with oil. Your country is desolate; your cities are burned with fire; your land, strangers devour it in your presence, and it is desolate, as overthrown by floods. And the daughter of Zion is left as a booth in a vineyard, as a lodge in a garden of cucumbers, as a besieged city. Except the Lord of hosts had left unto us a very small remnant, we should have been as Sodom, we should have been like unto Gomorrah. Hear the word of the Lord, ye rulers of Sodom; give ear unto the law of our God, ye people of Gomorrah. To what purpose is the multitude of your sacrifices unto Me? saith the Lord; I am full of the burnt offerings of rams, and the fat of fed beasts; and I delight not in the blood of bullocks, or of lambs, or of he goats.

When ye come to appear before Me, who hath required this at your hand to trample My courts? Bring no more vain oblations; it is an offering of abomination unto Me; new moon and sabbath, the holding of convocations, I cannot endure iniquity along with the solemn assembly. Your new moons and your appointed seasons my soul hateth, they are a burden unto Me; I am weary to bear them. And when ye spread forth your hands, I will hide Mine eyes from you; yea, when ye make many prayers, I will not hear; your hands are full of blood. Wash you, make you clean, put away the evil of your doings from before Mine eyes, cease to do evil, learn to do well; seek justice, relieve the oppressed, judge the fatherless, plead for the widow. Come now, and let us reason together, saith the Lord; though your sins be as scarlet, they shall be as white as snow; though they be red like crimson, they shall be as wool. If ye be willing and obedient, ye shall eat the good of the land; but if ye refuse and rebel, ye shall be devoured with the sword; for the mouth of the Lord hath spoken.

II

Let me sing of my well-beloved, a song of my beloved touching his vineyard. My well-beloved had a vineyard in a very fruitful hill; and he digged it, and cleared it of stones, and planted it with the choicest vine, and built a tower in the midst of it, and also hewed out a vat therein; and he looked that it should bring forth grapes, and it brought forth wild grapes. And now, O inhabitants of Jerusalem and men of Judah, judge, I pray you, betwixt me and my vineyard. What could have been done more to my vineyard, that I have not done in it? Wherefore, when I looked that it should bring forth grapes, brought it forth wild grapes? And now come, I will tell you what I will do to my vineyard: I will take away the hedge thereof, and it shall be trodden down and I will lay it waste: it shall not be pruned nor hoed, but there shall come up briers and thorns; I will also command the clouds that they rain no rain upon it. For the vineyard of the Lord of hosts is the house of Israel, and the men of Judah the plant of His delight; and He looked for justice, but behold violence; for righteousness but behold a cry. Woe unto them that join house to house, that lay field to field, till there be no room, and ye be made to dwell alone in the midst of the land. In mine ears said the Lord of hosts: Of a truth many houses shall be desolate, even great and fair, without inhabitant. For ten acres of vineyard shall yield one bath, and the seed of a homer shall yield an ephah. Woe unto them that rise up early in the morning, that they may follow strong drink; that tarry late into the night, till wine inflame them! And the harp and the psaltery, the tabret and the pipe, and wine, are in their feasts; but they regard not the work of the Lord, neither have they considered the operation of His hands. Therefore My people are gone into captivity, for want of knowledge; and their honorable men are famished, and their multitude are parched with thirst. Therefore the nether-world hath enlarged her desire, and opened her mouth without measure; and down goeth their glory, and their tumult and their uproar, and he that rejoiceth among them. And man is bowed down, and man is humbled, and the eyes of the lofty are humbled; but the Lord of hosts is exalted through justice, and God, the Holy One, is sanctified through righteousness. Then shall the lambs feed as in their pasture, and the waste place of the fat ones shall wanderers eat. Woe unto them that draw iniquity with cords of vanity, and sin as it were with a cart rope; that say: Let Him make speed, let Him hasten His work, that we may see it; and let the counsel of the Holy One of Israel draw nigh and come, that we may know it! Woe unto them that call evil good, and good evil; that change darkness into light, and light into darkness; that change bitter into sweet, and sweet into bitter! Woe unto them that are wise in their own eyes, and prudent in their own sight! Woe unto them that are mighty to drink wine, and men of strength to mingle strong drink; that justify the wicked for a reward, and take away the righteousness of the righteous from him! Therefore as the tongue of fire devoureth the stubble, and as the chaff is consumed in the flame, so their root shall be as rottenness, and their blossom shall go up as dust; because they have rejected the law of the Lord of hosts, and condemned the word of the Holy One of Israel. Therefore is the anger of the Lord kindled against His people, and He hath stretched forth His hand against them and hath smitten them, and the hills did tremble, and their carcasses were as refuse in the midst of the streets. For all this His anger is not turned away, but His hand is stretched out still. And He will lift up an ensign to the nations from afar, and will summon them from the end of the earth; and, behold, they shall come with speed swiftly; none shall be weary nor stumble among them; none shall slumber nor sleep; neither shall the girdle of their loins be loosed nor the latchet of their shoes be broken; whose arrows are sharp, and all their bows bent; their horses' hoofs shall be counted like flint, and their wheels like a whirlwind; their roaring shall be like a lion, they shall roar like young lions, yea, they shall roar, and lay hold of the prey, and carry it away safe, and there shall be none to deliver. And they shall roar against them in that day like the roaring of the sea; and if one look unto the land, behold darkness and distress, and the light is darkened in the skies thereof.

III

(Isaiah vi)

In the year that king Uzziah died, I saw the Lord sitting upon a throne high and lifted up, and His train filled the temple. Above Him stood the seraphim; each one had six wings: with twain he covered his face, and with twain he covered his feet, and with twain he did fly. And one called unto another, and said: Holy, holy, holy, is the Lord of hosts; the whole earth is full of His glory. And the posts of the door were moved at the voice of them that called, and the house was filled with smoke. Then said I: Woe is me! for I am undone; because I am a man of unclean lips, and I dwell in the midst of a people of unclean lips; for mine eyes have seen the King, the Lord of hosts.

Then flew unto me one of the seraphim, with a glowing stone in his hand, which he had taken with the tongs from off the altar; and he touched my mouth with it, and said: Lo, this hath touched thy lips; and thine iniquity is taken away, and thy sin expiated. And I heard the voice of the Lord, saying: Whom shall I send, and who will go for us? Then I said: Here am I; send me. And He said: Go, and tell this people: Hear ye indeed, but understand not; and see ye indeed, but perceive not. Make the heart of this people fat, and make their ears heavy, and shut their eyes, lest they, seeing with their eyes, and hearing with their ears, and understanding with their heart, return, and be healed. Then said I: Lord, how long? and He answered: Until cities be waste without inhabitant and houses without man, and the land become utterly waste, and the Lord have removed men far away, and the forsaken places be many in the midst of the land. And if there be yet a tenth in it, it shall again be eaten up; as a terebinth, and as an oak, whose stock remaineth, when they cast their leaves, so the holy seed shall be the stock thereof.

(Isaiah xlii, 1–7; lxi, 1–4, 8–11)

Behold My servant, whom I uphold; Mine elect, in whom My soul delighteth; I have put My spirit upon him; he shall make the right to go forth to the nations. He shall not cry, nor lift up, nor cause his voice to be heard in the street. A bruised reed shall he not break, and the dimly burning wick shall he not quench; he shall make the right to go forth according to the truth. He shall not fail nor be crushed, till he have set the right in the earth; and the isles shall wait for his teaching. Thus saith God the Lord, He that created the heavens, and stretched them forth, He that spread forth the earth and that which cometh out of it; He that giveth breath unto the people upon it, and spirit to them that walk therein: I, the Lord, have called thee in righteousness, and have taken hold of thy hand, and kept thee, and set thee for a covenant of the people, for a light of the nations; to open the blind eyes, to bring out the prisoners from the dungeon, and them that sit in darkness out of the prison-house.

The spirit of the Lord God is upon me; because the Lord hath anointed me to bring good tidings unto the humble; He hath sent me to bind up the brokenhearted, to proclaim liberty to the captives, and the opening of the eyes to them that are bound; to proclaim the year of the Lord's good pleasure, and the day of vengeance of our God; to comfort all that mourn; to appoint unto them that mourn in Zion, to give unto them a garland for ashes, the oil of joy for mourning, the mantle of praise for the spirit of heaviness, that they might be called terebinths of righteousness, the planting of the Lord, wherein He might glory. And they shall build the old wastes, they shall raise up the former desolations, and they shall renew the waste cities, the desolations of many generations.

For I the Lord love justice, I hate robbery with iniquity, and I will give them their recompense in truth, and I will make an everlasting covenant with them. And their seed shall be known among the nations, and their offspring among the peoples; all that see them shall acknowledge them, that they are the seed which the Lord hath blessed.

I will greatly rejoice in the Lord, my soul shall be joyful in my God; for He hath clothed me with the garments of salvation, He hath covered me with the robe of victory, as a bridegroom putteth on a priestly diadem, and as a bride adorneth herself with her jewels. For as the earth bringeth forth her growth, and as the garden causeth the things that are sown in it to spring forth; so the Lord God will cause victory and glory to spring forth before all the nations.

IV

(Jeremiah xxix–xxxi–xxxiii)

Now these are the words of the letter that Jeremiah
the prophet sent from Jerusalem unto the residue of
the leaders of the captivity, and to the priests, and to
the prophets, and to all the people, whom Nebuchad-
nezzar had carried away captive from Jerusalem to
Babylon. Build ye houses, and dwell in them, and
plant gardens, and eat the fruit of them; take ye wives,
and beget sons and daughters; and take wives for your
sons, and give your daughters to husbands, and multiply ye there, and be not diminished. And seek the
peace of the city whither I have caused you to be carried away captive, and pray unto the Lord for it; for
in the peace thereof shall ye have peace.

For thus saith the Lord of hosts, the God of Israel:
Let not your prophets that are in the midst of you,
and your diviners, beguile you, neither hearken ye to
your dreams which ye cause to be dreamed. For they
prophesy falsely unto you in My name; I have not sent
them, saith the Lord. For thus saith the Lord: After
seventy years are accomplished for Babylon, I will remember you, and perform My good word toward you,
in causing you to return to this place, for I know the
thoughts that I think toward you, saith the Lord,
thoughts of peace, and not of evil, to give you a future
and a hope. And ye shall call upon Me, and I will
hearken unto you. And ye shall seek Me, and find Me,
when ye shall search for Me with all your heart. And
I will be found of you, saith the Lord, and I will turn

your captivity, and gather you from all the nations, and from all the places whither I have driven you, saith the Lord; and I will bring you back unto the place whence I caused you to be carried away captive. Behold the days come, saith the Lord, that I will make a new covenant with the house of Israel, and with the house of Judah. This is the covenant that I will make with the house of Israel after those days, saith the Lord; I will put My law in their inward parts, and in their heart will I write it; and I will be their God, and they shall be My people; and they shall teach no more every man his neighbor, saying: Know the Lord; for they shall all know Me, from the least of them unto the greatest of them, saith the Lord; for I will forgive their iniquity, and their sin will I remember no more.

Thus saith the Lord: Yet again there shall be heard in this place, the voice of joy and the voice of gladness, the voice of the bridegroom and the voice of the bride, the voice of them that say: Give thanks to the Lord of hosts, for the Lord is good, for His mercy endureth forever.

V

(Ezekiel xviii)

And the word of the Lord came unto me, saying: What mean ye, that ye use this proverb in the land of Israel, saying: The fathers have eaten sour grapes, and the children's teeth are set on edge? As I live, saith the Lord God, ye shall not have occasion any more to use this proverb in Israel. Behold, all souls are Mine;

as the soul of the father, so also the soul of the son is Mine; the soul that sinneth, it shall die.

But if a man be just, and do that which is lawful and right, and hath not wronged any, but hath restored his pledge for a debt, hath taken nought by robbery, hath given his bread to the hungry, and hath covered the naked with a garment; he that hath not given forth upon interest, neither hath taken any increase, that hath withdrawn his hand from iniquity, hath executed true justice between man and man, hath walked in My statutes, and hath kept Mine ordinances, to deal truly; he is just, he shall surely live, saith the Lord God.

If he beget a son that is a robber, a shedder of blood, and that doeth to a brother any of these things, hath wronged the poor and needy; hath taken by robbery, hath not restored the pledge, and hath lifted up his eyes to the idols, hath committed abomination, hath given forth upon interest, and hath taken increase; shall he then live? He shall not live—he hath done all these abominations; he shall surely be put to death, his blood shall be upon him.

Now, lo, if he beget a son, that seeth all his father's sins which he hath done, and considereth, and doeth not such like, he shall not die for the iniquity of his father, he shall surely live. As for his father, because he cruelly oppressed, committed robbery on his brother, and did that which is not good among his people, behold, he dieth for his iniquity. Yet say ye: Why doth not the son bear the iniquity of the father with him? When the son hath done that which is lawful and right, and hath kept all My statutes, and hath done them, he shall surely live. The soul that sinneth, it shall die; the son shall not bear the iniquity of the father with him, neither shall the father bear the iniquity of the son with him; the righteousness of the righteous shall be upon him, and the wickedness of the wicked shall be upon him.

But if the wicked turn from all his sins that he hath committed, and keep all My statutes, and do that which is lawful and right, he shall surely live, he shall not die. When the righteous man turneth away from his righteousness, and committeth iniquity, he shall die therefor; for his iniquity that he hath done shall he die. Again when the wicked man turneth away from his wickedness that he hath committed, and doeth that which is lawful and right, he shall save his soul alive. Because he considereth and turneth away from all his transgressions that he hath committed, he shall surely live; he shall not die. Yet saith the house of Israel: The way of the Lord is not equal. O house of Israel, is it My ways that are not equal? Is it not your ways that are unequal? Therefore I will judge you, O house of Israel, every one according to his ways, saith the Lord God. Return ye, and turn yourselves from all your transgressions; so shall they not be a stumbling-block of iniquity unto you. Cast away from you all your transgressions, wherein ye have transgressed; and make you a new heart and a new spirit; for why will ye die, O house of Israel? For I have no pleasure in the death of him that dieth, saith the Lord God; wherefore turn yourselves, and live.

VI

(From Malachi)

A son honoreth his father, and a servant his master; if then I be a father, where is My honor? and if I be a master where is My fear? saith the Lord of hosts unto you, O priests, that despise My name. Know then that I have sent this commandment unto you, that My covenant might be with Levi, saith the Lord of hosts. My covenant was with him of life and peace, and I gave them to him, and of fear and he feared Me, and was afraid of My name. The law of truth was in his mouth, and unrighteousness was not found in his lips; he walked with me in peace and uprightness, and did turn many away from iniquity. For the priest's lips should keep knowledge, and they should seek the law at his mouth; for he is the messenger of the Lord of hosts. But ye are turned aside out of the way; ye have caused many to stumble in the law; ye have corrupted the covenant of Levi, saith the Lord of hosts. Therefore have I also made you contemptible and base before all the people, according as ye have not kept My ways, but have had respect of persons in the law. Have we not all one father? Hath not one God created us? Why do we deal treacherously every man against his brother, profaning the covenant of our fathers?

Remember ye the law of Moses My servant, which I commanded unto him in Horeb for all Israel, even statutes and ordinances. Behold, I will send you Elijah the prophet before the coming of the great and terrible day of the Lord. And he shall turn the heart of the fathers to the children, and the heart of the children to their fathers.

VII

(Job xxv–xxvi)

Dominion and fear are with Him; He maketh peace in His high places. Is there any number of His armies? And upon whom doth not His light arise?

The shades tremble beneath the waters and the inhabitants thereof. He stretcheth out the north over empty space, and hangeth the earth over nothing. He bindeth up the waters in His thick clouds; and the cloud is not rent under them. He closeth in the face of His throne, and spreadeth His cloud upon it. He hath described a boundary upon the face of the waters, unto the confines of light and darkness. The pillars of heaven tremble and are astonished at His rebuke. He stirreth up the sea with His power; by His breath the heavens are serene. Lo, these are but the outskirts of His ways; and how small a whisper is heard of Him! But the thunder of His mighty deeds who can understand?

VIII

(Job xxviii)

Man setteth an end to darkness, and searcheth out to the furthest bound the stones of thick darkness and of the shadow of death. He breaketh open a shaft away from where men sojourn; they are forgotten of the foot that passeth by; they hang afar from men, they swing to and fro. As for the earth, out of it cometh bread, and underneath it is turned up as it were by fire. The stones thereof are the place of sapphires, and it hath dust of gold. That path no bird of prey knoweth, neither hath the falcon's eye seen it; the proud beasts have not trodden it, nor hath the lion passed thereby.

He putteth forth his hand upon the flinty rock; he overturneth the mountains by the roots. He cutteth out channels among the rocks and his eye seeth every precious thing. He bindeth the streams that they trickle not; and the thing that is hid bringeth he forth to light.

But wisdom, where shall it be found? And where is the place of understanding? Man knoweth not the price thereof; neither is it found in the land of the living. The deep saith: It is not in me; and the sea saith: It is not with me. It cannot be gotten for gold. Neither shall silver be weighed for the price thereof. It cannot be valued with the gold of Ophir, with the precious onyx, or the sapphire. Gold and glass cannot equal it; neither shall the exchange thereof be vessels of fine gold. No mention shall be made of coral or of crystal; yea, the price of wisdom is above rubies. The topaz of Ethiopia shall not equal it, neither shall it be valued with pure gold. Whence then cometh wisdom, and where is the place of understanding, seeing it is hid from the eyes of all living, and kept close from the fowls of the air? Destruction and Death say: We have heard a rumor thereof with our ears. God understandeth the way thereof, and He knoweth the place thereof. For He looketh to the ends of the earth, and seeth under the whole heaven; when He maketh a weight for the wind, and meteth out the waters by measure. When He made a decree for the rain, and a way for the storm of thunders; then did He see it, and declare it; He established it, yea, and searched it out. And unto man He said: Behold, the fear of the Lord that is wisdom; and to depart from evil is understanding.

IX

(From Sirach)

The greater thou art, the more thou must humble thyself, then shalt thou find favor before the Lord. My son, make not the needy eyes to wait long, neither provoke a man in his distress. Add not more trouble to a heart that is vexed; reject not the supplication of the afflicted, neither turn away thy face from a poor man. Honor thy father with thy whole heart and forget not the sorrows of thy mother; how canst thou recompense them the things they have done for thee? Kindle not the coal of a sinner lest thou be burnt with the flame of his fire. Why is earth and ashes proud? When a man is dead he shall inherit worms. As the judge of the people is himself, so are his officers, and what manner of man the ruler of the city is, such are all they that dwell therein. Who will justify him that sinneth against his own soul and who will honor him that dishonoreth his own life? Blame not before thou hast examined the truth; understand first and then rebuke. Judge no one blessed before his death. Say not: It is through the Lord I fell away; for thou oughtest not to do the things that He hateth. He that buildeth his house with other men's money is like one that gathereth himself stones for his own tomb. The heart of fools is in their mouth, but the mouth of the wise is in their hearts. Oh, how comely a thing is judgment for gray hairs and for old men to know counsel! Much experience is the crown of old men and the fear of God is their glory. Whether a man be rich or poor, if he have a good heart toward the

Lord, he shall at all times rejoice with a cheerful countenance. Be not as a lion in thy house nor frantic among thy servants.

X

(From Sirach)

Whatsoever is brought upon thee take cheerfully and be patient when thou art brought to a low estate. For gold is tried in fire and acceptable men in adversity. They that fear God will prepare their hearts and humble their souls in His sight, saying: We will fall into His hand and not into the hands of men; for as His majesty is, so is His mercy. Seek not out the things that are too hard for thee, neither search the things that are above thy strength, but that which is commanded thee, think thereupon with reverence; for it is not needful to thee to see things with thine own eyes that are in secret. Be not curious in unnecessary matters, for more things are shown unto thee than men understand. Deliver him that suffereth wrong from the hand of the oppressor, and be not faint-hearted when thou sittest in judgment; observe the opportunity and beware of evil, and be never ashamed when it concerneth the soul; for there is a shame that bringeth sin and there is shame which is glory and grace. Accept no person's authority against thy soul and let no respect of any person cause thee to fall. Refrain not to speak when there is occasion to do good, and hide not thy wisdom; for by speech wisdom shall be known and learning by the word of the tongue. In no wise speak against the truth; but be ashamed of the error of thine ignorance. Be not hasty in thy tongue, whilst thou art slack and remiss in thy deeds. Say not: Who shall control me for my works? I have sinned and what harm hath happened to me? For though the Lord is long suffering yet will He in no wise let thee go unpunished. But neither do thou add sin upon sin and say: His mercy is great, He will be pacified for the multitude of my sins; for mercy and wrath both come from Him and His displeasure rests upon sinners. Let thy life be sincere; be swift to hear the words of the wise and learn from them to give all thine answers with patience. Honor and shame is in the speech and the tongue of man often causeth his fall. Be not known as a whisperer of slander and lie not in wait against thy neighbor with thy tongue.

XI

(From Sirach)

The beginning of pride is when one departeth from God, and his heart is turned away from his Maker. Pride is not made for man nor furious anger for them that are born of woman. Whether a man be rich and of high station, or poor and lowly, his glory is in the fear of the Lord. Great men and judges and potentates shall be honored; yet is there none of them greater than he that feareth the Lord. Forgive thy neighbor the hurt that he hath done unto thee; so shall thy sins also be forgiven when thou prayest. One man beareth hatred against the other, and doth he seek pardon for himself from the Lord? He showeth no mercy to a man who is like himself and doth he ask forgiveness of his own sins? If he that is but flesh, nourish hatred, who will entreat for pardon of his sins? Remember the commandments not to bear malice to thy neighbor; abstain from strife and thou shalt diminish thine own sins. A sinful man disquieteth friends and maketh debate amongst them that are at peace. Have thou patience with a man in poor estate and delay not to show him mercy. There is no riches above a sound body and no joy above the joy of the heart. He that taketh away his neighbor's living slayeth him and he that defraudeth the laborer of his hire is a shedder of blood. He that washeth himself after the touching of a dead body, if he touch it again, what availeth his washing? So is it with a man that fasteth for his sins and goeth again and doeth the same, will his prayer be heard? or what doth his humbling profit him? He that keepeth the law bringeth offerings enough; he that taketh heed to the commandments, a peace offering; he that requiteth a good turn, offereth fine flour; he that giveth alms sacrificeth praise-offering; to forsake unrighteousness is a propitiation. In all thy gifts show a cheerful countenance and dedicate thy tithes with gladness. Fear not the sentence of death; remember them that have been before thee and that come after thee; this is the sentence of the Lord over all flesh. Work thy work betimes and in His time He will give thee thy reward.

From the Talmud

XII

Life is a passing shadow, says the Scripture. Is it the shadow of a tower, or a tree? A shadow that prevails for a while? No, it is the shadow of a bird in his flight—away flies the bird and there is neither bird nor shadow. Repent one day before thy death, said a teacher to his pupils. How do we know the day of death? asked the pupils. Whereupon the teacher rejoined: Since any day may be the day of death, repent every day. A king bade all his servants to a great repast, but did not indicate the hour; some went home and put on their best garments and stood at the door of the palace; others said: There is ample time, the king will let us know beforehand. But the king summoned them of a sudden; and those that came in slovenly garb were turned away in disgrace. Repent today, lest ye be summoned tomorrow. The aim and end of all wisdom are repentance and good works. The truly repentant are more meritorious in the sight of God than the most righteous. One good deed brings another in its train, and the result of sin is sin. The dying benediction of a sage to his disciples was: May your fear of God be as great as your fear of man; as you avoid sin before man so avoid it also before God. A heathen asked Rabban Gamliel: If your God hates idols, why does He not destroy them? Whereupon he answered, Behold, men worship the sun, the moon and the stars; should you destroy this beautiful world on account of the foolish? If your God is a friend of the poor, Rabbi Akiba was asked, why does He not support them? Suppose I, being angry with one of my slaves, he replied, deny him food and drink, and some one gives it to him secretly, would I be pleased? No, answered the other. Suppose you are wroth with your only son and imprison him without food, and some good man takes pity on the child, and saves him from the pangs of hunger, would you be angry with him? Though we be called servants of God, we are also called His children.

XIII

He who gives charity in secret is greater even than Moses. Honor the children of the poor for they devote themselves to the pursuit of learning. Let the honor of thy neighbor be to thee as thine own. Rather let them cast thee into a fiery furnace than put any one to shame publicly. There are three crowns: the crown of the law, of the priesthood, and of royalty; but the crown of a good name excels them all. Iron breaks stone, fire melts iron, water extinguishes fire, the clouds drink up water, a storm dispels clouds, man withstands the storm, fear unmans man, wine removes fear, sleep overcomes wine, and death conquers all, even sleep; but Solomon the wise says: Charity saves from Death. How can you escape sin? By being mindful of three things: whence thou comest, whither thou goest, and to whom thou must give account for all thy deeds; to the King of kings, the All Holy, praised be He. Four shall not enter Paradise: the scoffer, the liar, the hypocrite, and the slanderer. To slander is to murder. He who has the sense of shame will not commit sin readily. There is a great difference between him who is ashamed before his own self and him who is ashamed only before others. It speaks well for a man if he have a keen sense of shame. Contrition in the heart is better far than much torturing of the flesh. He who humiliates himself will be lifted up; he who exalts himself will be humiliated. Honor avoids him who seeks honor; honor comes to him who shuns honor.

From Medieval Jewish Writers

XIV

(From Maimonides)
(12th Century)

Let no one say, lo, I will fulfil the precepts of the Torah, and labor to acquire the wisdom thereof in order that I may obtain all the blessings therein promised, or tha I may acquire eternal life in the world to come; or I will keep myself far from the sins condemned in the Torah, in order that I may be delivered from the penalties therein threatened, or that I may not be cut off from the life hereafter. God is not fittingly served from such motives, for it is fear that then prompts our actions. The service we render Him from fear differs widely from that of the prophets and sages, and though it may be found in those who stand upon the lowest steps of knowledge and virtue, it is excusable only as a preparation for that nobler service which springs from fuller knowledge and has its root in love.

He who serves God from love devotes himself to His law and to the observance of His commandments, and walks in the paths of wisdom, not because of any worldly advantage, nor to protect himself from evil, nor even to inherit good thereafter; he does the right because it is right, though in the end the blessing will not fail him. A very high degree of moral worth is this; not every wise man attains unto it. Such, however, was the distinction of our father Abraham, whom the Holy One, praised be He, called His friend, because he verily served Him from love alone; and after this same ideal He has bidden us to strive in the words: Thou shalt love the Lord thy God. Let but that true love of God fill the heart of man, and it will manifest itself in every duty done by him. The sages of old have said, Say not I will study the Law of God so that I may be called Rabbi and so that I may receive my reward in the world to come. Nay, but to love the Lord thy God with all thy heart, is its own reward. So also the Psalmist declared that man happy who delighteth greatly in God's commandments; that is, the truest happiness does not fall to him who aims at and secures the reward for obeying the commandments, but to him who delights in the commandments themselves, in accordance with the words of one of the ancient sages, Be not like slaves who serve their master for the sake of the reward.

XV

(From Maimonides)
(12th Century)

There are eight degrees or steps in the duty of charity. The first and lowest degree is to give, but with reluctance or regret. This is the gift of the hand, but not of the heart.

The second is, to give cheerfully, but not proportionately to the distress of the sufferer.

The third is, to give cheerfully and proportionately, but not until solicited.

The fourth is, to give cheerfully, proportionately, and even unsolicited; but to put it in the poor man's hand, thereby exciting in him the painful emotion of shame.

The fifth is, to give charity in such a way that the distressed may receive the bounty, and know their benefactor, without their being known to him. Such was the conduct of some of our ancestors, who used to tie up money in the corners of their cloaks, so that the poor might take it unperceived.

The sixth, which rises still higher is to know the objects of our bounty, but remain unknown to them. Such was the conduct of those of our ancestors, who used to convey their charitable gifts into poor people's dwellings; taking care that their own persons and names should remain unknown.

The seventh is still more meritorious, namely to bestow charity in such a way that the benefactor may not know the relieved persons, nor they the name of their benefactors, as was done by our charitable forefathers during the existence of the Temple. For there was in that holy building a place called the Chamber of the Silent, wherein the good deposited secretly whatever their generous hearts suggested, and from which the poor were maintained with equal secrecy.

Lastly, the eighth, and the most meritorious of all, is to anticipate charity, by preventing poverty; namely, to assist the reduced fellowman, either by a considerable gift, or a loan of money, or by teaching him a trade, or by putting him in the way of business, so that he may earn an honest livelihood; and not be forced to the dreadful alternative of holding out his hand for charity. To this Scripture alludes when it says: And if thy brother be waxen poor, and fallen in decay with thee, then thou shalt relieve him; yea, though he be a stranger or a sojourner; that he may live with thee. This is the highest step and the summit of charity's golden ladder.

XVI

(From Bachya Ibn Pakuda)
(11th Century)

Of all things the most necessary to him who would serve God, is trust in God. He who trusts in his own wisdom or capacity, or in the strength of his body, will labor in vain. He will weaken his powers. Trust in wealth may prove the destruction of the soul. He who trusts in God will be led to serve none other than Him, in that he will not build his hopes on men and will not rely, in anxious anticipation, on human beings; he will not serve them, nor curry favor with them. He will not play the hypocrite to please mankind, to the detriment of the service of God; he will have no fear of man nor of human fault-finding, but will be independent, and will doff the livery of human favor and benefaction.

The wealthy man who trusts in God will not find his wealth a hindrance to his faith; for he does not place his reliance upon his wealth, which is, in his eyes, a trust which has been placed in his keeping for a limited period to be used in various appointed ways. He will not be proud, nor will he make mention of his goodness to those to whom he has been commanded to give of his wealth, neither will he look for reward, or thanks, or praise; instead thereof he will render thanks to the Creator who has made him the agent of His beneficence. And if he loses his wealth, he will not be anxious, nor will he mourn, but he will rejoice in his portion, and not seek the injury of any one else, nor envy any other man his wealth.

XVII

(Solomon Ibn Gabirol)
(11th Century)

My thoughts astounded asked me why
Towards the whirling wheels on high
In ecstasy I rush and fly.

The living God is my desire,
It carries me on wings of fire,
Body and soul to Him aspire.

God is at once my joy and fate,
This yearning me He did create,
At thought of Him I palpitate.

Shall song with all its loveliness
Submerge my soul with happiness
Before the God of Gods it bless?

XVIII

(Solomon Ibn Gabirol)
(From the Royal Crown)

Wonderful are thy works, as my soul overwhelmingly knoweth.

Thine, O Lord, are the greatness and the might, the beauty, the triumph, and the splendor.

Thine, O Lord, is the Kingdom, and Thou art exalted as head over all.

Thine are all riches and honor: Thine the creatures of the heights and depths.

They bear witness that they perish, while Thou endurest.

Thine is the might in whose mystery our thoughts can find no stay, so far art Thou beyond us.

In Thee is the veiled retreat of power, the secret and the foundation.

Thine is the name concealed from the sages,

The force that sustaineth the world on naught,

And that can bring to light every hidden thing.

Thine is the loving-kindness that ruleth over all Thy creatures,

And the good treasured up for those who fear Thee.

Thine are the mysteries that transcend understanding and thought.

Thine is the life over which extinction holdeth no sway,

And Thy throne is exalted above every sovereignty,

And Thy habitation hidden in the shrouded height.

Thou art Light celestial, and the eyes of the pure shall
  behold Thee;
But the clouds of sin shall veil Thee from the eyes of
  the sinners.
Thou art Light, hidden in this world but to be revealed
  in the visible world on high.
"On the mount of the Lord shall it be seen."
Light Eternal art Thou, and the eye of the intellect
  longeth and yearneth for Thee.
"Yet only a part shall it see, the whole it shall not
  behold."
Thou art the God of Gods, and the Lord of Lords,
Ruler of beings celestial and terrestrial,
For all creatures are Thy witnesses
And by the glory of this, Thy name, every creature is
  bound to Thy service.
Thou art God, and all things formed are Thy servants
  and worshipers.
Yet is not Thy glory diminished by reason of those
  that worship aught beside Thee,
For the yearning of them all is to draw nigh Thee,
But they are like the blind,
Setting their faces forward on the King's highway,
Yet still wandering from the path.
One sinketh into the well of a pit
And another falleth into a snare,
But all imagine they have reached their desire,
Albeit they have suffered in vain.
But Thy servants are as those walking cleareyed in the
  straight path,

Turning neither to the right nor the left
Till they come to the court of the King's palace.
Thou art God, by Thy Godhead sustaining all that hath
  been formed,
And upholding in Thy Unity all creatures.
Thou art God, and there is no distinction 'twixt Thy
  Godhead and Thy Unity, Thy pre-existence and Thy
  existence,
For 'tis all one mystery.
And although the name of each be different,
Yet they are all proceeding to one place.

XIX

(From R. Meir of Rothenburg)

Lo, as the potter molds his clay,
Shaping and forming it from day to day,
Thus in Thy hand, O Lord, are we,
O Thou whose mercies never pass away.

E'en as the mason hews the stone,
And one is carv'd and wrought, and shattered one,
Thus in Thy hand, O Lord, are we,
Thou who of life and death art Lord alone.

Lo, as amidst the fiery glow
The smith his iron forges blow on blow,
Thus in Thy hand, O Lord, are we,
O Thou who savest those by care laid low.

Lo, as the silver seven times tried
Is in the smelter's furnace purified,
Thus in Thy hand, O Lord, are we,
O Thou who balm and healing scatterest wide.

Services for Day of Atonement

EVENING SERVICE

MORNING SERVICE

AFTERNOON SERVICE

MEMORIAL SERVICE

CONCLUDING SERVICE

THOUGHTS ON YOM KIPPUR

The gates of repentance are always open.

—Pesikta of Rab Kahana, p. 142b

Yet even now, saith the Lord,
Turn ye unto Me with all your heart,
And with fasting, and with weeping, and with lamentation;
And rend your heart, and not your garments,
And turn unto the Lord your God.

—Joel 2: 12–13

Forgive thy neighbor the injury done to thee;
Then, when thou prayest, thy sins will be forgiven.
Shall a man nurse anger against another
And yet seek healing from God?
On a man like himself, he hath no mercy;
And doth he make supplication for his own sins?
He, being flesh, nourisheth wrath;
Who will grant atonement for his sins?
Remember thy latter end, and cease from enmity;
Remember decay and death, and abide in the commandments.

—Sirach 28: 2–6

Rabbi Akiba said: Blessed are ye, O Israel! Before whom are you cleansed, and who purifies you? Your Father in heaven.

—Mishnah Yoma 8: 9

When all within is dark,
    And former friends misprise;
From them I turn to Thee,
    And find love in Thine eyes.

When all within is dark,
    And I my soul despise;
From me I turn to Thee,
    And find love in Thine eyes.

When all Thy face is dark,
    And Thy just angers rise;
From Thee I turn to Thee,
    And find love in Thine eyes.

—Israel Abrahams, Based on Solomon Ibn Gabirol.

When thou prayest, remove all worldly considerations from thy heart. Set thy heart right before God, cleanse thine inmost thoughts and meditate before uttering thy devotions. Act thus all thy days, in all things, and thou wilt not sin. By this course thy deeds will all be upright, and thy prayer pure and devout, and acceptable before the Lord.

—Nahmanides, Ethical Wills, edited by Israel Abrahams, I, p. 98

THE RABBI'S PRAYER

(Immediately after organ prelude, the Rabbi approaches the open Ark,
the congregation standing, and prays:)

Father of mercies, in awe and deep humility, I stand before Thee on this Atonement Eve. In the midst of Thy people who look to me to lead them I approach the holy Ark. I have erred and sinned. Forgive me, I pray Thee. May my people not be put to shame because of me nor I because of them.

In this solemn moment, O God, I lift up mine eyes unto Thee. Help me in the great task to which I have dedicated my life. Show me Thy way, and teach me to lead Thy children nearer to Thee. Help me to find the way to their hearts that I may win them for Thy service.

Heavenly Father, let me hear Thy voice saying: Be strong and of good courage. Give me strength, give me understanding, give me faith, for Thou alone art my hope, O God, my Rock and my Redeemer.

Congregation: Amen.

(Congregation is seated)

HYMN

O come, day of God,
And fill all our spirits
With peace and with gladness from heaven.
From eventide to eventide
Let all earthly thoughts be sanctified
In prayer.
Upward to God, upward to God,
Sons of earth, together!

Lift the voice of prayer and song,
Heavenward borne on the current strong,
Upward all aspire.
In the angel choir
Blend our prayers and praises.

Lord God, see—
See Thou our heart's contrition,
And bow Thine ear.
Hear, O hear, the voice of petition.
Banish our fear,
Blot out our evil ways,
Open the door of grace,
Bid us enter there!

Evening Service for the
Day of Atonement

Choir

(Psalm xcvii, 11)

אוֹר זָרֻעַ לַצַּדִּיק
וּלְיִשְׁרֵי־לֵב שִׂמְחָה:

Light is sown for the
righteous and gladness
for the upright in heart.

Reader

Great and holy God, who inhabitest eternity, Thine everlasting arms uphold the universe and support the lowliest of Thy creatures. In this solemn hour we bring to Thine altar humble hearts and contrite spirits. From eventide to eventide we tarry in Thy courts. We unite with our brethren of the household of Israel in penitence and in prayer and, turning away from worldly pursuits, we direct our souls unto Thee. Thou who probest the heart and knowest our inmost thoughts, help us to examine ourselves in the light of Thy truth. Let neither complacency nor sinfulness separate us from Thy presence.

Life and Light of the world, from of old Thou hast

been our redeemer. Thou art the hope of the prisoner in the dungeon, the help of the storm-tossed at sea, the guide of the wanderer astray in the desert. Free all Thy children from the fetters of tyranny and oppression. Be near, we pray Thee, unto the grief-stricken and afflicted. Endow us with renewed courage to face our tasks unafraid, and strengthen us to do Thy will with perfect hearts.

Reader

(Psalm cxxx)

Out of the depths I cry unto Thee, O Lord, listen to my voice, let Thine ear be attentive to my supplication. If Thou shouldst mark transgressions, O Lord, who shall stand before Thy judgment? But with Thee is forgiveness, that Thou mayest be feared. I wait for the Lord; my soul doth wait, and in His word do I hope. My soul waiteth for the Lord more than they who watch for the morning—I say, more than they who watch for the morning. Let Israel hope in the Lord; for with the Lord there is mercy, and with Him is plenteous redemption. He shall redeem Israel from all his iniquities.

(Congregation rises. The Rabbi takes the scrolls from the ark and hands them to those who assist him, retaining one himself. Returning to the pulpit, the Rabbi reads:)

Reader

All prayers which the children of Israel offer unto Thee, O our Father, that they may depart from sin, from guilt and from wickedness, and follow the ways of Thy Torah, the ways of justice and of righteousness; yea, all the resolutions which we make from this Day of Atonement until the coming Day of Atonement— may they be acceptable before Thee, and may we be given strength to fulfil them. We have come to seek atonement and to ask Thy pardon and forgiveness. Turn us in full repentance unto Thee, and teach us to undo the wrongs which we have committed. Thus will thy great and revered name be sanctified among us.

(Congregation is seated)

כָּל נִדְרֵי

(The Kol Nidre Chant)

Reader

סְלַח־נָא לַעֲוֹן הָעָם הַזֶּה כְּגֹדֶל חַסְדֶּךָ: וְכַאֲשֶׁר
נָשָׂאתָה לָעָם הַזֶּה מִמִּצְרַיִם וְעַד־הֵנָּה:

Forgive, I beseech Thee, the iniquity of this people
according to the greatness of Thy love, even as Thou
hast borne with this people from Egypt until now.

Choir

וַיֹּאמֶר יְהֹוָה סָלַחְתִּי כִּדְבָרֶךָ:

And the Lord said, I have pardoned according to
Thy word.

Reader

בָּרוּךְ אַתָּה יְיָ אֱלֹהֵינוּ מֶלֶךְ הָעוֹלָם. שֶׁהֶחֱיָנוּ
וְקִיְּמָנוּ וְהִגִּיעָנוּ לַזְּמַן הַזֶּה:

Praise be to Thee, O God, Ruler of the world, who
hast granted us life, hast preserved and sustained us
and brought us unto this day.

Choir: Amen.

(Congregation rises)
(The scrolls are returned to the ark. The congregation remains standing:)

Reader

Praise ye the Lord, to whom all praise is due.

Choir and Congregation

Praised be the Lord to whom all praise is due forever and ever.

(Congregation is seated)

Reader

Praised be Thou, O Lord our God, ruler of the world, by whose law the shadows of evening fall and the gates of morn are opened. Thy wisdom established the changes of times and seasons and ordered the ways of the stars in their heavenly courses. The heavens shall vanish like smoke, and the earth shall wax old like a garment; thus, too, they that dwell therein shall die, but Thy salvation shall be forever, and Thy favor shall not fail. O ever living God, Creator of heaven and earth, rule Thou over us forever. Praised be Thou, O Lord, for the day and its work and for the night and its rest.

Congregation and Reader

Infinite as is Thy power so is Thy love. Thou didst manifest it through Israel Thy servant. By laws and commandments, by statutes and ordinances hast Thou led us in the way of righteousness and brought us to the light of truth. Happy are they who are upright in the way, who walk in the law of the Lord. Happy are they who keep His testimonies, who seek Him with a whole heart. Therefore at our lying down and our rising up, let us meditate on Thy teachings and find in Thy laws true life and length of days. O that Thy love may never depart from our hearts. Praised be Thou, O Lord, who hast revealed Thy love through Israel.

(Congregation rises)
(The scrolls are returned to the ark. The congregation remains standing:

Reader

בָּרְכוּ אֶת יְיָ הַמְבֹרָךְ:

Choir and Congregation

בָּרוּךְ יְיָ הַמְבֹרָךְ לְעוֹלָם וָעֶד:

(Congregation is seated)

Reader

בָּרוּךְ אַתָּה יְיָ אֱלֹהֵינוּ מֶלֶךְ הָעוֹלָם. אֲשֶׁר
בִּדְבָרוֹ מַעֲרִיב עֲרָבִים. בְּחָכְמָה פּוֹתֵחַ שְׁעָרִים.
וּבִתְבוּנָה מְשַׁנֶּה עִתִּים וּמַחֲלִיף אֶת הַזְּמַנִּים. וּמְסַדֵּר
אֶת הַכּוֹכָבִים בְּמִשְׁמְרוֹתֵיהֶם בָּרָקִיעַ כִּרְצוֹנוֹ.
בּוֹרֵא יוֹם וָלָיְלָה. יְיָ צְבָאוֹת שְׁמוֹ. אֵל חַי וְקַיָּם
תָּמִיד יִמְלֹךְ עָלֵינוּ לְעוֹלָם וָעֶד. בָּרוּךְ אַתָּה יְיָ
הַמַּעֲרִיב עֲרָבִים:

אַהֲבַת עוֹלָם בֵּית יִשְׂרָאֵל עַמְּךָ אָהָבְתָּ. תּוֹרָה
וּמִצְוֹת חֻקִּים וּמִשְׁפָּטִים אוֹתָנוּ לִמַּדְתָּ. עַל כֵּן יְיָ
אֱלֹהֵינוּ בְּשָׁכְבֵנוּ וּבְקוּמֵנוּ נָשִׂיחַ בְּחֻקֶּיךָ. וְנִשְׂמַח
בְּדִבְרֵי תוֹרָתֶךָ וּבְמִצְוֹתֶיךָ לְעוֹלָם וָעֶד. כִּי הֵם
חַיֵּינוּ וְאֹרֶךְ יָמֵינוּ. וּבָהֶם נֶהְגֶּה יוֹמָם וָלָיְלָה.
וְאַהֲבָתְךָ אַל־תָּסִיר מִמֶּנּוּ לְעוֹלָמִים. בָּרוּךְ אַתָּה
יְיָ אוֹהֵב עַמּוֹ יִשְׂרָאֵל:

(Congregation rises)

Reader

Hear, O Israel: The Lord our God, the Lord is One. Praised be His name whose glorious kingdom is forever and ever.

(Congregation is seated)

Congregation and Reader

Thou shalt love the Lord, thy God, with all thy heart, with all thy soul, and with all thy might. And these words, which I command thee this day, shall be upon thy heart. Thou shalt teach them diligently unto thy children, and shalt speak of them when thou sittest in thy house, when thou walkest by the way, when thou liest down, and when thou risest up. Thou shalt bind them for a sign upon thy hand, and they shall be for frontlets between thine eyes. Thou shalt write them upon the doorposts of thy house and upon thy gates: That ye may remember and do all my commandments and be holy unto your God.

Responsive Reading

Reader
Eternal truth it is that Thou alone art God, and there is none else.

Congregation
Thy righteousness is like the mighty mountains; Thy judgments are like the great deep.

Forever, O Lord, Thy word standeth fast;
Thy faithfulness is unto all generations.
Unless Thy law had been my delight, I should then have perished in mine affliction.

(Congregation rises)

Reader, then Choir and Congregation

שְׁמַע יִשְׂרָאֵל יְהֹוָה אֱלֹהֵינוּ יְהֹוָה אֶחָד:

בָּרוּךְ שֵׁם כְּבוֹד מַלְכוּתוֹ לְעוֹלָם וָעֶד:

(Congregation is seated)

Reader

וְאָהַבְתָּ אֵת יְיָ אֱלֹהֶיךָ בְּכָל־לְבָבְךָ וּבְכָל־נַפְשְׁךָ
וּבְכָל־מְאֹדֶךָ: וְהָיוּ הַדְּבָרִים הָאֵלֶּה אֲשֶׁר אָנֹכִי
מְצַוְּךָ הַיּוֹם עַל־לְבָבֶךָ: וְשִׁנַּנְתָּם לְבָנֶיךָ וְדִבַּרְתָּ
בָּם. בְּשִׁבְתְּךָ בְּבֵיתֶךָ וּבְלֶכְתְּךָ בַדֶּרֶךְ וּבְשָׁכְבְּךָ
וּבְקוּמֶךָ: וּקְשַׁרְתָּם לְאוֹת עַל־יָדֶךָ. וְהָיוּ לְטֹטָפֹת
בֵּין עֵינֶיךָ: וּכְתַבְתָּם עַל־מְזֻזוֹת בֵּיתֶךָ וּבִשְׁעָרֶיךָ:
לְמַעַן תִּזְכְּרוּ וַעֲשִׂיתֶם אֶת־כָּל־מִצְוֹתָי וִהְיִיתֶם
קְדֹשִׁים לֵאלֹהֵיכֶם: אֲנִי יְיָ אֱלֹהֵיכֶם:

For Alternate Reading or Chanting

אֱמֶת וֶאֱמוּנָה כָּל־זֹאת וְקַיָּם עָלֵינוּ. כִּי־הוּא יְיָ
אֱלֹהֵינוּ וְאֵין זוּלָתוֹ. וַאֲנַחְנוּ יִשְׂרָאֵל עַמּוֹ.

צִדְקָתְךָ כְּהַרְרֵי־אֵל מִשְׁפָּטֶיךָ תְּהוֹם רַבָּה
לְעוֹלָם יְהֹוָה דְּבָרְךָ נִצָּב בַּשָּׁמָיִם:
לְדוֹר וָדוֹר אֱמוּנָתֶךָ

Thy word is a lamp unto my feet, and a light unto my
  path.
Thy love has watched over us in the night of oppression; and Thy mercy has sustained us in the
  hour of trial.
And now that we live in a land of freedom, may we
  continue to be faithful to Thee and Thy word.
May Thy love rule in the hearts of all Thy children,
  and Thy truth unite them in the bonds of
  fellowship.
Let the righteous of all nations rejoice in Thy grace,
  and exult in Thy justice.
O God, Thou art our refuge and our hope; we glorify
  Thy name now, as did our fathers in the ancient
  days:

Choir and Congregation

Who is like unto Thee, O God, among the mighty?
  Who is like unto Thee, glorious in holiness, extolled in praises, working wonders?

Reader

Thy children acknowledged Thy Sovereign power, and
  exclaimed:

Choir

The Lord shall reign forever and ever.

Reader

As Thou hast redeemed Israel and saved him from
arms stronger than his, so mayest Thou redeem all who
are oppressed and persecuted. Praised art Thou, O
God, Redeemer of Israel.

Choir

For on this day He will grant you atonement to
purify you from all your sins. Before the Lord shall
ye be pure.

לוּלֵי תוֹרָתְךָ שַׁעֲשֻׁעָי אָז אָבַדְתִּי בְעָנְיִי

נֵר לְרַגְלִי דְבָרֶךָ וְאוֹר לִנְתִיבָתִי:

הָעוֹשֶׂה גְדֹלוֹת עַד־אֵין חֵקֶר. וְנִפְלָאוֹת עַד־אֵין

מִסְפָּר.

הַשָּׂם נַפְשֵׁנוּ בַּחַיִּים. וְלֹא נָתַן לַמּוֹט רַגְלֵנוּ.

הָעוֹשֶׂה לָנוּ נִסִּים בְּמִצְרָיִם. אוֹתֹת וּמֹפְתִים

בְּאַדְמַת בְּנֵי־חָם.

וַיִּרְאוּ בָנָיו גְּבוּרָתוֹ. שִׁבְּחוּ וְהוֹדוּ לִשְׁמוֹ.

Choir and Congregation

מִי־כָמֹכָה בָּאֵלִם יְיָ. מִי כָּמֹכָה נֶאְדָּר בַּקֹּדֶשׁ.

נוֹרָא תְהִלֹּת עֹשֵׂה פֶלֶא:

Reader

מַלְכוּתְךָ רָאוּ בָנֶיךָ. זֶה אֵלִי עָנוּ וְאָמְרוּ:

Choir and Congregation

יְיָ יִמְלֹךְ לְעֹלָם וָעֶד:

Reader

וְנֶאֱמַר כִּי פָדָה יְהֹוָה אֶת יַעֲקֹב וּגְאָלוֹ מִיַּד חָזָק

מִמֶּנּוּ. בָּרוּךְ אַתָּה יְיָ גָּאַל יִשְׂרָאֵל:

Choir

כִּי בַיּוֹם הַזֶּה יְכַפֵּר עֲלֵיכֶם לְטַהֵר אֶתְכֶם מִכָּל

חַטֹּאתֵיכֶם לִפְנֵי יְיָ תִּטְהָרוּ:

Reader

Praised be Thou, O Lord, God of our fathers, God of Abraham, Isaac and Jacob, great, mighty and exalted. Thou bestowest lovingkindness upon all Thy children. Thou rememberest the devotion of the fathers. In Thy love Thou bringest redemption to their descendants for the sake of Thy name.

Remember us unto life, O King, who delightest in life, and inscribe us in the book of life, for Thy sake, O God of life. Thou, O King, art our Helper, Savior and Protector. Praised be Thou, O Lord, Shield of Abraham.

Eternal is Thy power, O Lord, Thou art mighty to save. In lovingkindness Thou sustainest the living; in the multitude of Thy mercies Thou preservest all. Thou upholdest the falling and healest the sick; freest the captives and keepest faith with Thy children in death as in life. Who is like unto Thee, Almighty God, Author of life and death, Source of salvation?

Who is like unto Thee, O merciful Father, who rememberest Thy creatures unto life. Praised be Thou, O Lord, who hast implanted within us eternal life. Thou art holy, Thy name is holy, and Thy worshipers proclaim Thy holiness.

Reader

בָּרוּךְ אַתָּה יְיָ אֱלֹהֵינוּ וֵאלֹהֵי אֲבוֹתֵינוּ. אֱלֹהֵי
אַבְרָהָם אֱלֹהֵי יִצְחָק וֵאלֹהֵי יַעֲקֹב. הָאֵל הַגָּדוֹל
הַגִּבּוֹר וְהַנּוֹרָא. אֵל עֶלְיוֹן. גּוֹמֵל חֲסָדִים טוֹבִים.
וְקֹנֵה הַכֹּל וְזוֹכֵר חַסְדֵּי אָבוֹת. וּמֵבִיא גֹאֲלָה לִבְנֵי
בְנֵיהֶם. לְמַעַן שְׁמוֹ בְּאַהֲבָה:

זָכְרֵנוּ לַחַיִּים. מֶלֶךְ חָפֵץ בַּחַיִּים. וְכָתְבֵנוּ בְּסֵפֶר
הַחַיִּים. לְמַעַנְךָ אֱלֹהִים חַיִּים:

מֶלֶךְ עוֹזֵר וּמוֹשִׁיעַ וּמָגֵן. בָּרוּךְ אַתָּה יְיָ מָגֵן
אַבְרָהָם:

אַתָּה גִּבּוֹר לְעוֹלָם אֲדֹנָי. רַב לְהוֹשִׁיעַ. מְכַלְכֵּל
חַיִּים בְּחֶסֶד. מְחַיֶּה הַכֹּל בְּרַחֲמִים רַבִּים. סוֹמֵךְ
נוֹפְלִים וְרוֹפֵא חוֹלִים וּמַתִּיר אֲסוּרִים. וּמְקַיֵּם
אֱמוּנָתוֹ לִישֵׁנֵי עָפָר. מִי כָמוֹךָ בַּעַל גְּבוּרוֹת. וּמִי
דּוֹמֶה לָּךְ. מֶלֶךְ מֵמִית וּמְחַיֶּה. וּמַצְמִיחַ יְשׁוּעָה:

מִי כָמוֹךָ אַב הָרַחֲמִים. זוֹכֵר יְצוּרָיו לַחַיִּים
בְּרַחֲמִים: בָּרוּךְ אַתָּה יְיָ נֹטֵעַ בְּתוֹכֵנוּ חַיֵּי עוֹלָם:

אַתָּה קָדוֹשׁ וְשִׁמְךָ קָדוֹשׁ וּקְדוֹשִׁים בְּכָל־יוֹם
יְהַלְלוּךָ סֶּלָה:

Reader

O Lord, our God, let Thy presence be manifest to us in all Thy works, that reverence for Thee may fill the hearts of all Thy creatures. May all the children of men come before Thee in humility and unite to do Thy will with perfect heart, that all may acknowledge that Thine are power, dominion and majesty, and that Thy name is exalted above all.

Grant honor, O Lord, to them that revere Thee, inspire with courage those who wait for Thee, and fulfil the hope of all who trust in Thy name. Hasten the day that will bring gladness to all who dwell on earth and victory of the spirit to those who bear witness to Thy unity. Then the just shall see and exult, the righteous be glad, and the pious sing for joy. Then shall iniquity be made dumb, and wickedness vanish like smoke; for the dominion of arrogance shall have passed away from the earth.

Thou alone, O Lord, shalt reign over all Thy works, as it is written in Thy holy word: The Lord shall reign forever, thy God, O Zion, from generation to generation, Hallelujah.

Holy art Thou, awe-inspiring is Thy name, there is no God but Thee. The Lord of hosts is exalted through justice, and the holy God is sanctified through righteousness. Praised be Thou, O Lord, King of holiness.

Reader

וּבְכֵן תֵּן פַּחְדְּךָ יְיָ אֱלֹהֵינוּ עַל כָּל־מַעֲשֶׂיךָ
וְאֵימָתְךָ עַל כָּל־מַה־שֶּׁבָּרֵאתָ. וְיִירָאוּךָ כָּל־הַמַּעֲשִׂים
וְיִשְׁתַּחֲווּ לְפָנֶיךָ כָּל־הַבְּרוּאִים. וְיֵעָשׂוּ כֻלָּם אֲגֻדָּה
אַחַת לַעֲשׂוֹת רְצוֹנְךָ בְּלֵבָב שָׁלֵם. כְּמוֹ שֶׁיָּדַעְנוּ יְיָ
אֱלֹהֵינוּ שֶׁהַשָּׁלְטוֹן לְפָנֶיךָ עֹז בְּיָדְךָ וּגְבוּרָה בִּימִינֶךָ
וְשִׁמְךָ נוֹרָא עַל כָּל־מַה־שֶּׁבָּרֵאתָ:

וּבְכֵן תֵּן כָּבוֹד יְיָ לְעַמֶּךָ תְּהִלָּה לִירֵאֶיךָ וְתִקְוָה
לְדוֹרְשֶׁיךָ וּפִתְחוֹן פֶּה לַמְיַחֲלִים לָךְ. שִׂמְחָה לְכָל־
יוֹשְׁבֵי תֵבֵל וּצְמִיחַת קֶרֶן לְמִיַחֲדֵי שְׁמֶךָ. בִּמְהֵרָה
בְיָמֵינוּ:

וּבְכֵן צַדִּיקִים יִרְאוּ וְיִשְׂמָחוּ וִישָׁרִים יַעֲלֹזוּ
וַחֲסִידִים בְּרִנָּה יָגִילוּ וְעוֹלָתָה תִּקְפָּץ־פִּיהָ. וְכָל־
הָרִשְׁעָה כֻּלָּהּ כְּעָשָׁן תִּכְלֶה. כִּי תַעֲבִיר מֶמְשֶׁלֶת
זָדוֹן מִן־הָאָרֶץ:

וְתִמְלוֹךְ אַתָּה יְיָ לְבַדֶּךָ עַל כָּל־מַעֲשֶׂיךָ. כַּכָּתוּב
בְּדִבְרֵי קָדְשֶׁךָ יִמְלֹךְ יְיָ לְעוֹלָם אֱלֹהַיִךְ צִיּוֹן לְדֹר
וָדֹר הַלְלוּיָהּ:

קָדוֹשׁ אַתָּה וְנוֹרָא שְׁמֶךָ. וְאֵין אֱלוֹהַּ מִבַּלְעָדֶיךָ.
כַּכָּתוּב. וַיִּגְבַּהּ יְיָ צְבָאוֹת בַּמִּשְׁפָּט. וְהָאֵל הַקָּדוֹשׁ
נִקְדַּשׁ בִּצְדָקָה. בָּרוּךְ אַתָּה יְיָ הַמֶּלֶךְ הַקָּדוֹשׁ:

We give thanks unto Thee that Thou hast called us to Thy service and entrusted us with Thy commandments. In love Thou hast given us this Day of Atonement, that we may obtain forgiveness for our sins and become reconciled to Thee and our fellowmen.

May this day lead us to search the hidden recesses of our hearts. May it arouse us to examine all our thoughts and deeds in the light of Thy truth, that we may know wherein we have strayed from Thy way. And when we have learned our shortcomings and the burden of our sins weighs us down, grant us the strength and courage to turn from the evil of our ways and to seek the shelter of Thy fatherly love.

O Lord, enter not into judgment with us, for in Thy sight can no living man be justified. Show us Thy mercy; grant us Thy favor. Aid us as we seek to purify our spirits; in Thy lovingkindness protect us for we put our trust in Thee.

Reader

Our God and God of our fathers, pardon our transgressions on this Day of Atonement; remove our guilt and blot out our iniquities. May we, sanctified through Thy commandments, become sharers in the blessings of Thy word. Teach us to be satisfied with the gifts of Thy goodness and gratefully to rejoice in all Thy mercies. Purify our hearts that we may serve Thee in truth. In all ages, Thy people Israel turned unto Thee for forgiveness and received assurance of Thy pardon. We, too, seek forgiveness for our sins by turning unto Thee. Praised be Thou, O Lord, who forgivest transgressions; Ruler of the world, who sanctifiest (the Sabbath) Israel and the Day of Atonement.

Reader

אֱלֹהֵינוּ וֵאלֹהֵי אֲבוֹתֵינוּ מְחַל לַעֲוֹנוֹתֵינוּ בְּיוֹם

(הַשַּׁבָּת הַזֶּה וּבְיוֹם) הַכִּפֻּרִים הַזֶּה. מְחֵה וְהַעֲבֵר

פְּשָׁעֵינוּ (וְחַטֹּאתֵינוּ) מִנֶּגֶד עֵינֶיךָ. כָּאָמוּר אָנֹכִי אָנֹכִי

הוּא מֹחֶה פְשָׁעֶיךָ לְמַעֲנִי וְחַטֹּאתֶיךָ לֹא־אֶזְכֹּר:

(אֱלֹהֵינוּ וֵאלֹהֵי אֲבוֹתֵינוּ רְצֵה בִמְנוּחָתֵנוּ) קַדְּשֵׁנוּ

בְּמִצְוֹתֶיךָ. וְתֵן חֶלְקֵנוּ בְּתוֹרָתֶךָ שַׂבְּעֵנוּ מִטּוּבֶךָ

וְשַׂמְּחֵנוּ בִּישׁוּעָתֶךָ. (וְהַנְחִילֵנוּ יְיָ אֱלֹהֵינוּ בְּאַהֲבָה

וּבְרָצוֹן שַׁבַּת קָדְשֶׁךָ וְיָנוּחוּ בָהּ יִשְׂרָאֵל מְקַדְּשֵׁי

שְׁמֶךָ) וְטַהֵר לִבֵּנוּ לְעָבְדְּךָ בֶּאֱמֶת. כִּי אַתָּה סָלְחָן

לְיִשְׂרָאֵל וּמָחֳלָן לְשִׁבְטֵי יְשֻׁרוּן בְּכָל־דּוֹר וָדוֹר

וּמִבַּלְעָדֶיךָ אֵין לָנוּ מֶלֶךְ מוֹחֵל וְסוֹלֵחַ (אֶלָּא

אָתָּה). בָּרוּךְ אַתָּה יְיָ מֶלֶךְ מוֹחֵל וְסוֹלֵחַ לַעֲוֹנוֹתֵינוּ

וְלַעֲוֹנוֹת עַמּוֹ בֵּית יִשְׂרָאֵל. וּמַעֲבִיר אַשְׁמוֹתֵינוּ

בְּכָל־שָׁנָה וְשָׁנָה. מֶלֶךְ עַל־כָּל־הָאָרֶץ מְקַדֵּשׁ

(הַשַּׁבָּת וְ)יִשְׂרָאֵל וְיוֹם הַכִּפֻּרִים:

Choir: Amen.

Reader

Look with favor, O Lord, upon us, and may our service ever be acceptable unto Thee. Praised be Thou, O God, whom alone we serve in reverence.

Congregation and Reader

We gratefully acknowledge, O Lord, our God, that Thou art our Creator and Preserver, the Rock of our life and the Shield of our help. We render thanks unto Thee for our lives which are in Thy hand, for our souls which are ever in Thy keeping, for Thy wondrous providence and for Thy continuous goodness, which Thou bestowest upon us day by day. Truly, Thy mercies never fail and Thy lovingkindness never ceases. Therefore do we forever put our trust in Thee.

Reader

רְצֵה יְיָ אֱלֹהֵינוּ בְּעַמְּךָ יִשְׂרָאֵל. וּתְפִלָּתָם
בְּאַהֲבָה תְקַבֵּל. וּתְהִי לְרָצוֹן תָּמִיד עֲבוֹדַת יִשְׂרָאֵל
עַמֶּךָ: בָּרוּךְ אַתָּה יְיָ שֶׁאוֹתְךָ לְבַדְּךָ בְּיִרְאָה נַעֲבוֹד:

מוֹדִים אֲנַחְנוּ לָךְ. שֶׁאַתָּה הוּא יְיָ אֱלֹהֵינוּ וֵאלֹהֵי
אֲבוֹתֵינוּ לְעוֹלָם וָעֶד. צוּר חַיֵּינוּ מָגֵן יִשְׁעֵנוּ אַתָּה
הוּא לְדוֹר וָדוֹר. נוֹדֶה לְךָ וּנְסַפֵּר תְּהִלָּתֶךָ. עַל
חַיֵּינוּ הַמְּסוּרִים בְּיָדֶךָ. וְעַל נִשְׁמוֹתֵינוּ הַפְּקוּדוֹת
לָךְ. וְעַל נִסֶּיךָ שֶׁבְּכָל-יוֹם עִמָּנוּ. וְעַל נִפְלְאוֹתֶיךָ
שֶׁבְּכָל-עֵת. עֶרֶב וָבֹקֶר וְצָהֳרָיִם. הַטּוֹב כִּי לֹא-
כָלוּ רַחֲמֶיךָ. וְהַמְרַחֵם כִּי לֹא-תַמּוּ חֲסָדֶיךָ.
מֵעוֹלָם קִוִּינוּ לָךְ:

Reader

Grant us peace, Thy most precious gift, O Thou eternal source of peace, and enable Israel to be its messenger unto the peoples of the earth. Bless our country that it may ever be a stronghold of peace, and its advocate in the council of nations. May contentment reign within its borders, health and happiness within its homes. Strengthen the bonds of friendship and fellowship among the inhabitants of all lands. Plant virtue in every soul, and may the love of Thy name hallow every home and every heart. Praised be Thou, O Lord, Giver of peace.

Choir: Amen.

Reader

Our God and God of our fathers, pardon our transgressions, on this Day of Atonement, remove our guilt and blot out our iniquities, as Thou hast promised: I, even I, blot out thine iniquities for Mine own sake, and thy sins will I remember no more. I have made thy sins to vanish like a cloud and thy transgressions like a mist; return to me for I have redeemed thee. For on this day shall ye be forgiven and cleansed from all your sins; before the Lord shall ye be pure.

(Congregation rises)

Reader and Congregation, then Choir

Our God and God of our fathers, let our prayers come
before Thee. Turn not away from our supplication, for we are not so presumptuous and stiff-
necked as to say before Thee that we are wholly

Reader

שָׁלוֹם רָב עַל יִשְׂרָאֵל עַמְּךָ תָּשִׂים לְעוֹלָם. כִּי
אַתָּה הוּא מֶלֶךְ אָדוֹן לְכָל הַשָּׁלוֹם. וְטוֹב בְּעֵינֶיךָ
לְבָרֵךְ אֶת־עַמְּךָ יִשְׂרָאֵל בְּכָל־עֵת וּבְכָל־שָׁעָה
בִּשְׁלוֹמֶךָ:

Reader

אֱלֹהֵינוּ וֵאלֹהֵי אֲבוֹתֵינוּ. מְחַל לַעֲוֹנוֹתֵינוּ בְּיוֹם
הַכִּפֻּרִים הַזֶּה. מְחֵה וְהַעֲבֵר פְּשָׁעֵינוּ וְחַטֹּאתֵינוּ
מִנֶּגֶד עֵינֶיךָ. כָּאָמוּר. אָנֹכִי אָנֹכִי הוּא מֹחֶה פְשָׁעֶיךָ
לְמַעֲנִי וְחַטֹּאתֶיךָ לֹא אֶזְכֹּר: וְנֶאֱמַר. מָחִיתִי כָעָב
פְּשָׁעֶיךָ. וְכֶעָנָן חַטֹּאתֶיךָ. שׁוּבָה אֵלַי כִּי גְאַלְתִּיךָ:
וְנֶאֱמַר. כִּי בַיּוֹם הַזֶּה יְכַפֵּר עֲלֵיכֶם. לְטַהֵר אֶתְכֶם
מִכֹּל חַטֹּאתֵיכֶם. לִפְנֵי יְיָ תִּטְהָרוּ:

(Congregation rises)

Reader and Congregation, then Choir

אֱלֹהֵינוּ וֵאלֹהֵי אֲבוֹתֵינוּ.

תָּבֹא לְפָנֶיךָ תְּפִלָּתֵנוּ. וְאַל תִּתְעַלַּם מִתְּחִנָּתֵנוּ. שֶׁאֵין
אֲנַחְנוּ עַזֵּי פָנִים וּקְשֵׁי עֹרֶף. לוֹמַר לְפָנֶיךָ יְיָ אֱלֹהֵינוּ

righteous and have not sinned, but verily, we have sinned.

We have sinned; we have transgressed; we have done perversely.

Reader

We have turned aside from Thy commandments and from Thy beneficent ordinances, and it hath not availed us. Thou art righteous in all that has befallen us, for Thou doest justice, but we have wrought evil.

What shall we say before Thee, who art on high, and what shall we recount unto Thee, who dwellest in the heavens? Dost Thou not know all things; both the hidden and the revealed? Thou knowest the secrets of eternity and the hidden thoughts of every living being.

Thou searchest the innermost recesses and probest the deepest impulses of the heart. Naught is concealed from Thee nor hidden from Thine eyes.

O Lord our God, help us to see ourselves as Thou seest us. Make us conscious of our sins and failings; cause us to turn from our evil ways. Give us strength to make amends for our wrongdoings, and grant us pardon for our sins.

Reader, then Congregation

For the sin which we have sinned against Thee under stress or through choice;

For the sin which we have sinned against Thee openly or in secret;

וֵאלֹהֵי אֲבוֹתֵינוּ. צַדִּיקִים אֲנַחְנוּ וְלֹא חָטָאנוּ. אֲבָל
אֲנַחְנוּ חָטָאנוּ:

חָטָאנוּ. עָוִינוּ. פָּשַׁעְנוּ:

(Congregation is seated)

Reader

סַרְנוּ מִמִּצְוֹתֶיךָ וּמִמִּשְׁפָּטֶיךָ הַטּוֹבִים וְלֹא שָׁוָה
לָנוּ. וְאַתָּה צַדִּיק עַל־כָּל־הַבָּא עָלֵינוּ. כִּי־אֱמֶת
עָשִׂיתָ וַאֲנַחְנוּ הִרְשָׁעְנוּ:

מַה־נֹּאמַר לְפָנֶיךָ יוֹשֵׁב מָרוֹם. וּמַה־נְּסַפֵּר לְפָנֶיךָ
שׁוֹכֵן שְׁחָקִים. הֲלֹא כָּל־הַנִּסְתָּרוֹת וְהַנִּגְלוֹת אַתָּה
יוֹדֵעַ:

אַתָּה יוֹדֵעַ רָזֵי עוֹלָם. וְתַעֲלוּמוֹת סִתְרֵי כָל־חָי.
אַתָּה חוֹפֵשׂ כָּל־חַדְרֵי בָטֶן. וּבוֹחֵן כְּלָיוֹת וָלֵב. אֵין
דָּבָר נֶעְלָם מִמֶּךָּ. וְאֵין נִסְתָּר מִנֶּגֶד עֵינֶיךָ:

וּבְכֵן יְהִי רָצוֹן מִלְּפָנֶיךָ יְיָ אֱלֹהֵינוּ וֵאלֹהֵי
אֲבוֹתֵינוּ שֶׁתִּסְלַח לָנוּ עַל־כָּל־חַטֹּאתֵינוּ. וְתִמְחַל
לָנוּ עַל־כָּל־עֲוֹנוֹתֵינוּ. וּתְכַפֶּר לָנוּ עַל־כָּל־פְּשָׁעֵינוּ:

Reader, then Congregation

עַל חֵטְא שֶׁחָטָאנוּ לְפָנֶיךָ בְּאֹנֶס וּבְרָצוֹן:

עַל חֵטְא שֶׁחָטָאנוּ לְפָנֶיךָ בְּגָלוּי וּבַסָּתֶר:

For the sin which we have sinned against Thee in stubbornness or in error;

For the sin which we have sinned against Thee in the evil meditations of the heart;

For the sin which we have sinned against Thee by word of mouth;

For the sin which we have sinned against Thee by abuse of power;

For the sin which we have sinned against Thee by the profanation of Thy name;

For the sin which we have sinned against Thee by disrespect for parents and teachers;

For the sin which we have sinned against Thee by exploiting and dealing treacherously with our neighbor,

For all these sins, O God of forgiveness, bear with us! pardon us! forgive us!

Choir

For all these sins, O God of forgiveness, bear with us! pardon us! forgive us!

Reader

Our God and God of our fathers, forsake us not. Let us not be put to shame. Lead us to the knowledge of Thy law, that we may understand Thy ways. Direct our thoughts to revere Thy name. Incline our hearts to love Thee, that we may return to Thee in truth and sincerity. Forgive our sins for the sake of Thy great name.

עַל חֵטְא שֶׁחָטֶאנוּ לְפָנֶיךָ בְּזָדוֹן וּבִשְׁגָגָה:

עַל חֵטְא שֶׁחָטֶאנוּ לְפָנֶיךָ בְּהַרְהוֹר הַלֵּב:

עַל חֵטְא שֶׁחָטֶאנוּ לְפָנֶיךָ בְּדִבּוּר פֶּה:

עַל חֵטְא שֶׁחָטֶאנוּ לְפָנֶיךָ בְּחוֹזֶק יָד:

עַל חֵטְא שֶׁחָטֶאנוּ לְפָנֶיךָ בְּחִלּוּל הַשֵּׁם:

עַל חֵטְא שֶׁחָטֶאנוּ לְפָנֶיךָ בְּזִלְזוּל הוֹרִים וּמוֹרִים:

עַל חֵטְא שֶׁחָטֶאנוּ לְפָנֶיךָ בְּהוֹנָאַת וּצְדִיַת רֵעַ:

וְעַל כֻּלָּם אֱלוֹהַּ סְלִיחוֹת. סְלַח לָנוּ. מְחַל לָנוּ. כַּפֶּר־לָנוּ:

Reader

אֱלֹהֵינוּ וֵאלֹהֵי אֲבוֹתֵינוּ. אַל תַּעַזְבֵנוּ. וְאַל תִּטְּשֵׁנוּ. וְאַל תַּכְלִימֵנוּ. וְאַל תָּפֵר בְּרִיתְךָ אִתָּנוּ. קָרְבֵנוּ לְתוֹרָתֶךָ. לַמְּדֵנוּ מִצְוֹתֶיךָ. הוֹרֵנוּ דְּרָכֶיךָ. הַט לִבֵּנוּ לְיִרְאָה אֶת־שְׁמֶךָ. וּמוֹל אֶת־לְבָבֵנוּ לְאַהֲבָתֶךָ. וְנָשׁוּב אֵלֶיךָ בֶּאֱמֶת וּבְלֵב שָׁלֵם. וּלְמַעַן שִׁמְךָ הַגָּדוֹל תִּמְחוֹל וְתִסְלַח לַעֲוֹנֵינוּ:

Choir

Unto Thee, with contrite spirits,
Do we come this eventide;
And throughout the morrow's passing
We will in Thy presence bide.
O that ere the great Day closeth
We be cleansed and purified!

How this solemn evening's advent
Bids us search and look within,
And until the morrow's twilight,
To confront our secret sin!
O that ere the great Day closeth
Our true penitence begin!

We of guilt, alas, are conscious
As we usher in this night;
And we would make full confession
Through the lengthened morrow's flight.
O that ere the great Day closeth
To our souls will come the light!

Our petitions and our prayers
Yearning rise to Thee this eve,
And until the morrow's twilight
Will our chastened spirits grieve.
O that ere the great Day closeth
Thy forgiveness we receive.

Choir

יַעֲלֶה תַּחֲנוּנֵנוּ מֵעֶֽרֶב. וְיָבֹא שַׁוְעָתֵֽנוּ מִבֹּֽקֶר.
וְיֵרָאֶה רִנּוּנֵֽנוּ. עַד עָֽרֶב:

יַעֲלֶה קוֹלֵֽנוּ מֵעֶֽרֶב. וְיָבֹא צִדְקָתֵֽנוּ מִבֹּֽקֶר.
וְיֵרָאֶה פִּדְיוֹנֵֽנוּ. עַד עָֽרֶב:

יַעֲלֶה עִנּוּיֵֽנוּ מֵעֶֽרֶב. וְיָבֹא סְלִיחָתֵֽנוּ מִבֹּֽקֶר.
וְיֵרָאֶה נַאֲקָתֵֽנוּ. עַד עָֽרֶב:

יַעֲלֶה מְנוּסֵֽנוּ מֵעֶֽרֶב. וְיָבֹא לְמַעֲנוֹ מִבֹּֽקֶר.
וְיֵרָאֶה כִּפּוּרֵֽנוּ. עַד עָֽרֶב:

יַעֲלֶה יִשְׁעֵֽנוּ מֵעֶֽרֶב. וְיָבֹא טָהֳרֵֽנוּ מִבֹּֽקֶר.
וְיֵרָאֶה חִנּוּנֵֽנוּ. עַד עָֽרֶב:

יַעֲלֶה זִכְרוֹנֵֽנוּ מֵעֶֽרֶב. וְיָבֹא וְעוּדֵֽנוּ מִבֹּֽקֶר.
וְיֵרָאֶה הַדְרָתֵֽנוּ. עַד עָֽרֶב:

יַעֲלֶה דָפְקֵֽנוּ מֵעֶֽרֶב. וְיָבֹא גִּילֵֽנוּ מִבֹּֽקֶר.
וְיֵרָאֶה בַּקָּשָׁתֵֽנוּ. עַד עָֽרֶב:

יַעֲלֶה אֶנְקָתֵֽנוּ מֵעֶֽרֶב. וְיָבֹא אֵלֶֽיךָ מִבֹּֽקֶר.
וְיֵרָאֶה אֵלֵֽינוּ. עַד עָֽרֶב:

Responsive Reading

Reader

O Thou, who hearest prayer, unto Thee shall all flesh
come.

Congregation

*All flesh shall come to worship before Thee, O Lord,
and to do honor to Thy name.*

With Thee is the fountain of life; in Thy light do we
see light.

*Thy righteousness is an everlasting righteousness, and
Thy law is truth.*

Listen to the voice of my supplication, my King and
my God, for to Thee do I pray.

*Give ear to my words, O Lord, have regard to my
prayer.*

Lead me, O Lord, in Thy righteousness, make Thy
path straight before me.

*Order my steps by Thy word; let not iniquity have
dominion over me.*

Turn away mine eyes from beholding vanity, and
quicken me in Thy ways.

*Deliver me in Thy righteousness and rescue me; in-
cline thine ear unto me and save me.*

In Thee did our fathers trust; in Thee did they trust
and were not ashamed.

Choir

Prepare to meet thy God, O Israel! Seek ye the Lord
and ye shall live. Let justice flow forth as water,
and righteousness as a mighty stream.

Reader

Be gracious unto me, O God, according to Thy lovingkindness.

Congregation

In Thine endless mercy, blot out my transgressions.

Cleanse me, O Lord, and I shall be clean; purify me
and I shall be whiter than snow.

Behold Thou desirest truth in our innermost heart;
so teach me wisdom and right understanding.

I acknowledge my transgressions and my sin is ever
before me.

Create in me a clean heart, O God, renew a steadfast
spirit within me.

Cast me not away from Thy presence and take not Thy
holy spirit from me.

The soul is Thine and the body is Thine; O, have
compassion on Thy handiwork.

For Thy name's sake, O merciful God, pardon our iniquities, though they be many.

Let us search and try our ways and return again unto
the Lord.

For Thee, O Lord, do we wait; in Thee, O Lord, do we
hope, for with the Lord there is mercy and with
Him is plenteous redemption.

Choir

Like as a father pitieth his children so the Lord pitieth
them that fear Him. High as the heaven is above
the earth, so great is His mercy toward them that
revere Him.

Responsive Reading

Reader

Hear our cry, O Lord our God, and be gracious unto us.

Congregation

In Thy mercy favorably accept our prayers.

Forsake us not, O Lord our God, be not far from us.

Forsake us not when our own strength fails us.

We are Thy people, Thou art our King.

We are Thy children, Thou art our Father.

We are Thy possession, Thou art our Portion.

We are Thy flock, Thou art our Shepherd.

We are Thy vineyard, Thou art our Keeper.

We are Thy beloved, Thou art our Friend.

Choir

כִּי אָנוּ עַמֶּךָ וְאַתָּה מַלְכֵּנוּ:

אָנוּ בָנֶיךָ וְאַתָּה אָבִינוּ:

אָנוּ נַחֲלָתֶךָ וְאַתָּה גוֹרָלֵנוּ:

אָנוּ צֹאנֶךָ וְאַתָּה רוֹעֵנוּ:

אָנוּ כַרְמֶךָ וְאַתָּה נוֹטְרֵנוּ:

אָנוּ רַעְיָתֶךָ וְאַתָּה דוֹדֵנוּ:

Silent Prayer

(Psalm cxxxix)

O Lord! Thou hast searched me, and known me; Thou
knowest my down-sitting and mine up-rising;
Thou understandest my thought afar off.

Thou measurest my going about and my lying down,
and art acquainted with all my ways.

Whither shall I go from Thy spirit, or whither shall I
flee from Thy presence?

If I ascend up into heaven, Thou art there; if I make
my bed in the netherworld, behold, Thou art
there.

If I take the wings of the morning, and dwell in the
uttermost part of the sea; even there would Thy
hand lead me, and Thy right hand would hold
me.

And if I say: Surely the darkness shall envelop me,
and the light about me shall be night;

Even the darkness is not too dark for Thee, but the
night shineth as the day; the darkness is even
as the light.

How weighty also are Thy thoughts unto me, O God!
how great is the sum of them!

Search me, O God! and know my heart; try me and
know my thoughts.

And see if there be any way in me that is grievous, and
lead me in the way everlasting.

Choir

May the words of my mouth and the meditations of
my heart be acceptable in Thy sight, O Lord, my Rock
and my Redeemer.

(Congregation rises)

Reader, then Congregation

Our Father, our King, we have sinned before Thee.

Our Father, our King, inscribe us for blessing in the book of life.

Our Father, our King, grant us a year of happiness.

Our Father, our King, bestow upon us an abundance of Thy blessings.

Our Father, our King, have mercy upon us and upon our children.

Our Father, our King, keep far from our country, pestilence, war and famine.

Our Father, our King, cause every oppressor and reviler of men to vanish from our midst.

Our Father, our King, cause us to return unto Thee in perfect repentance.

Our Father, our King, forgive and pardon all our iniquities.

Our Father, our King, may this hour reveal to us Thy mercy and Thy favor.

Our Father, our King, be merciful and answer us; though we can plead no merit, deal with us according to Thy lovingkindness and help us.

Choir: Amen.

(Congregation is seated)

SERMON

HYMN

(Congregation rises)

Reader, then Congregation

אָבִינוּ מַלְכֵּנוּ חָטָאנוּ לְפָנֶיךָ:

אָבִינוּ מַלְכֵּנוּ כָּתְבֵנוּ בְּסֵפֶר חַיִּים טוֹבִים:

אָבִינוּ מַלְכֵּנוּ חַדֵּשׁ עָלֵינוּ שָׁנָה טוֹבָה:

אָבִינוּ מַלְכֵּנוּ כָּתְבֵנוּ בְּסֵפֶר פַּרְנָסָה וְכַלְכָּלָה:

אָבִינוּ מַלְכֵּנוּ חֲמוֹל עָלֵינוּ וְעַל־עוֹלָלֵינוּ וְטַפֵּינוּ:

אָבִינוּ מַלְכֵּנוּ כַּלֵּה דֶּבֶר וְחֶרֶב וְרָעָב מֵעָלֵינוּ:

אָבִינוּ מַלְכֵּנוּ סְתוֹם פִּיוֹת מַשְׂטִינֵינוּ וּמְקַטְרִיגֵנוּ:

אָבִינוּ מַלְכֵּנוּ הַחֲזִירֵנוּ בִּתְשׁוּבָה שְׁלֵמָה לְפָנֶיךָ:

אָבִינוּ מַלְכֵּנוּ סְלַח וּמְחַל לְכָל־עֲוֹנוֹתֵינוּ:

אָבִינוּ מַלְכֵּנוּ תְּהִי הַשָּׁעָה הַזֹּאת שַׁעַת רַחֲמִים וְעֵת רָצוֹן מִלְּפָנֶיךָ:

אָבִינוּ מַלְכֵּנוּ חָנֵּנוּ וַעֲנֵנוּ כִּי אֵין בָּנוּ מַעֲשִׂים עֲשֵׂה עִמָּנוּ צְדָקָה וָחֶסֶד וְהוֹשִׁיעֵנוּ:

Choir: Amen.

(Congregation is seated)

SERMON

HYMN

ADORATION

(Congregation rises)

Congregation and Reader

Let us adore the ever-living God, and render praise
unto Him who spread out the heavens and established
the earth, whose glory is revealed in the heavens above
and whose greatness is manifest throughout the world.
He is our God; there is none else.

We bow the head in reverence, and worship the
King of kings, the Holy One, praised be He.

Choir and Congregation

וַאֲנַחְנוּ כֹּרְעִים וּמִשְׁתַּחֲוִים וּמוֹדִים לִפְנֵי מֶלֶךְ
מַלְכֵי הַמְּלָכִים הַקָּדוֹשׁ בָּרוּךְ הוּא:

(Congregation is seated)

Reader

May the time not be distant, O God, when Thy
name shall be worshiped in all the earth, when unbelief
shall disappear and error be no more. We fervently
pray that the day may come when all men shall invoke
Thy name, when corruption and evil shall give way to
purity and goodness, when superstition shall no longer
enslave the mind, nor idolatry blind the eye, when all
who dwell on earth shall know that to Thee alone every
knee must bend and every tongue give homage. O

may all, created in Thine image, recognize that they are brethren, so that, one in spirit and one in fellowship, they may be forever united before Thee. Then shall Thy kingdom be established on earth and the word of Thine ancient seer be fulfilled: The Lord will reign forever and ever.

Congregation (or Choir)

On that day the Lord shall be One and His name shall be One.

בַּיּוֹם הַהוּא יִהְיֶה יְיָ אֶחָד וּשְׁמוֹ אֶחָד:

Reader

This solemn service of Atonement hallows and deepens the memory of our beloved dead. The searchings of the heart which lead us to Thee, O God, lead us also to thoughts of them. As we examine the record of our lives in the light of Thy truth, we acknowledge the justice of Thine eternal law; we realize that death itself, deep mystery though it be, also reveals Thy justice and love. Thou wilt not suffer Thy children to see destruction; our beloved, who have passed through the portals of death, live on with Thee. Into Thy hands we commit our lives, as we entrust the spirits of those we love. On this solemn day death as well as life is revealed to us in the light of an unfaltering faith.

With bowed heads and mourning hearts, yet with abiding trust in Thy justice and lovingkindness, we repeat the words hallowed by centuries of devotion:

(Mourners rise)

Reader

Extolled and hallowed be the name of God throughout the world which He has created according to His will. And may He speedily establish His kingdom of righteousness on earth. Amen.

Congregation

Praised be His glorious name unto all eternity.

Reader

Praised and glorified be the name of the Holy One, though He be above all the praises which we can utter. Our guide is He in life and our redeemer through all eternity.

Congregation

Our help cometh from Him, the creator of heaven and earth.

Reader

The departed whom we now remember have entered into the peace of life eternal. They still live on earth in the acts of goodness they performed and in the hearts of those who cherish their memory. May the beauty of their life abide among us as a loving benediction.

Congregation: Amen.

Reader

May the Father of peace send peace to all who mourn, and comfort all the bereaved among us.

Congregation: Amen.

(Mourners are seated)

(Mourners rise)

Reader

יִתְגַּדַּל וְיִתְקַדַּשׁ שְׁמֵהּ רַבָּא. בְּעָלְמָא דִי־בְרָא
כִרְעוּתֵהּ. וְיַמְלִיךְ מַלְכוּתֵהּ. בְּחַיֵּיכוֹן וּבְיוֹמֵיכוֹן
וּבְחַיֵּי דְכָל־בֵּית יִשְׂרָאֵל. בַּעֲגָלָא וּבִזְמַן קָרִיב.
וְאִמְרוּ אָמֵן:

Congregation

יְהֵא שְׁמֵהּ רַבָּא מְבָרַךְ לְעָלַם וּלְעָלְמֵי עָלְמַיָּא:

Reader

יִתְבָּרַךְ וְיִשְׁתַּבַּח וְיִתְפָּאַר וְיִתְרוֹמַם וְיִתְנַשֵּׂא
וְיִתְהַדָּר וְיִתְעַלֶּה וְיִתְהַלָּל שְׁמֵהּ דְּקוּדְשָׁא. בְּרִיךְ
הוּא. לְעֵלָּא מִן כָּל בִּרְכָתָא וְשִׁירָתָא. תֻּשְׁבְּחָתָא
וְנֶחָמָתָא. דַּאֲמִירָן בְּעָלְמָא. וְאִמְרוּ אָמֵן:

עַל יִשְׂרָאֵל וְעַל צַדִּיקַיָּא. וְעַל־כָּל־מַן דְּאִתְפְּטַר
מִן עָלְמָא הָדֵין כִּרְעוּתֵהּ דֶּאֱלָהָא. יְהֵא לְהוֹן
שְׁלָמָא רַבָּא וְחִנָּא וְחִסְדָּא מִן־קֳדָם מָרֵא שְׁמַיָּא
וְאַרְעָא. וְאִמְרוּ אָמֵן:

יְהֵא שְׁלָמָא רַבָּא מִן־שְׁמַיָּא וְחַיִּים. עָלֵינוּ וְעַל־
כָּל־יִשְׂרָאֵל. וְאִמְרוּ אָמֵן:

עֹשֶׂה שָׁלוֹם בִּמְרוֹמָיו. הוּא יַעֲשֶׂה שָׁלוֹם עָלֵינוּ
וְעַל כָּל־יִשְׂרָאֵל. וְאִמְרוּ אָמֵן:

(Mourners are seated)

CLOSING HYMN

Give glory to the living God, and praise
God who reigneth beyond the end of days.
Thou only One, who is like unto Thee!
Beyond man's ken throughout eternity.
Bodied not in figure, in form not found,
No living thing Thy holiness can sound.
Thou wast ere the world its grandeur began,
Nor lies it with time Thy being to span.
God of the universe, source of all light,
Thy works all reveal Thy glory and might.
The power prophetic Thy word to make clear,
Gavest Thou unto those to Thy service drawn near.
Like unto Moses no prophet has been,
Who more than all men Thy glory has seen.
Through Thy faithful servants, the prophets, O Lord,
Didst Thou Thy message of truth accord.
Neither God nor His law will ever change,
Throughout all time will they endlessly range.
From Him there is nothing veiled or concealed
From beginning to end, all things are revealed.
Both the just and the unjust their portion receive;
None faileth; none can Omniscience deceive.
In His own time, in His appointed way
Will come His salvation for which we pray.
He redeems the dead to life that endeth never,
Praised be His name forever and ever.

BENEDICTION

CLOSING HYMN

יִגְדַּל אֱלֹהִים חַי וְיִשְׁתַּבַּח. נִמְצָא וְאֵין עֵת אֶל־
מְצִיאוּתוֹ:

אֶחָד וְאֵין יָחִיד כְּיִחוּדוֹ. נֶעְלָם וְגַם אֵין סוֹף לְאַחְדּוּתוֹ:

אֵין לוֹ דְּמוּת הַגּוּף וְאֵינוֹ גוּף. לֹא נַעֲרוֹךְ אֵלָיו קְדֻשָּׁתוֹ:

קַדְמוֹן לְכָל־דָּבָר אֲשֶׁר נִבְרָא. רִאשׁוֹן וְאֵין רֵאשִׁית
לְרֵאשִׁיתוֹ:

הִנּוֹ אֲדוֹן עוֹלָם. לְכָל־נוֹצָר יוֹרֶה גְּדֻלָּתוֹ וּמַלְכוּתוֹ:

שֶׁפַע נְבוּאָתוֹ נְתָנוֹ אֶל־אַנְשֵׁי סְגֻלָּתוֹ וְתִפְאַרְתּוֹ:

לֹא קָם בְּיִשְׂרָאֵל כְּמֹשֶׁה עוֹד נָבִיא. וּמַבִּיט אֶת־
תְּמוּנָתוֹ:

תּוֹרַת אֱמֶת נָתַן לְעַמּוֹ אֵל. עַל־יַד נְבִיאוֹ נֶאֱמַן בֵּיתוֹ:

לֹא יַחֲלִיף הָאֵל וְלֹא יָמִיר דָּתוֹ לְעוֹלָמִים לְזוּלָתוֹ:

צוֹפֶה וְיוֹדֵעַ סְתָרֵינוּ. מַבִּיט לְסוֹף דָּבָר בְּקַדְמָתוֹ:

גּוֹמֵל לְאִישׁ חֶסֶד כְּמִפְעָלוֹ. נוֹתֵן לְרָשָׁע רַע
כְּרִשְׁעָתוֹ:

יִשְׁלַח לְקֵץ יָמִין פְּדוּת עוֹלָם כָּל־חַי וְיֵשׁ יַכִּיר
יְשׁוּעָתוֹ:

חַיֵּי עוֹלָם נָטַע בְּתוֹכֵנוּ. בָּרוּךְ עֲדֵי־עַד שֵׁם תְּהִלָּתוֹ:

BENEDICTION

Morning Service for the
Day of Atonement

Meditation for the Day of Atonement

O God and Father, I come into Thy benign presence to lift my voice in penitent prayer. This Day of Atonement is a messenger from on high, calling me in love to return to Thee. May it be Thy will, O Master of the universe, that I may hear and heed Thy voice. Thou hast given me the understanding to distinguish between good and evil and hast bestowed upon me freedom of will to choose between them. Often have I disregarded Thy words and strayed from Thy path. But in Thy mercy dost Thou give me the means of turning from my evil ways and of coming back unto the path on which Thou desirest me to go.

Give me strength, O my God, to cast out the complacency and self-righteousness that have blinded mine eyes and led me to my failings and misconduct. Forgive my sins, O merciful Father! May I find tranquility for my troubled soul. Help me to look into mine own heart and thus come to know myself. Let me seek and find reconciliation with those of my fellowmen whom I have grieved. May I be worthy of their renewed affection and confidence. Remove malice and hatred from my heart against those who wish me ill. May I seek to be reconciled, O Lord, with my fellowmen and with Thee. O Thou who art the loving Father of all, hear my prayer, and in Thy mercy answer me. Amen.

Morning Service for the Day of Atonement

Choir

How goodly are thy tents, O Jacob, thy dwellings, O Israel! Through Thy great mercy, O God, I come to Thy house and bow down in Thy holy temple in the fear of Thee. O Lord, I love the place of Thy house and the abode in which Thy glory dwelleth. And so I bow down, and adore Thee, O God, my Maker. May my prayer be offered in an acceptable time; mayest Thou, in the greatness of Thy mercy, answer me according to Thy faithfulness.

מַה־טֹּבוּ אֹהָלֶיךָ יַעֲקֹב מִשְׁכְּנֹתֶיךָ יִשְׂרָאֵל: וַאֲנִי בְּרֹב חַסְדְּךָ אָבֹא בֵיתֶךָ אֶשְׁתַּחֲוֶה אֶל־הֵיכַל קָדְשְׁךָ בְּיִרְאָתֶךָ: יְיָ אָהַבְתִּי מְעוֹן בֵּיתֶךָ וּמְקוֹם מִשְׁכַּן כְּבוֹדֶךָ: וַאֲנִי אֶשְׁתַּחֲוֶה וְאֶכְרָעָה אֶבְרְכָה לִפְנֵי־יְיָ עֹשִׂי: וַאֲנִי תְפִלָּתִי לְךָ יְיָ עֵת רָצוֹן אֱלֹהִים בְּרָב חַסְדֶּךָ עֲנֵנִי בֶּאֱמֶת יִשְׁעֶךָ:

Reader

This is the day of God. On this day we are called to the sanctuary by a summons as exalting and enduring as the everlasting hills: Prepare to meet Thy God, O Israel.

This is the day of awe. What are we as we stand in the presence of God—a leaf in the storm, a fleeting moment in the tide of time, a whisper lost in the vastness of creation.

This is the day of decision. On this day we invoke God as the Master of our destiny. We vow that we will mend the evil of our ways and pray that He may judge us in mercy and inscribe us in the book of life for a year of blessing.

This is the day of our atonement. We would return to God as penitent children long to return to a loving father. Before God we confess our sins knowing that the gates of repentance are always open. We yearn to be at one again with God's holy law and blessed with His forgiving love.

Reader

God and Father! On this great day, the Sabbath of the soul, Thy children, wherever they dwell, gather in Thy sanctuaries to rededicate themselves unto Thee. We come into Thy presence with a sense of our unworthiness. We have yielded to temptations and gone astray after the devices of our hearts, heedless of Thy holy will. O Thou, who art glorious in holiness and whose love is boundless, purify our hearts and direct our thoughts unto Thee. Kindle within us a steadfast faith that shall dispel the darkness of doubt and confusion.

Father of mercies! We do not pray for ourselves alone, but for all Thy children. May the recognition of our own failings lead us to be patient with the shortcomings of others, and may every virtue which Thou hast implanted within us reveal to us the dignity and sanctity of each human being. Every soul is precious in Thy sight; every life is Thy gift. Though man is often set against man and nation against nation, teach us the common kinship of all men. Cleanse us from falsehood and selfishness; remove from us hatred and cruelty which blight human life. Unite us in a brotherhood of service to Thee and to our fellowmen.

Congregation and Reader

Grant that this day bring renewal of spirit to us and to all Israel. May our worship direct the hearts of parents to their children and the hearts of children to their parents, and the heart of Israel unto Thee, O heavenly Father! Open within our souls the springs of hope and of joy in Thy salvation, and vouchsafe unto us Thy blessings of atonement and reconciliation. Amen.

Choir

The Lord of all, who reigned supreme
   Ere first creation's form was framed;
When all was finished by His will
   His name Almighty was proclaimed.

When this, our world, shall be no more,
   In majesty He still shall reign,
Who was, who is, who will for aye
   In endless glory still remain.

Alone is He beyond compare,
   Without division or ally,
Without initial date or end,
   Omnipotent He rules on high.

He is my God, my Savior He,
   To whom I turn in sorrow's hour;
My banner proud, my refuge sure,
   Who hears and answers with His power.

Then in His hand myself I lay,
   And trusting sleep, and wake with cheer;
My soul and body are His care;
   The Lord doth guard, I have no fear.

Choir

אֲדוֹן עוֹלָם אֲשֶׁר מָלַךְ. בְּטֶרֶם כָּל־יְצִיר נִבְרָא:
לְעֵת נַעֲשָׂה בְחֶפְצוֹ כֹּל. אֲזַי מֶלֶךְ שְׁמוֹ נִקְרָא:

וְאַחֲרֵי כִּכְלוֹת הַכֹּל. לְבַדּוֹ יִמְלוֹךְ נוֹרָא:
וְהוּא הָיָה וְהוּא הֹוֶה. וְהוּא יִהְיֶה בְּתִפְאָרָה:

וְהוּא אֶחָד וְאֵין שֵׁנִי. לְהַמְשִׁיל לוֹ לְהַחְבִּירָה:
בְּלִי רֵאשִׁית בְּלִי תַכְלִית. וְלוֹ הָעֹז וְהַמִּשְׂרָה:

וְהוּא אֵלִי וְחַי גּוֹאֲלִי. וְצוּר חֶבְלִי בְּעֵת צָרָה:
וְהוּא נִסִּי וּמָנוֹס־לִי. מְנָת כּוֹסִי בְּיוֹם אֶקְרָא:

בְּיָדוֹ אַפְקִיד רוּחִי. בְּעֵת אִישָׁן וְאָעִירָה:
וְעִם־רוּחִי גְּוִיָּתִי. יְיָ לִי וְלֹא אִירָא:

Reader

The soul which Thou, O God, hast given unto me came pure from Thee. Thou hast created it, Thou hast formed it, Thou hast breathed it into me; Thou hast preserved it in this body and, at the appointed time, Thou wilt take it from this earth that it may enter upon life everlasting. While the breath of life is within me, I will worship Thee, Sovereign of the world and Lord of all souls. Praised be Thou, O God, in whose hands are the souls of all the living and the spirits of all flesh.

Congregation and Reader

Praised be Thou, O Lord our God, who openest the eyes of the blind. Amen.

Praised be Thou, O Lord our God, who freest the captive. Amen.

Praised be Thou, O Lord our God, who liftest up those who are bowed down. Amen.

Praised be Thou, O Lord our God, who givest strength to the weary. Amen.

Praised be Thou, O Lord our God, who hast crowned Israel with the glory of Thy spirit. Amen.

Reader

אֱלֹהַי. נְשָׁמָה שֶׁנָּתַתָּ בִּי טְהוֹרָה הִיא. אַתָּה
בְרָאתָהּ אַתָּה יְצַרְתָּהּ אַתָּה נְפַחְתָּהּ בִּי. וְאַתָּה
מְשַׁמְּרָהּ בְּקִרְבִּי. וְאַתָּה עָתִיד לִטְּלָהּ מִמֶּנִּי
וּלְהַחֲזִירָהּ בִּי לֶעָתִיד לָבֹא: כָּל־זְמַן שֶׁהַנְּשָׁמָה
בְקִרְבִּי מוֹדֶה אֲנִי לְפָנֶיךָ יְיָ אֱלֹהַי וֵאלֹהֵי אֲבוֹתַי
רִבּוֹן כָּל־הַמַּעֲשִׂים אָדוֹן כָּל־הַנְּשָׁמוֹת:

Congregation and Reader

בָּרוּךְ אַתָּה יְיָ אֱלֹהֵינוּ מֶלֶךְ הָעוֹלָם פּוֹקֵחַ עִוְרִים:

בָּרוּךְ אַתָּה יְיָ אֱלֹהֵינוּ מֶלֶךְ הָעוֹלָם מַתִּיר אֲסוּרִים:

בָּרוּךְ אַתָּה יְיָ אֱלֹהֵינוּ מֶלֶךְ הָעוֹלָם זוֹקֵף כְּפוּפִים:

בָּרוּךְ אַתָּה יְיָ אֱלֹהֵינוּ מֶלֶךְ הָעוֹלָם הַנּוֹתֵן לַיָּעֵף
כֹּחַ:

בָּרוּךְ אַתָּה יְיָ אֱלֹהֵינוּ מֶלֶךְ הָעוֹלָם עוֹטֵר יִשְׂרָאֵל
בְּתִפְאָרָה:

Reader

רבון כל העולמים

Lord of all worlds, not in reliance upon our own merit do we lay our supplications before Thee, but trusting in Thine infinite mercy alone. For what are we, what is our life, what our goodness, what our power? What can we say in Thy presence? Are not all the mighty men as naught before Thee and those of great renown as though they had never been; the wisest as if without knowledge, and men of understanding as if without discernment? Many of our works are vain, and our days pass away like a shadow. Our life would be altogether vanity were it not for the soul which, fashioned in Thine own image, gives us assurance of our higher destiny and imparts to our fleeting days an abiding value.

Help us, O God, to banish from our hearts all vainglory, pride of worldly possessions, and self-sufficient leaning upon our own reason. Fill us with the spirit of meekness and the grace of modesty that we may grow in wisdom and in reverence. May we never forget that all we have and prize is but lent to us, a trust for which we must render account to Thee. O heavenly Father, put into our hearts the love and awe of Thee, that we may consecrate our lives to Thy service and glorify Thy name in the eyes of all men.

Reader

How shall I come before God, the Most High? And
how shall I bow before the God of old?

If the mountains were an altar, and all the wood of
Lebanon were laid thereon;

If all cattle and all beasts were slain, and laid as sacrifice upon the wood;

All Lebanon would not suffice for fuel, nor all its beasts
for burnt-offering—

Lo! all these were not enough to serve, to come there-
with before the God of glory,

For Thou, our King, art exceeding glorious: how then
should we bow down before our Lord.

Verily none living can honor Thee—how can I, Thy
servant?

For Thou hast multiplied good things for me—
for Thou hast magnified Thy mercy unto me.

Great are the debts I owe Thee for the good Thou hast
wrought for me.

I have not served Thee in accordance with Thy benefits: one in ten thousand I have not repaid Thee.

If I say, I will declare their number, I know not how to
count them.

And what shall I return unto Thee, seeing that Thine
are the heavens, and the earth also is Thine?

It is written: I, the Lord, will not reprove thee for
lack of sacrifices or thy burnt offerings.

Concerning your sacrifices and your burnt offerings I
   commanded not your fathers.

What have I asked, and what have I sought of Thee but
   to fear me?

To serve with joy and a good heart; behold, to hearken
   is better than sacrifice,

And a broken heart than a whole offering. The sacrifices of God are a broken spirit.

I will build an altar of the broken fragments of my
   heart, and will bow my spirit within me.

My broken spirit—that is Thy sacrifice; let it be acceptable upon Thine altar.

I will proclaim aloud Thy praise, I will declare all Thy
   wonders.

(From *Hymn of Unity*, 12th Century)

Congregation and Choir

Early will I seek Thee,
God, my refuge strong;
Late prepare to meet Thee
With my evening song.

שַׁחַר אֲבַקֶּשְׁךָ צוּרִי
וּמִשְׂגַּבִּי
אֶעֱרוֹךְ לְפָנֶיךָ שַׁחֲרִי
וְגַם עַרְבִּי:

Though unto Thy greatness
I with trembling soar,—
Yet my inmost thinking
Lies Thine eyes before.

לְפָנֵי גְדֻלָּתְךָ אֶעֱמֹד
וְאֶבָּהֵל
כִּי עֵינְךָ תִרְאֶה כָּל
מַחְשְׁבוֹת לִבִּי:

What this frail heart dreameth
And my tongue's poor speech,
Can they even distant
To Thy greatness reach?

מַה־זֶּה אֲשֶׁר יוּכַל הַלֵּב
וְהַלָּשׁוֹן
לַעֲשׂוֹת וּמַה כֹּחַ רוּחִי
בְּתוֹךְ קִרְבִּי:

Being great in mercy,
Thou wilt not despise
Praises which till death's hour
From my soul shall rise.

הִנֵּה לְךָ תִיטַב זִמְרַת
אֱנוֹשׁ עַל־כֵּן
אוֹדְךָ בְּעוֹד תִּהְיֶה
נִשְׁמַת אֱלוֹהַּ בִּי:

Reader

Praised be He who by His creative word called the universe into being. Praised be He who sustains it by His might. Praised be He who orders it in His wisdom and establishes the world in righteousness. Praised be Thou who hast given us the (Sabbath and the) Day of Atonement, on which we may draw nigh unto Thee and rejoice in Thy pardon and grace.

Congregation and Reader

Praised be Thou, O God, for Thy manifold mercies unto us, for our heritage of faith, for visions of truth and of duty and for the courage to remain true to our higher nature amid trials and temptations. Thy servants in all generations have found joy in worshiping Thee with pure hearts. With psalms and songs they glorified Thy name. We too would adore Thee with prayers of thanksgiving and with deeds of lovingkindness.

Reader

בָּרוּךְ שֶׁאָמַר וְהָיָה הָעוֹלָם. בָּרוּךְ הוּא. בָּרוּךְ
עֹשֶׂה בְרֵאשִׁית. בָּרוּךְ אוֹמֵר וְעֹשֶׂה. בָּרוּךְ גּוֹזֵר
וּמְקַיֵּם. בָּרוּךְ מְרַחֵם עַל־הָאָרֶץ. בָּרוּךְ מְרַחֵם עַל
הַבְּרִיּוֹת. בָּרוּךְ מְשַׁלֵּם שָׂכָר טוֹב לִירֵאָיו. בָּרוּךְ
חַי לָעַד וְקַיָּם לָנֶצַח. בָּרוּךְ פּוֹדֶה וּמַצִּיל. בָּרוּךְ
שֶׁנָּתַן לְעַמּוֹ יִשְׂרָאֵל אֶת (יוֹם הַשַּׁבָּת וְאֶת) יוֹם
הַכִּפּוּרִים הַזֶּה. אֶת־יוֹם סְלִיחַת הֶעָוֹן הַזֶּה. וְאֶת
יוֹם מִקְרָא קֹדֶשׁ הַזֶּה. בָּרוּךְ הוּא וּבָרוּךְ שְׁמוֹ.
בָּרוּךְ אַתָּה יְיָ אֱלֹהֵינוּ מֶלֶךְ הָעוֹלָם. הָאֵל הָאָב
הָרַחֲמָן. הַמְהֻלָּל בְּפִי עַמּוֹ. מְשֻׁבָּח וּמְפֹאָר
בִּלְשׁוֹן חֲסִידָיו וַעֲבָדָיו. וּבְשִׁירֵי דָוִד עַבְדֶּךָ.
נְהַלֶּלְךָ יְיָ אֱלֹהֵינוּ בִּשְׁבָחוֹת וּבִזְמִרוֹת נְגַדֶּלְךָ
וּנְשַׁבֵּחֲךָ וּנְפָאֶרְךָ וְנַזְכִּיר שִׁמְךָ וְנַמְלִיכְךָ מַלְכֵּנוּ
אֱלֹהֵינוּ. יָחִיד חֵי הָעוֹלָמִים. מֶלֶךְ מְשֻׁבָּח וּמְפֹאָר
עֲדֵי עַד שְׁמוֹ הַגָּדוֹל. בָּרוּךְ אַתָּה יְיָ מֶלֶךְ מְהֻלָּל
בַּתִּשְׁבָּחוֹת:

Responsive Reading

(Psalm xix)

Reader

The heavens declare the glory of God, and the firmament showeth His handiwork.

Congregation

Day unto day uttereth speech, and night unto night revealeth knowledge.

There is no speech, there are no words, neither is their voice heard.

Their line is gone out through all the earth, and their words to the end of the world.

In them hath He set a tent for the sun, which is as a bridegroom coming out of his chamber;

And rejoiceth, as a strong man, to run his course.

His going forth is from the end of the heaven, and his circuit unto the ends of it;

And there is nothing hid from the heat thereof.

The law of the Lord is perfect, restoring the soul;

The testimony of the Lord is sure, making wise the simple.

The precepts of the Lord are right, rejoicing the heart;

The commandment of the Lord is pure, enlightening the eyes.

The fear of the Lord is clean, enduring forever;

The ordinances of the Lord are true, they are righteous altogether:

Choir

May the words of my mouth and the meditation of my heart be acceptable unto Thee, O Lord, my Rock and my Redeemer.

(Psalm xix)

הַשָּׁמַיִם מְסַפְּרִים כְּבוֹד אֵל. וּמַעֲשֵׂה יָדָיו מַגִּיד הָרָקִיעַ:

יוֹם לְיוֹם יַבִּיעַ אֹמֶר. וְלַיְלָה לְלַיְלָה יְחַוֶּה דָּעַת:

אֵין אֹמֶר וְאֵין דְּבָרִים. בְּלִי נִשְׁמָע קוֹלָם:

בְּכָל־הָאָרֶץ יָצָא קַוָּם. וּבִקְצֵה תֵבֵל מִלֵּיהֶם. לַשֶּׁמֶשׁ שָׂם אֹהֶל בָּהֶם:

וְהוּא כְּחָתָן יֹצֵא מֵחֻפָּתוֹ. יָשִׂישׂ כְּגִבּוֹר לָרוּץ אֹרַח:

מִקְצֵה הַשָּׁמַיִם מוֹצָאוֹ. וּתְקוּפָתוֹ עַל־קְצוֹתָם. וְאֵין נִסְתָּר מֵחַמָּתוֹ:

תּוֹרַת יְיָ תְּמִימָה. מְשִׁיבַת נָפֶשׁ. עֵדוּת יְיָ נֶאֱמָנָה. מַחְכִּימַת פֶּתִי:

פִּקּוּדֵי יְיָ יְשָׁרִים. מְשַׂמְּחֵי־לֵב. מִצְוַת יְיָ בָּרָה. מְאִירַת עֵינָיִם:

יִרְאַת יְיָ טְהוֹרָה. עוֹמֶדֶת לָעַד. מִשְׁפְּטֵי־יְיָ אֱמֶת. צָדְקוּ יַחְדָּו:

Choir

יִהְיוּ לְרָצוֹן אִמְרֵי־פִי. וְהֶגְיוֹן לִבִּי לְפָנֶיךָ. יְיָ צוּרִי וְגֹאֲלִי:

(Psalm xxxiii)

Reader

Rejoice in the Lord, O ye righteous, praise is comely for the upright.

Congregation

Give thanks unto the Lord with harp, sing praises unto Him with the psaltery of ten strings.

For the word of the Lord is upright; and all His work is done in faithfulness.

He loveth righteousness and justice; the earth is full of the lovingkindness of the Lord.

By the word of the Lord were the heavens made; and all the hosts of them by the breath of His mouth.

He gathereth the waters of the sea together as a heap; He layeth up the deeps in storehouses.

Let all the earth fear the Lord; let all the inhabitants of the world stand in awe of Him.

For He spoke, and it was; He commanded, and it stood.

The counsel of the Lord standeth forever; the thoughts of His heart to all generations.

Happy is the nation whose God is the Lord; the people whom He hath chosen for His own inheritance.

The Lord looketh from heaven; He beholdeth all the sons of men;

Congregation and Reader

(Psalm xxxiii)

רַנְּנוּ צַדִּיקִים בַּיְיָ. לַיְשָׁרִים נָאוָה תְהִלָּה:

הוֹדוּ לַיְיָ בְּכִנּוֹר. בְּנֵבֶל עָשׂוֹר זַמְּרוּ לוֹ:

שִׁירוּ לוֹ שִׁיר חָדָשׁ. הֵיטִיבוּ נַגֵּן בִּתְרוּעָה:

כִּי יָשָׁר דְּבַר־יְיָ. וְכָל־מַעֲשֵׂהוּ בֶּאֱמוּנָה:

אֹהֵב צְדָקָה וּמִשְׁפָּט. חֶסֶד יְיָ מָלְאָה הָאָרֶץ:

בִּדְבַר יְיָ שָׁמַיִם נַעֲשׂוּ. וּבְרוּחַ פִּיו כָּל־צְבָאָם:

כֹּנֵס כַּנֵּד מֵי הַיָּם. נֹתֵן בְּאוֹצָרוֹת תְּהוֹמוֹת:

יִירְאוּ מֵיְיָ כָּל־הָאָרֶץ. מִמֶּנּוּ יָגוּרוּ כָּל יֹשְׁבֵי תֵבֵל:

כִּי־הוּא אָמַר וַיֶּהִי. הוּא צִוָּה וַיַּעֲמֹד:

יְיָ הֵפִיר עֲצַת גּוֹיִם. הֵנִיא מַחְשְׁבוֹת עַמִּים:

עֲצַת יְיָ לְעוֹלָם תַּעֲמֹד. מַחְשְׁבוֹת לִבּוֹ לְדֹר וָדֹר:

אַשְׁרֵי הַגּוֹי אֲשֶׁר יְיָ אֱלֹהָיו. הָעָם בָּחַר לְנַחֲלָה לוֹ:

מִשָּׁמַיִם הִבִּיט יְיָ. רָאָה אֶת־כָּל־בְּנֵי הָאָדָם:

He that fashioneth the hearts of them all, that considereth all their doings.

A king is not saved by the multitude of a host, a mighty man is not delivered by great strength.

Behold the eye of the Lord is toward them that fear Him, toward them that wait for His mercy.

To deliver their soul from death, and to keep them alive in famine.

Our soul hath waited for the Lord; He is our help and our shield.

For in Him doth our heart rejoice, because we have trusted in His holy name.

Choir

Let Thy mercy, O Lord, be upon us, according as we have waited for Thee.

(Psalm cxlvi)

Reader

Hallelujah, praise the Lord, O my soul.

Congregation

I will praise the Lord as long as I live; I will sing praises to my God while I have my being.

Put not your trust in princes, in the son of man, in whom there is no help.

His breath goeth forth; he returneth to the dust; in that very day his plans perish.

Happy is he that hath the God of Jacob for his help;

Whose hope is in the Lord his God;

Who made heaven and earth, the sea, and all that is therein; who keepeth truth forever;

Who executeth judgment for the oppressed; who giveth food to the hungry.

מִמְּכוֹן שִׁבְתּוֹ הִשְׁגִּיחַ. אֶל־כָּל־יֹשְׁבֵי הָאָרֶץ:

הַיֹּצֵר יַחַד לִבָּם. הַמֵּבִין אֶל־כָּל־מַעֲשֵׂיהֶם:

אֵין הַמֶּלֶךְ נוֹשָׁע בְּרָב־חָיִל. גִּבּוֹר לֹא יִנָּצֵל בְּרָב־
כֹּחַ:

שֶׁקֶר הַסּוּס לִתְשׁוּעָה. וּבְרֹב חֵילוֹ לֹא יְמַלֵּט:

הִנֵּה עֵין יְיָ אֶל־יְרֵאָיו. לַמְיַחֲלִים לְחַסְדּוֹ:

לְהַצִּיל מִמָּוֶת נַפְשָׁם. וּלְחַיּוֹתָם בָּרָעָב:

נַפְשֵׁנוּ חִכְּתָה לַיְיָ. עֶזְרֵנוּ וּמָגִנֵּנוּ הוּא:

כִּי־בוֹ יִשְׂמַח לִבֵּנוּ. כִּי בְשֵׁם קָדְשׁוֹ בָטָחְנוּ:

Choir

יְהִי חַסְדְּךָ יְיָ עָלֵינוּ. כַּאֲשֶׁר יִחַלְנוּ לָךְ:

(Psalm cxlvi)

הַלְלוּיָהּ הַלְלִי נַפְשִׁי אֶת־יְהֹוָה:

אֲהַלְלָה יְהֹוָה בְּחַיָּי. אֲזַמְּרָה לֵאלֹהַי בְּעוֹדִי:

אַל־תִּבְטְחוּ בִנְדִיבִים. בְּבֶן־אָדָם שֶׁאֵין־לוֹ תְשׁוּעָה:

תֵּצֵא רוּחוֹ יָשֻׁב לְאַדְמָתוֹ. בַּיּוֹם הַהוּא אָבְדוּ
עֶשְׁתֹּנֹתָיו:

אַשְׁרֵי שֶׁאֵל יַעֲקֹב בְּעֶזְרוֹ. שִׂבְרוֹ עַל־יְיָ אֱלֹהָיו:

עֹשֶׂה שָׁמַיִם וָאָרֶץ. אֶת־הַיָּם וְאֶת־כָּל־אֲשֶׁר בָּם.
הַשֹּׁמֵר אֱמֶת לְעוֹלָם:

The Lord setteth free the prisoners; the Lord openeth the eyes of the blind.

 The Lord raiseth up them that are bowed down; the Lord loveth the righteous.

The Lord preserveth the strangers; he relieveth the fatherless and the widow.

Choir

The Lord shall reign forever; thy God, O Zion, to all generations!   Praise ye the Lord!

Responsive Reading
(From Psalm cxlv)

Reader

Happy are they who dwell in Thy house, they are continually praising Thee.

Congregation

 Happy are they who thus know Him; happy is the people whose God is the Lord.

I will extol Thee, my God, O King, and I will bless Thy name forever and ever.

 Every day I will bless Thee, and I will praise Thy name forever and ever.

Great is the Lord and highly to be praised; and His greatness is beyond our finding out.

 One generation shall praise Thy works to another, and shall declare Thy mighty acts.

I will speak of the splendor of Thy majesty and of Thy wondrous works

 And men shall tell of Thy mighty acts, and I will tell of Thy greatness.

עֹשֶׂה מִשְׁפָּט לַעֲשׁוּקִים. נֹתֵן לֶחֶם לָרְעֵבִים. יְיָ מַתִּיר
אֲסוּרִים:

יְיָ פֹּקֵחַ עִוְרִים. יְיָ זֹקֵף כְּפוּפִים. יְיָ אֹהֵב צַדִּיקִים:

יְהוָֹה שֹׁמֵר אֶת־גֵּרִים. יָתוֹם וְאַלְמָנָה יְעוֹדֵד. וְדֶרֶךְ
רְשָׁעִים יְעַוֵּת:

Choir

יִמְלֹךְ יְיָ לְעוֹלָם אֱלֹהַיִךְ צִיּוֹן לְדֹר וָדֹר הַלְלוּיָהּ:

Reader and Congregation

אַשְׁרֵי יוֹשְׁבֵי בֵיתֶךָ. עוֹד יְהַלְלוּךָ סֶּלָה:

אַשְׁרֵי הָעָם שֶׁכָּכָה לּוֹ. אַשְׁרֵי הָעָם שֶׁיְיָ אֱלֹהָיו:

(Psalm cxlv)

אֲרוֹמִמְךָ אֱלוֹהַי הַמֶּלֶךְ. וַאֲבָרְכָה שִׁמְךָ לְעוֹלָם
וָעֶד:

בְּכָל־יוֹם אֲבָרְכֶךָּ. וַאֲהַלְלָה שִׁמְךָ לְעוֹלָם וָעֶד:

גָּדוֹל יְיָ וּמְהֻלָּל מְאֹד. וְלִגְדֻלָּתוֹ אֵין חֵקֶר:

דּוֹר לְדוֹר יְשַׁבַּח מַעֲשֶׂיךָ. וּגְבוּרֹתֶיךָ יַגִּידוּ:

הֲדַר כְּבוֹד הוֹדֶךָ וְדִבְרֵי נִפְלְאֹתֶיךָ אָשִׂיחָה:

וֶעֱזוּז נוֹרְאֹתֶיךָ יֹאמֵרוּ. וּגְדֻלָּתְךָ אֲסַפְּרֶנָּה:

They shall herald Thy great goodness, and shall sing of Thy righteousness.

The Lord is gracious and full of compassion, slow to anger and of great mercy.

The Lord is good to all, and His tender mercies are over all his works.

Thy kingdom is a kingdom for all ages, and Thy dominion endureth throughout all generations.

The Lord upholdeth those who fall, and raiseth up those who are bowed down.

The eyes of all wait upon Thee, and Thou givest them their food in due season.

Thou openest Thy hand and satisfiest the desire of every living being.

The Lord is righteous in all His ways, and gracious in all His works.

The Lord is near unto all who call upon Him, to all who call upon Him in truth.

Choir

My mouth shall utter the praise of the Lord; and let all flesh bless His holy name forever and ever.

זֵכֶר רַב־טוּבְךָ יַבִּיעוּ. וְצִדְקָתְךָ יְרַנֵּנוּ:

חַנּוּן וְרַחוּם יְיָ. אֶרֶךְ אַפַּיִם וּגְדָל־חָסֶד:

טוֹב יְיָ לַכֹּל. וְרַחֲמָיו עַל־כָּל־מַעֲשָׂיו:

יוֹדוּךָ יְיָ כָּל־מַעֲשֶׂיךָ. וַחֲסִידֶיךָ יְבָרְכוּכָה:

כְּבוֹד מַלְכוּתְךָ יֹאמֵרוּ. וּגְבוּרָתְךָ יְדַבֵּרוּ:

לְהוֹדִיעַ לִבְנֵי הָאָדָם גְּבוּרֹתָיו. וּכְבוֹד הֲדַר
מַלְכוּתוֹ:

מַלְכוּתְךָ מַלְכוּת כָּל־עֹלָמִים. וּמֶמְשַׁלְתְּךָ בְּכָל־
דּוֹר וָדֹר:

סוֹמֵךְ יְיָ לְכָל־הַנֹּפְלִים. וְזוֹקֵף לְכָל־הַכְּפוּפִים:

עֵינֵי כֹל אֵלֶיךָ יְשַׂבֵּרוּ וְאַתָּה נוֹתֵן־לָהֶם אֶת־אָכְלָם
בְּעִתּוֹ:

פּוֹתֵחַ אֶת־יָדֶךָ. וּמַשְׂבִּיעַ לְכָל־חַי רָצוֹן:

צַדִּיק יְיָ בְּכָל־דְּרָכָיו. וְחָסִיד בְּכָל־מַעֲשָׂיו:

קָרוֹב יְיָ לְכָל־קֹרְאָיו. לְכֹל אֲשֶׁר יִקְרָאֻהוּ בֶאֱמֶת:

Choir

תְּהִלַּת יְיָ יְדַבֶּר־פִּי. וִיבָרֵךְ כָּל־בָּשָׂר שֵׁם קָדְשׁוֹ
לְעוֹלָם וָעֶד:

Reader

(I Chronicles xxix, 10–13)

Wherefore David blessed the Lord before all the congregation; and David said: Blessed be Thou, O Lord, the God of Israel our father, forever and ever. Thine, O Lord, is the greatness, and the power, and the glory, and the victory, and the majesty; for all that is in the heaven and in the earth is Thine; Thine is the kingdom, O Lord, and Thou art exalted as head above all. Both riches and honor come of Thee, and Thou rulest over all; and in Thy hand is power and might; and in Thy hand it is to make great, and to give strength unto all. Now therefore, our God, we thank Thee, and praise Thy glorious name.

Reader

O Lord, where shall I find Thee?
    Hid is Thy lofty place;
And where shall I not find Thee,
    Whose glory fills all space?
Who formed the world, abideth
    Within man's soul alway;
Refuge to them that seek Him,
    Ransom for them that stray.

O, how shall mortals praise Thee,
    When angels strive in vain

Or build for Thee a dwelling,
  Whom worlds cannot contain?
Longing to draw anear Thee
  With all my heart I pray
Then going forth to seek Thee
  Thou meetest me on the way.

I find Thee in the marvels
  Of Thy creative might,
In visions in Thy Temple,
  In dreams that bless the night.
Who saith he hath not seen Thee?
  Thy heavens refute his word;
Their hosts declare Thy glory,
  Though never voice be heard.

(Jehuda Halevi, 11th–12th Century)

Reader

Every living soul shall praise Thee; the spirit of all flesh shall glorify Thy name. Thou art God from everlasting to everlasting and besides Thee there is no redeemer nor savior. Thou art the first and the last, the Lord of all generations. Thou rulest the world in kindness and all Thy creatures in mercy. Thou art our guardian who sleepeth not and slumbereth not. To Thee alone we give thanks. Yet, though our lips should overflow with song, and our tongues with joyous praise, we should still be unable to thank Thee even for a thousandth part of the bounties which Thou hast bestowed upon our fathers and upon us. Thou hast been our protector and our savior in every trial and peril. Thy mercy has watched over us, and Thy lovingkindness has never failed us.

Congregation and Reader

Praised be Thy holy name. Thou hast made Thine eternal law our portion, and hast given us a goodly heritage. Open our eyes to the beauty of Thy truth and help us so to exemplify it in our lives that we may win all men for Thy law of righteousness. Gather all Thy children around Thy banner of truth that Thy name may be hallowed through us in all the world and the entire human family may be blessed with truth and peace. Amen.

Reader

נִשְׁמַת כָּל־חַי תְּבָרֵךְ אֶת־שִׁמְךָ יְיָ אֱלֹהֵינוּ. וְרוּחַ
כָּל־בָּשָׂר תְּפָאֵר וּתְרוֹמֵם זִכְרְךָ מַלְכֵּנוּ תָּמִיד: מִן
הָעוֹלָם וְעַד־הָעוֹלָם אַתָּה אֵל. וּמִבַּלְעָדֶיךָ אֵין
לָנוּ מֶלֶךְ גּוֹאֵל וּמוֹשִׁיעַ פּוֹדֶה וּמַצִּיל. וּמְפַרְנֵס
וּמְרַחֵם. בְּכָל־עֵת צָרָה וְצוּקָה. אֵין לָנוּ מֶלֶךְ אֶלָּא
אָתָּה: אֱלֹהֵי הָרִאשׁוֹנִים וְהָאַחֲרוֹנִים. הַמְנַהֵג עוֹלָמוֹ
בְּחֶסֶד וּבְרִיּוֹתָיו בְּרַחֲמִים. לְךָ לְבַדְּךָ אֲנַחְנוּ
מוֹדִים: אִלּוּ פִינוּ מָלֵא שִׁירָה כַּיָּם וּלְשׁוֹנֵנוּ רִנָּה
כַּהֲמוֹן גַּלָּיו. וְשִׂפְתוֹתֵינוּ שֶׁבַח כְּמֶרְחֲבֵי רָקִיעַ. אֵין
אֲנַחְנוּ מַסְפִּיקִים לְהוֹדוֹת לְךָ יְיָ אֱלֹהֵינוּ וֵאלֹהֵי
אֲבוֹתֵינוּ. עַל־כָּל־הַטּוֹבוֹת שֶׁעָשִׂיתָ עִם־אֲבוֹתֵינוּ
וְעִמָּנוּ: מִמִּצְרַיִם גְּאַלְתָּנוּ יְיָ אֱלֹהֵינוּ וּמִבֵּית עֲבָדִים
פְּדִיתָנוּ. בְּרָעָב זַנְתָּנוּ. וּבְשָׂבָע כִּלְכַּלְתָּנוּ: מֵחֶרֶב
הִצַּלְתָּנוּ וּמִדֶּבֶר מִלַּטְתָּנוּ. וּמֵחֳלָיִם רָעִים וְנֶאֱמָנִים
דִּלִּיתָנוּ: עַד־הֵנָּה עֲזָרוּנוּ רַחֲמֶיךָ. וְלֹא־עֲזָבוּנוּ
חֲסָדֶיךָ. וְאַל־תִּטְּשֵׁנוּ יְיָ אֱלֹהֵינוּ לָנֶצַח: עַל־כֵּן
נְהַלֶּלְךָ וּנְשַׁבֵּחַךָ וּנְפָאֶרְךָ וּנְבָרֵךְ אֶת־שֵׁם קָדְשֶׁךָ:
בָּרוּךְ אַתָּה יְיָ. אֵל מֶלֶךְ גָּדוֹל בַּתִּשְׁבָּחוֹת. אֵל
הַהוֹדָאוֹת. אֲדוֹן הַנִּפְלָאוֹת. הַבּוֹחֵר בְּשִׁירֵי זִמְרָה,
מֶלֶךְ אֵל חֵי הָעוֹלָמִים:

(Congregation rises)

Reader

Praise ye the Lord to whom all praise is due.

Choir and Congregation

Praised be the Lord to whom all praise is due forever and ever.

(Congregation is seated)

Reader

Praised be Thou, O Lord our God, Ruler of the world, who openest for us the gates of mercy and makest glad the heart of them that wait for Thy forgiveness. How manifold are Thy works, O Lord! In wisdom hast Thou made them all. The heavens declare Thy glory. The earth reveals Thy creative power. Thou formest light and darkness, ordainest good out of evil, bringest harmony into nature and peace to the heart of man.

Great has been Thy love for us and Thy compassion boundless. Our fathers put their trust in Thee and Thou didst teach them the law of life. Be gracious also unto us that we may understand and fulfil the teachings of Thy word. Enlighten our eyes in Thy law that we may cling unto Thy commandments. Unite our hearts to love and revere Thee. We trust in Thee

(Congregation rises)

Reader

בָּרְכוּ אֶת־יְיָ הַמְבֹרָךְ:

Choir and Congregation

בָּרוּךְ יְיָ הַמְבֹרָךְ לְעוֹלָם וָעֶד:

(Congregation is seated)

Reader

בָּרוּךְ אַתָּה יְיָ אֱלֹהֵינוּ מֶלֶךְ הָעוֹלָם. יוֹצֵר אוֹר
וּבוֹרֵא חֹשֶׁךְ. עֹשֶׂה שָׁלוֹם וּבוֹרֵא אֶת־הַכֹּל:

הַמֵּאִיר לָאָרֶץ וְלַדָּרִים עָלֶיהָ בְּרַחֲמִים. וּבְטוּבוֹ
מְחַדֵּשׁ בְּכָל־יוֹם תָּמִיד מַעֲשֵׂה בְרֵאשִׁית: מָה
רַבּוּ מַעֲשֶׂיךָ יְיָ. כֻּלָּם בְּחָכְמָה עָשִׂיתָ. מָלְאָה
הָאָרֶץ קִנְיָנֶךָ: תִּתְבָּרַךְ יְיָ אֱלֹהֵינוּ עַל־שֶׁבַח מַעֲשֵׂה
יָדֶיךָ. וְעַל־מְאוֹרֵי־אוֹר שֶׁעָשִׂיתָ יְפָאֲרוּךָ סֶּלָה:
בָּרוּךְ אַתָּה יְיָ יוֹצֵר הַמְּאוֹרוֹת:

אַהֲבָה רַבָּה אֲהַבְתָּנוּ יְיָ אֱלֹהֵינוּ. חֶמְלָה גְדוֹלָה
וִיתֵרָה חָמַלְתָּ עָלֵינוּ: אָבִינוּ מַלְכֵּנוּ. בַּעֲבוּר
אֲבוֹתֵינוּ שֶׁבָּטְחוּ בְךָ וַתְּלַמְּדֵם חֻקֵּי חַיִּים. כֵּן
תְּחָנֵּנוּ וּתְלַמְּדֵנוּ: הָאֵר עֵינֵינוּ בְּתוֹרָתֶךָ. וְדַבֵּק לִבֵּנוּ
בְּמִצְוֹתֶיךָ. וְיַחֵד לְבָבֵנוּ לְאַהֲבָה וּלְיִרְאָה שְׁמֶךָ:

and rejoice in Thy saving power, for from Thee cometh our help. Thou hast called us and drawn us nigh unto Thee to serve Thee in faithfulness. Joyfully do we lift up our voices and proclaim Thy unity. Praised be Thou, O God, who in Thy love hast called Thy people Israel to serve Thee.

(Congregation rises)

Reader

Hear, O Israel: The Lord our God, the Lord is One. Praised be His name whose glorious kingdom is forever and ever.

(Congregation is seated)

Congregation and Reader

Thou shalt love the Lord, thy God, with all thy heart, with all thy soul, and with all thy might. And these words, which I command thee this day, shall be upon thy heart. Thou shalt teach them diligently unto thy children, and shalt speak of them when thou sittest in thy house, when thou walkest by the way, when thou liest down, and when thou risest up. Thou shalt bind them for a sign upon thy hand and they shall be for frontlets between thine eyes. Thou shalt write them upon the doorposts of thy house and upon thy gates: That ye may remember and do all My commandments and be holy unto your God.

כִּי בְשֵׁם קָדְשְׁךָ בָּטֶחְנוּ. נָגִילָה וְנִשְׂמְחָה בִּישׁוּעָתֶךָ.
כִּי אֵל פּוֹעֵל יְשׁוּעוֹת אָתָּה. וּבָנוּ בָחַרְתָּ וְקֵרַבְתָּנוּ
לְשִׁמְךָ הַגָּדוֹל סֶלָה בֶּאֱמֶת לְהוֹדוֹת לְךָ וּלְיַחֶדְךָ
בְּאַהֲבָה. בָּרוּךְ אַתָּה יְיָ הַבּוֹחֵר בְּעַמּוֹ יִשְׂרָאֵל
בְּאַהֲבָה:

(Congregation rises)

Reader, then Choir and Congregation

שְׁמַע יִשְׂרָאֵל יְהֹוָה אֱלֹהֵינוּ יְהֹוָה אֶחָד:
בָּרוּךְ שֵׁם כְּבוֹד מַלְכוּתוֹ לְעוֹלָם וָעֶד:

(Congregation is seated)

Reader

וְאָהַבְתָּ אֵת יְיָ אֱלֹהֶיךָ בְּכָל־לְבָבְךָ וּבְכָל־נַפְשְׁךָ
וּבְכָל־מְאֹדֶךָ: וְהָיוּ הַדְּבָרִים הָאֵלֶּה אֲשֶׁר אָנֹכִי
מְצַוְּךָ הַיּוֹם עַל־לְבָבֶךָ: וְשִׁנַּנְתָּם לְבָנֶיךָ וְדִבַּרְתָּ
בָּם. בְּשִׁבְתְּךָ בְּבֵיתֶךָ וּבְלֶכְתְּךָ בַדֶּרֶךְ וּבְשָׁכְבְּךָ
וּבְקוּמֶךָ: וּקְשַׁרְתָּם לְאוֹת עַל־יָדֶךָ. וְהָיוּ לְטֹטָפֹת
בֵּין עֵינֶיךָ: וּכְתַבְתָּם עַל־מְזֻזוֹת בֵּיתֶךָ וּבִשְׁעָרֶיךָ:
לְמַעַן תִּזְכְּרוּ וַעֲשִׂיתֶם אֶת־כָּל־מִצְוֹתָי וִהְיִיתֶם
קְדֹשִׁים לֵאלֹהֵיכֶם: אֲנִי יְיָ אֱלֹהֵיכֶם:

Responsive Reading

Reader

True and enduring is Thy word which Thou hast spoken through Thy prophets.

Congregation

Thou art the living God, Thy words bring life and light to the soul.

Thou art the strength of our life, the rock of our salvation; Thy kingdom and Thy truth abide forever.

Thou hast been the help of our fathers in time of trouble and art our refuge in all generations.

Thou art the first and the last, and besides Thee there is no redeemer nor helper.

As Thou hast saved Israel from Egyptian bondage, so mayest Thou send Thy help to all who are oppressed.

May Thy law rule in the hearts of all Thy children, and Thy truth unite them in bonds of fellowship.

May the righteous of all nations rejoice in Thy grace and triumph by Thy power.

O God, who art our refuge and our hope, we glorify Thy name now as did our fathers in ancient days:

Choir

Who is like unto Thee, O Lord? Who is like unto Thee, glorious in holiness, awe-inspiring, working wonders?

Responsive Reading

אֱמֶת. אֱלֹהֵי עוֹלָם מַלְכֵּנוּ. צוּר יַעֲקֹב מָגֵן יִשְׁעֵנוּ:

לְדוֹר וָדוֹר הוּא קַיָּם וּשְׁמוֹ קַיָּם. וּמַלְכוּתוֹ
וֶאֱמוּנָתוֹ לָעַד קַיָּמֶת:

וּדְבָרָיו חַיִּים וְקַיָּמִים. נֶאֱמָנִים וְנֶחֱמָדִים לָעַד
וּלְעוֹלְמֵי עוֹלָמִים:

עֶזְרַת אֲבוֹתֵינוּ אַתָּה הוּא מֵעוֹלָם. מָגֵן וּמוֹשִׁיעַ
לִבְנֵיהֶם אַחֲרֵיהֶם בְּכָל־דּוֹר וָדוֹר:

אַשְׁרֵי אִישׁ שֶׁיִּשְׁמַע לְמִצְוֹתֶיךָ וְתוֹרָתְךָ וּדְבָרְךָ
יָשִׂים עַל־לִבּוֹ:

אֱמֶת. שָׁאַתָּה הוּא יְיָ אֱלֹהֵינוּ. צוּר יְשׁוּעָתֵנוּ.
פּוֹדֵנוּ וּמַצִּילֵנוּ מֵעוֹלָם שְׁמֶךָ. אֵין אֱלֹהִים זוּלָתֶךָ:

אַתָּה הוּא רִאשׁוֹן וְאַתָּה הוּא אַחֲרוֹן. וּמִבַּלְעָדֶיךָ
אֵין לָנוּ מֶלֶךְ גּוֹאֵל וּמוֹשִׁיעַ:

מִמִּצְרַיִם גְּאַלְתָּנוּ יְיָ אֱלֹהֵינוּ. וּמִבֵּית עֲבָדִים
פְּדִיתָנוּ:

עַל־זֹאת שִׁבְּחוּ אֲהוּבִים וְרוֹמְמוּ אֵל:

Choir

מִי כָמֹכָה בָּאֵלִים יְיָ. מִי כָּמֹכָה נֶאְדָּר בַּקֹּדֶשׁ
נוֹרָא תְהִלֹּת עֹשֵׂה־פֶלֶא:

Reader

A new song the redeemed sang unto Thy name.
They proclaimed Thy sovereignty and said:

Choir

The Lord shall reign forever and ever.

Reader

O Rock of Israel, redeem those who are oppressed
and deliver those who are persecuted. Praised be
Thou, our Redeemer, the Holy One of Israel.

Choir: Amen

Reader

Praised be Thou, O Lord, God of our fathers, God
of Abraham, Isaac and Jacob, great, mighty, and exalted. Thou bestowest lovingkindness upon all Thy
children. Thou rememberest the devotion of the fathers. In Thy love Thou bringest redemption to their
descendants for the sake of Thy name.

Remember us unto life, O King, who delightest in
life, and inscribe us in the book of life, for Thy sake,
O God of life. Thou, O King, art our helper, savior
and protector. Praised be Thou, O Lord, Shield of
Abraham.

Eternal is Thy power, O Lord, Thou art mighty to
save. In lovingkindness Thou sustainest the living; in
the multitude of Thy mercies, Thou preservest all.
Thou upholdest the falling, healest the sick; bringest
freedom to the captives and keepest faith with Thy
children in death as in life. Who is like unto Thee,

Reader

שִׁירָה חֲדָשָׁה שִׁבְּחוּ גְאוּלִים לְשִׁמְךָ עַל־שְׂפַת
הַיָּם יַחַד כֻּלָּם הוֹדוּ וְהִמְלִיכוּ וְאָמְרוּ:

Choir and Congregation

יְיָ יִמְלֹךְ לְעֹלָם וָעֶד:

Reader

צוּר יִשְׂרָאֵל. קוּמָה בְּעֶזְרַת יִשְׂרָאֵל. וּפְדֵנוּ יְיָ
צְבָאוֹת. שְׁמוֹ קְדוֹשׁ יִשְׂרָאֵל. בָּרוּךְ אַתָּה יְיָ גָּאַל
יִשְׂרָאֵל:

Choir: Amen.

Reader

בָּרוּךְ אַתָּה יְיָ אֱלֹהֵינוּ וֵאלֹהֵי אֲבוֹתֵינוּ. אֱלֹהֵי
אַבְרָהָם אֱלֹהֵי יִצְחָק וֵאלֹהֵי יַעֲקֹב. הָאֵל הַגָּדוֹל
הַגִּבּוֹר וְהַנּוֹרָא. אֵל עֶלְיוֹן. גּוֹמֵל חֲסָדִים טוֹבִים.
וְקוֹנֵה הַכֹּל וְזוֹכֵר חַסְדֵי אָבוֹת. וּמֵבִיא גְאֻלָּה לִבְנֵי
בְנֵיהֶם לְמַעַן שְׁמוֹ בְּאַהֲבָה:

זָכְרֵנוּ לַחַיִּים. מֶלֶךְ חָפֵץ בַּחַיִּים. וְכָתְבֵנוּ בְּסֵפֶר
הַחַיִּים. לְמַעַנְךָ אֱלֹהִים חַיִּים: מֶלֶךְ עוֹזֵר וּמוֹשִׁיעַ
וּמָגֵן. בָּרוּךְ אַתָּה יְיָ מָגֵן אַבְרָהָם:

אַתָּה גִבּוֹר לְעוֹלָם אֲדֹנָי. רַב לְהוֹשִׁיעַ. מְכַלְכֵּל
חַיִּים בְּחֶסֶד. מְחַיֶּה הַכֹּל בְּרַחֲמִים רַבִּים. סוֹמֵךְ
נוֹפְלִים וְרוֹפֵא חוֹלִים וּמַתִּיר אֲסוּרִים. וּמְקַיֵּם

Almighty God, Author of life and death, Source of salvation?

Who is like unto Thee, O merciful Father, who rememberest Thy children unto life? Praised be Thou, O Lord, who hast implanted within us immortal life.

SANCTIFICATION

(Congregation rises)

Congregation and Reader

We sanctify Thy name on earth, as the heavens glorify Thee on high; and in the words of the prophet we say:

Holy, holy, holy is the Lord of hosts; the whole earth is full of His glory.

Reader

God our Strength, God our Lord, how excellent is Thy name in all the earth.

Congregation and Reader

Praised be the glory of God throughout the world.

Reader

Our God is one; He is our Father, He is our King, He is our Helper and in His mercy He will answer our prayers in the sight of all the living.

Congregation and Reader

The Lord will reign forever, thy God, O Zion, from generation to generation. Hallelujah.

(Congregation is seated)

אֱמוּנָתוֹ לִישֵׁנֵי עָפָר. מִי כָמוֹךָ בַּעַל גְּבוּרוֹת. וּמִי
דוֹמֶה־לָּךְ. מֶלֶךְ מֵמִית וּמְחַיֶּה. וּמַצְמִיחַ יְשׁוּעָה:
מִי כָמוֹךָ אַב הָרַחֲמִים. זוֹכֵר יְצוּרָיו לַחַיִּים
בְּרַחֲמִים: בָּרוּךְ אַתָּה יְיָ נֹטֵעַ בְּתוֹכֵנוּ חַיֵּי עוֹלָם:

SANCTIFICATION
(Congregation rises)

נְקַדֵּשׁ אֶת שִׁמְךָ בָּעוֹלָם. כְּשֵׁם שֶׁמַּקְדִּישִׁים אוֹתוֹ
בִּשְׁמֵי מָרוֹם. כַּכָּתוּב עַל־יַד נְבִיאֶךָ. וְקָרָא זֶה אֶל־
זֶה וְאָמַר:

Choir and Congregation

קָדוֹשׁ קָדוֹשׁ קָדוֹשׁ יְיָ צְבָאוֹת. מְלֹא כָל־הָאָרֶץ
כְּבוֹדוֹ:

Reader

אַדִּיר אַדִּירֵנוּ יְיָ אֲדוֹנֵנוּ מָה־אַדִּיר שִׁמְךָ בְּכָל־
הָאָרֶץ:

Congregation and Choir

בָּרוּךְ כְּבוֹד יְיָ מִמְּקוֹמוֹ:

Reader

אֶחָד הוּא אֱלֹהֵינוּ. הוּא אָבִינוּ. הוּא מַלְכֵּנוּ.
הוּא מוֹשִׁיעֵנוּ: וְהוּא יַשְׁמִיעֵנוּ בְּרַחֲמָיו לְעֵינֵי כָּל־
חָי:

Congregation and Choir

יִמְלֹךְ יְיָ לְעוֹלָם אֱלֹהַיִךְ צִיּוֹן לְדֹר וָדֹר
הַלְלוּיָהּ:

(Congregation is seated)

Reader

Thou art holy, awe-inspiring is Thy name. There is no God besides Thee. As it is written, the Lord of hosts is exalted through justice, and the holy God is sanctified through righteousness.

Our God, and God of our fathers! Let Thy presence be manifest to us in all Thy works, so that reverence for Thee may fill the hearts of all Thy creatures. May all the children of men bow before Thee in humility and unite to do Thy will with one heart, that all may acknowledge that Thine are power, dominion and majesty, and that Thy name is exalted above all.

Grant honor, O Lord, to them that fear Thee, inspire with courage all who wait for Thee, and fulfil the hope of all who trust in Thy name. Hasten the day that will bring gladness to all the dwellers on earth and victory of the spirit to those who bear witness to Thy unity. Then shall the just see and exult, the righteous be glad and the pious sing for joy; then shall iniquity be made dumb and all wickedness shall vanish like smoke, for the reign of evil shall have passed away from the earth.

Lord our God, may Thy kingdom come speedily, so that the worship of Thy name and obedience to Thy law may unite all men in brotherhood and peace; that every creature may know that Thou art its Creator, and every living being exclaim: The Lord, the God of Israel, ruleth and His dominion endureth forever. Praised be Thou, O Lord, who rulest in holiness.

Choir: Amen.

Reader

קָדוֹשׁ אַתָּה וְנוֹרָא שְׁמֶךָ. וְאֵין אֱלוֹהַּ מִבַּלְעָדֶיךָ. כַּכָּתוּב. וַיִּגְבַּהּ יְיָ צְבָאוֹת בַּמִּשְׁפָּט. וְהָאֵל הַקָּדוֹשׁ נִקְדַּשׁ בִּצְדָקָה:

וּבְכֵן תֵּן פַּחְדְּךָ יְיָ אֱלֹהֵינוּ עַל כָּל־מַעֲשֶׂיךָ וְאֵימָתְךָ עַל כָּל־מַה־שֶּׁבָּרֵאתָ. וְיִירָאוּךָ כָּל־הַמַּעֲשִׂים וְיִשְׁתַּחֲווּ לְפָנֶיךָ כָּל־הַבְּרוּאִים. וְיֵעָשׂוּ כֻלָּם אֲגֻדָּה אַחַת לַעֲשׂוֹת רְצוֹנְךָ בְּלֵבָב שָׁלֵם. כְּמוֹ שֶׁיָּדַעְנוּ יְיָ אֱלֹהֵינוּ שֶׁהַשָּׁלְטוֹן לְפָנֶיךָ עֹז בְּיָדְךָ וּגְבוּרָה בִּימִינֶךָ וְשִׁמְךָ נוֹרָא עַל כָּל־מַה־שֶּׁבָּרֵאתָ:

וּבְכֵן תֵּן כָּבוֹד יְיָ לְעַמֶּךָ תְּהִלָּה לִירֵאֶיךָ וְתִקְוָה לְדוֹרְשֶׁיךָ וּפִתְחוֹן פֶּה לַמְיַחֲלִים לָךְ. שִׂמְחָה לְכָל־ יוֹשְׁבֵי תֵבֵל וּצְמִיחַת קֶרֶן לִמְיַחֲדֵי שְׁמֶךָ. בִּמְהֵרָה בְיָמֵינוּ: וּבְכֵן צַדִּיקִים יִרְאוּ וְיִשְׂמָחוּ וִישָׁרִים יַעֲלֹזוּ וַחֲסִידִים בְּרִנָּה יָגִילוּ וְעוֹלָתָה תִּקְפָּץ־פִּיהָ. וְכָל־ הָרִשְׁעָה כֻּלָּהּ כְּעָשָׁן תִּכְלֶה. כִּי תַעֲבִיר מֶמְשֶׁלֶת זָדוֹן מִן־הָאָרֶץ:

וְתִמְלוֹךְ אַתָּה יְיָ לְבַדֶּךָ עַל כָּל־מַעֲשֶׂיךָ. כַּכָּתוּב בְּדִבְרֵי קָדְשֶׁךָ יִמְלֹךְ יְיָ לְעוֹלָם אֱלֹהַיִךְ צִיּוֹן לְדֹר וָדֹר הַלְלוּיָהּ: בָּרוּךְ אַתָּה יְיָ הַמֶּלֶךְ הַקָּדוֹשׁ:

Choir: Amen.

Congregation and Reader

אֱלֹהֵֽינוּ וֵאלֹהֵי אֲבוֹתֵֽינוּ. קַדְּשֵֽׁנוּ בְּמִצְוֹתֶֽיךָ. וְתֵן
חֶלְקֵֽנוּ בְּתוֹרָתֶֽךָ. שַׂבְּעֵֽנוּ מִטּוּבֶֽךָ. וְשַׂמְּחֵֽנוּ בִּישׁוּעָתֶֽךָ.
וְטַהֵר לִבֵּֽנוּ לְעָבְדְּךָ בֶּאֱמֶת. כִּי אַתָּה סָלְחָן
לְיִשְׂרָאֵל וּמְבַּלְעָדֶֽיךָ אֵין לָֽנוּ מֶֽלֶךְ מוֹחֵל וְסוֹלֵֽחַ:

Congregation and Reader

Our God and God of our fathers, pardon our transgressions on this Day of Atonement, remove our guilt
and blot out our iniquities. May we, sanctified through
Thy commandments, become sharers in the blessings
of Thy word. Teach us to be satisfied with the gifts
of Thy goodness and gratefully to rejoice in all Thy
mercies. Purify our hearts that we may serve Thee in
truth. In all ages, Thy people Israel have turned unto
Thee for forgiveness and felt assured of Thy pardon.
We too seek forgiveness for our sins by turning unto
Thee.

Responsive Reading

Reader

Come and let us return unto the Lord;

Congregation

    For He hath torn, and He will heal us, He hath
      smitten, and He will bind us up.

Let us earnestly strive to know the Lord.

    He will raise us up, that we may live in His presence.

Return, O Israel, unto the Lord thy God,

For thou hast stumbled in thine iniquity.
The ways of the Lord are right, and the just do walk
    in them;
    But transgressors do stumble therein.
Who is like Thee, O God, that pardoneth iniquity and
    forgiveth transgressions?
    He retaineth not His anger forever, because He de-
    lighteth in mercy.
He will again have compassion upon us;
    He will pardon our sins and blot out our iniquities.
If thou wilt return unto Me, O Israel, saith the Lord,
    thou shalt stand before Me.

Choir

Turn us again to Thee, O Lord, that we may be re-
    stored; renew our life as in the days of yore.

Reader
Let us search and try our ways, and turn again to the
    Lord.

Congregation
    Let us lift up our hearts unto God and say: We have
    sinned, we have transgressed, we have rebelled
    against Thy word.
Heal me, O Lord, and I shall be healed;
    Save me, O Lord, and I shall be saved;
The Lord is my strength and my shield.
    In Him doth my heart trust, and I am helped.
Let us seek good and not evil, that we may live.
    Then shall the Lord, the God of hosts, be with us.
The Lord is good to them that trust in Him;
    To the soul that seeketh Him;

Good and upright is the Lord;
Therefore doth He instruct sinners in the way.
All the paths of the Lord are mercy and truth.
Unto such as keep His covenant and His testimonies.
Wait for the Lord, and keep His way.
The salvation of the righteous is of the Lord.
The Lord will not cast off forever; though He causeth
grief, yet will He have compassion.

Choir

I, the Lord, search the heart, and try the thoughts,
to give to every man according to his ways, and according to the fruit of his doings.

Reader

אנוש מה יזכה

What is man, O God, that Thou art mindful of him,
and the son of man that Thou thinkest of him? How
can mortal man appear pure and blameless before Thee
in whose sight even the hosts of heaven are not perfect?
How can he whose life is as a passing shadow, account
himself worthy to stand in Thy presence, O Thou
Eternal One.

Though we appear virtuous in the sight of men, yet
who of us can stand before Thee who searchest the
heart, to whom darkness is as light, and from whose
eye nothing is hid? Thou art veiled from the eyes of
all creatures; but their inmost ways lie open to Thee.
Even that which shall be is known unto Thee, and

Thou readest the future as Thou dost the past. As Thou seest and knowest all, so art Thou the judge of all. Who shall question Thy judgments, or who shall say to Thee, what doest Thou? Over men and nations Thou stretchest the line, and who can stay Thy measurements? O that man would think of this, so that he might seek that which is good, and turn from that which is evil! O that he might consider whither he goeth, and to whom he must give account at last! His days are as vanity, and his nights bring him no peace. His plans run to naught; he walketh as in a dream, and findeth no rest until the grave closes over him. But why should man murmur at his lot? Though he be called to toil and to trouble, his faithfulness shall not fail of reward. Happy, therefore, is the man who maketh divine wisdom his guide, and whose reverence for God is from the heart.

For all things stand revealed at last, and all men will be called to render account for their doings. Then truth will be made manifest, and deception will be ended forever. He who worketh righteousness and showeth mercy will find everlasting peace. His reward surpasses all earthly treasures and honors. A good name is his here below, and the crown of immortal life beyond. For him the day of death is better than the day of birth. Therefore until the day of a man's death, Thou dost wait for him to repent so that he may live the life eternal.

CONFESSION

Silent Devotion

In deep humility and contrition I make supplication unto Thee, my God and my Father, on this holiest of days. Conscious of my frailties and my shortcomings, I seek Thee with the hope in my heart that I shall find forgiveness for my sins for I know that Thou art merciful and loving, long suffering and abundant in pardoning.

As I ponder upon the years that lie behind me, I recognize how I have failed to make them count in Thy service and the service of my fellowmen. I have often been selfish when I should have been self-sacrificing, harsh when I should have been gentle, hard when I should have been kind, thoughtless when I should have been considerate. Day after day I have sought my own pleasure and gain without a thought of the higher purpose of my life. Again and again I have turned a deaf ear to the promptings of my better nature and have permitted the evil inclination to swerve me from the path of purity and right.

I know how often I have chosen the worse, conscious though I was of the better. I confess this before Thee in this hour of self-searching and self-examination. I know how frail I am.

Out of the depths I cry unto Thee. Attend to my supplication. Help me to be true to my best self. Hear Thou my voice, give ear to my prayer for forgiveness. Help me to live a life rich in deeds pleasing unto Thee. Strengthen me in the endeavor to fulfil my duties toward the beloved in my home, toward my friends and companions, and toward my fellowmen in the larger sphere of my activities. Be Thou my stay and support, for in Thee do I put my trust.

Thou desirest not the death of the sinner, but that he return from his evil way and live before Thee. Deep as I may have fallen, this day assures me that I can rise to the heights if I so will. Thou hast placed before me the good and the evil, and hast given me the power to choose between them. As mine is this power, so is mine also the responsibility. Give me the strength in the coming days to withstand folly and temptation, evil and wickedness. In all my doings make me to recognize every day and every hour that I am shaping for weal or for woe the destiny of my immortal soul.

Create in me a pure heart, O my God, and renew a right spirit within me. May reverence for Thee fill my waking hours. May I seek Thee more earnestly than I have done hitherto. Too often have I forgotten my divine endowment as a child of Thine. O that I may be constantly mindful of this in all my ways and all my works. May I seek Thee in the hours of joy as well as in the days of sorrow, that Thou mayest be a living Presence nigh unto me at all times.

Help me and I shall be helped, save me and I shall be saved. I yearn to undo the evil I may have done consciously or unconsciously, to correct fault and failing, to change bitter to sweet, to bring light where there is darkness, truth where there is falsehood, and good where there is evil. I would make atonement for all the lapses from the right of which I have been guilty. Open mine eyes that I may see clearly where I have gone astray. Give me the courage to ask forgiveness of all whom I have wronged. Remove from my heart all rancor and hardness, that I may forgive freely even as I hope to be forgiven. Accept Thou with favor my prayer for forgiveness, my confession which I make before Thee. May the words of my mouth and the meditation of my heart be acceptable before Thee, my Rock and my Redeemer. Amen.

SPECIAL MEDITATIONS

A PRAYER FOR THE AGED

The earnest meditations of this sacred day, O God, awaken my soul to grateful acknowledgement of Thy grace which has bestowed upon me the gift of life; of Thy loving Providence, which has prolonged my days. By Thy mercy I have been permitted to pass through the dangers and difficulties that beset my pathway and have come in safety to the coveted goal of a ripe old age.

And now as I look back over the years that have gone, the whole past shines out before me revealing my inmost self. I humbly confess before Thee in this solemn hour the sins and errors that cast their shadows over my life—the wilfulness of childhood, the way-wardness of youth, the selfishness and vanity of mature years and the frailties of even these later days. How far, alas, have I fallen from those noble ideals and pure motives in character and conduct which Thou hast set as the aim of life! How often have I failed to make use of those divine powers Thou has implanted within me! In the lengthening shadows of life's decline, all my sins and failures loom up reprovingly and I devoutly pray for thy pardoning favor and forgiveness.

Grant me clearness of vision to see life as a whole from youth to age and to be comforted in the faith that the best is yet to be. In moments of doubt and despondency when, like the patriarch, I count my days as few and evil and when the waning of my bodily powers makes me declare with the sage, I have no pleasure in them, oh, then sustain me with a realization of these blessings which the maturity of age alone can bring and the ripeness of experience alone can yield. Give me the sweetness of that joy which is reserved for those who serve others through the counsel and guidance learned in the school of life's experience.

Out of the lessons drawn from my own toils and trials, disappointments and sorrows, may I be able to help others find the true values in life's struggles and the joys and triumphs that endure. Grant me the calmness and serenity of a truly chastened spirit that I may thus bless others and serve Thee. May time not lessen but deepen within me the spirit of wisdom and understanding, the spirit of knowledge and the fear of God.

Enable me to hold fast, however old I may grow, to the spirit of youth. Suffer me not to lose that sense of wonder which stirs within me in the presence of Thy creation. O, quicken me from day to day with that power of communion with Thee which restores my soul.

I crave the power to see ever more clearly that other half of life's plan, which youth can not discern. Sustain me with the faith that wrong, cruelty and injustice cannot prevail but that the right, the pure and true shall endure. And may the imperishable worth of life uphold me in the deathless hope of the hereafter.

Let me not be afraid! As one by one my bodily powers weaken, may my soul enter into greater freedom and be purified and atoned in Thy sight. Let me die the death of the righteous and let mine end be like his. Amen!

A PRAYER FOR WOMEN

We come into Thy holy presence, O our heavenly Father, on this Day of Atonement to consecrate our thoughts and to chasten our lives. Stirred by the sentiments and memories of this sacred season, we feel keenly the blessedness of our opportunity for service in Thy cause. Our very being is warmed by the breath of Thy Fatherly love. We rejoice to pour forth our prayers and songs to Thee, and to draw nigh in humility before Thy throne of grace.

Yom Kippur comes with a special appeal to us as women. Its message of forgiveness touches the very root of our souls. We feel its melting tenderness no less than its demand for earnest self-scrutiny. Our domestic relations move in a circle of affection and responsibility. Thus hast Thou placed a particular task upon us, as mothers, wives, and daughters. We are proud to be witnesses of Thy truth and to be privileged to radiate Thy love wherever we may dwell. We thank Thee that Thou hast made us especially sensitive to the emotions and purposes of religion. Throughout the ages have our ancestors laid upon us the injunction to foster and promote the teachings of Thy Law. They have taught us to make our home a sanctuary and our table an altar unto Thee. Ours it is to fill our homes with the light of religious truth. Ours it is to strengthen ourselves by the power of prayer. Ours it is to train our children in the loyalties of our faith.

On a day so searching in its monitions, we realize that we have not fulfilled the high religious duties of our Jewish womanhood. Often we have weakened under the task. Often we have yielded to the allurements of the hour. At times we have treated things sacred in the spirit of levity. At times in utter forgetfulness of Thy many blessings, we have questioned the dispensation of Thy justice. Conscious that we have not reached the high mark which Thou hast set for us, we crave Thy pardoning love. Sincere in our remorse, we pray Thee to help us rise to our responsibilities.

Grant that we may use aright the enlarged opportunities which have come to women. Make us feel a new pride and dignity as workers for Thy kingdom of righteousness. Make us strong in our faith that we may be an inspiration to all who come within the circle of our influence. Imbue us with such unwavering trust in Thee as shall enable us to perform our duties in the home and in the world. Make us steadfast in our reliance upon Thee, that in sorrow and in joy we may cling to Thee and proclaim Thee as the God of life and love. Amen!

A PRAYER FOR YOUNG PEOPLE

Thou, my Maker, knowest my life, my thoughts, my conduct. Thou knowest the longings and ideals, the pains and hopes that urge and impel me. Thou knowest also that I would make my life acceptable unto

Thee, a source of pride to those who care for me, a source of blessing to my fellowmen.

There are moments when the vision of my better self animates my soul. I dream of a life of character and high achievement, a life of worth and service. But I also have my hours of temptation and struggle, when the vision fades and the will weakens. Be with me, O God, in those hours. Strengthen me, that I may realize the finer potentialities with which Thou hast endowed me. When in the pressure of daily living, when in the pursuit after pleasure and success, I lose sight of my better self, fortify me with a sense of the purposefulness and holiness of life. I ask not that my path be easy, that all temptation and struggle be removed from my way. But I pray Thee to strengthen within me the conviction that I can make of my life what I will. Cause me to feel that if Thou art with me, sustaining and encouraging me, no victory of the spirit is impossible. Oh, let me know the joy of moral conquest.

Often I am overwhelmed by the vastness of the world and my own littleness and insignificance in it. I seem so pitifully small, a mere atom in a measureless world of existence. I seem unable to find my place in all this bewildering scheme of things. My life appears meaningless, my work seems useless. Yet I know that Thou hast placed me here and hast allotted me a task that is useful and necessary. I beseech Thee, O my God, to reveal to me the high dignity of the part Thou hast assigned to me. Let me feel that in Thine eyes my efforts are worth while. Deepen within me the consciousness of the obligation I owe to my friends and loved ones, the responsibility I have to Thee and to my fellowmen. Give me the strength so to mould and purify my character that my life may be counted a blessing. I cannot find words to utter all that is within my heart. Thou art with me, I have no fear. Amen.

A PRAYER FOR CHILDREN

O Lord, on this Day of Atonement, I offer my prayer unto Thee. I am glad to be in Thy house in the company of those dear to me. Their prayers and praises make me feel the holiness of this day. I too lift my heart to Thee. Thy people are asking Thee to forgive their sins and failings. I too want to be forgiven. I know that at times I have failed to do my best. At times I have done wrong. I have not always obeyed my parents, and I have not always shown respect to my teachers. Often I have not been helpful enough to my family and my friends. Help me, O God, to grow ever better in my ways, and to cling to what is right. May the example of good men and women be my guide always. Keep me, O Lord, from all manner of sin, that they may gain no hold over me. Thine eye is upon all our doings. May I do nothing that will put me to shame.

O Father, as the years go on and life opens before me, keep Thou my heart true to Thy Law, and my eyes open to its teachings. Help me so to live as to add more and more to the joy of the world, the honor of Israel, and the glory of Thy name. Amen!

Reader

Our God and Father, Thou hast summoned us to appear before Thy judgment seat, to render account before Thee, the All-just and All-holy. What shall we say in Thy presence? How can we justify ourselves? We blush with shame and are bowed down with humiliation, for we know our unworthiness. Thou, O Father, searchest and knowest us; Thou compassest our paths and art acquainted with all our ways; our most secret thoughts are not hidden before Thee. Therefore, Thou dost not call upon us to justify ourselves, but to examine our conduct, acknowledge our sins, and forsake the evil. Thou hast summoned us this day that we may judge ourselves in the light of truth. Not to punish, but to pardon is Thy holy will; not to destroy us in Thine anger, but to forgive us in Thy love, hast Thou appointed this Day of Atonement. Lord our God, though trembling before Thee, we hope in Thee; though stricken with awe at the call of Thy judgment, we look for the light of Thy compassion. Judge us, O Father, in Thy mercy. Let each day be to us a day of repentance, and every hour as the hour of death, which calls us to appear before Thy throne of judgment.

Reader and Congregation

Before the hour has passed, let us in deep humility and contrition make confession to God, and with sincere vows resolve so to mend our ways that we shall not be moved from His path. Amen.

Reader

Our God and God of our fathers, pardon our transgressions, remove our guilt and blot out our iniquities on this Day of Atonement, as Thou hast promised: I, even I, blot out thine iniquities for Mine own sake, and thy sins will I remember no more. I have made thy sins to vanish like a cloud and thy transgressions like a mist; return to Me for I have redeemed thee. For on this day shall ye be forgiven and cleansed from all your sins; before the Lord shall ye be pure.

(Congregation rises)

Reader and Congregation, then Choir

Our God and God of our fathers, let our prayers come before Thee. Turn not away from our supplication, for we are not so presumptuous and stiff-necked as to say before Thee that we are wholly righteous and have not sinned, but verily, we have sinned.

We have sinned; we have transgressed; we have done perversely.

(Congregation is seated)

Reader

אֱלֹהֵינוּ וֵאלֹהֵי אֲבוֹתֵינוּ. מְחַל לַעֲוֹנוֹתֵינוּ בְּיוֹם
הַכִּפֻּרִים הַזֶּה. מְחֵה וְהַעֲבֵר פְּשָׁעֵינוּ וְחַטֹּאתֵינוּ
מִנֶּגֶד עֵינֶיךָ. כָּאָמוּר. אָנֹכִי אָנֹכִי הוּא מֹחֶה פְשָׁעֶיךָ
לְמַעֲנִי וְחַטֹּאתֶיךָ לֹא אֶזְכֹּר: וְנֶאֱמַר. מָחִיתִי כָעָב
פְּשָׁעֶיךָ. וְכֶעָנָן חַטֹּאתֶיךָ. שׁוּבָה אֵלַי כִּי גְאַלְתִּיךָ:
וְנֶאֱמַר. כִּי־בַיּוֹם הַזֶּה יְכַפֵּר עֲלֵיכֶם. לְטַהֵר אֶתְכֶם
מִכֹּל חַטֹּאתֵיכֶם. לִפְנֵי יְיָ תִּטְהָרוּ:

(Congregation rises)

Reader and Congregation, then Choir

אֱלֹהֵינוּ וֵאלֹהֵי אֲבוֹתֵינוּ.

תָּבֹא לְפָנֶיךָ תְּפִלָּתֵנוּ. וְאַל תִּתְעַלַּם מִתְּחִנָּתֵנוּ. שֶׁאֵין
אֲנַחְנוּ עַזֵּי פָנִים וּקְשֵׁי עֹרֶף. לוֹמַר לְפָנֶיךָ יְיָ אֱלֹהֵינוּ
וֵאלֹהֵי אֲבוֹתֵינוּ. צַדִּיקִים אֲנַחְנוּ וְלֹא חָטָאנוּ. אֲבָל
אֲנַחְנוּ חָטָאנוּ:

חָטָאנוּ. עָוִינוּ. פָּשָׁעְנוּ:

(Congregation is seated)

Reader

We have turned aside from Thy commandments and from Thy beneficent ordinances, and it hath not availed us. Thou art righteous in all that has befallen us, for Thou doest justice, but we have wrought evil.

What shall we say before Thee, who art on high, and what shall we recount unto Thee, who dwellest in the heavens? Dost Thou not know all things; both the hidden and the revealed? Thou knowest the secrets of eternity and the hidden thoughts of every living being.

Thou searchest the innermost recesses and probest the deepest impulses of the heart. Nought is concealed from Thee nor hidden from Thine eyes.

O Lord our God, help us to see ourselves as Thou seest us. Make us conscious of our sins and failings; cause us to turn from our evil ways, and give us strength to make amends for our wrong doings, and grant us pardon for our sins.

Reader, then Congregation

For the sin which we have sinned against Thee under stress or through choice;

For the sin which we have sinned against Thee openly or in secret;

For the sin which we have sinned against Thee in stubbornness or in error.

Reader

סַרְנוּ מִמִּצְוֹתֶיךָ וּמִמִּשְׁפָּטֶיךָ הַטּוֹבִים וְלֹא שָׁוָה
לָנוּ. וְאַתָּה צַדִּיק עַל־כָּל־הַבָּא עָלֵינוּ. כִּי אֱמֶת
עָשִׂיתָ וַאֲנַחְנוּ הִרְשָׁעְנוּ:

מַה־נֹּאמַר לְפָנֶיךָ יוֹשֵׁב מָרוֹם. וּמַה־נְּסַפֵּר לְפָנֶיךָ
שׁוֹכֵן שְׁחָקִים. הֲלֹא כָּל־הַנִּסְתָּרוֹת וְהַנִּגְלוֹת אַתָּה
יוֹדֵעַ:

אַתָּה יוֹדֵעַ רָזֵי עוֹלָם. וְתַעֲלוּמוֹת סִתְרֵי כָל־חָי.
אַתָּה חוֹפֵשׂ כָּל־חַדְרֵי בָטֶן. וּבוֹחֵן כְּלָיוֹת וָלֵב. אֵין
דָּבָר נֶעְלָם מִמֶּךָ. וְאֵין נִסְתָּר מִנֶּגֶד עֵינֶיךָ:

וּבְכֵן יְהִי רָצוֹן מִלְּפָנֶיךָ יְיָ אֱלֹהֵינוּ וֵאלֹהֵי
אֲבוֹתֵינוּ. שֶׁתִּסְלַח לָנוּ עַל־כָּל־חַטֹּאתֵינוּ. וְתִמְחַל
לָנוּ עַל־כָּל־עֲוֹנוֹתֵינוּ. וּתְכַפֵּר לָנוּ עַל־כָּל־פְּשָׁעֵינוּ:

Reader, then Congregation

עַל חֵטְא שֶׁחָטָאנוּ לְפָנֶיךָ בְּאֹנֶס וּבְרָצוֹן:
עַל חֵטְא שֶׁחָטָאנוּ לְפָנֶיךָ בְּגָלוּי וּבַסֵּתֶר:
עַל חֵטְא שֶׁחָטָאנוּ לְפָנֶיךָ בְּזָדוֹן וּבִשְׁגָגָה:

For the sin which we have sinned against Thee in the evil meditations of the heart;

For the sin which we have sinned against Thee by the word of mouth;

For the sin which we have sinned against Thee by abuse of power;

For the sin which we have sinned against Thee by the profanation of Thy name;

For the sin which we have sinned against Thee by disrespect for parents and teachers;

For the sin which we have sinned against Thee by exploiting or dealing treacherously with our neighbor.

For all these sins, O God of forgiveness, bear with us! pardon us! forgive us!

Choir

For all these sins, O God of forgiveness, bear with us! pardon us! forgive us!

Reader

Our God and God of our fathers, forsake us not. Let us not be put to shame. Lead us to the knowledge of Thy law, that we may understand Thy ways. Direct our thoughts to revere Thy name. Incline our hearts to love Thee, that we may return to Thee in truth and sincerity. Forgive our sins for the sake of Thy great name.

Hear our cry, O Lord our God, be gracious unto us, and with mercy favorably accept our prayers.

עַל חֵטְא שֶׁחָטָאנוּ לְפָנֶיךָ בְּהַרְהוֹר הַלֵּב:

עַל חֵטְא שֶׁחָטָאנוּ לְפָנֶיךָ בְּדִבּוּר פֶּה:

עַל חֵטְא שֶׁחָטָאנוּ לְפָנֶיךָ בְּחִזּוּק יָד:

עַל חֵטְא שֶׁחָטָאנוּ לְפָנֶיךָ בְּחִלּוּל הַשֵּׁם:

עַל חֵטְא שֶׁחָטָאנוּ לְפָנֶיךָ בְּזִלְזוּל הוֹרִים וּמוֹרִים:

עַל חֵטְא שֶׁחָטָאנוּ לְפָנֶיךָ בְּהוֹנָאַת וּצְדִיַּת רֵעַ:

וְעַל כֻּלָּם אֱלוֹהַּ סְלִיחוֹת. סְלַח לָנוּ. מְחַל לָנוּ.
כַּפֶּר לָנוּ:

וְעַל כֻּלָּם אֱלוֹהַּ סְלִיחוֹת. סְלַח לָנוּ. מְחַל לָנוּ.
כַּפֶּר לָנוּ:

אֱלֹהֵינוּ וֵאלֹהֵי אֲבוֹתֵינוּ. אַל תַּעַזְבֵנוּ. וְאַל
תִּטְּשֵׁנוּ. וְאַל תַּכְלִימֵנוּ. וְאַל תָּפֵר בְּרִיתְךָ אִתָּנוּ.
קָרְבֵנוּ לְתוֹרָתֶךָ. לַמְּדֵנוּ מִצְוֹתֶיךָ. הוֹרֵנוּ דְרָכֶיךָ.
הַט לִבֵּנוּ לְיִרְאָה אֶת־שְׁמֶךָ. וּמוֹל אֶת־לְבָבֵנוּ
לְאַהֲבָתֶךָ. וְנָשׁוּב אֵלֶיךָ בֶּאֱמֶת וּבְלֵב שָׁלֵם. וּלְמַעַן
שִׁמְךָ הַגָּדוֹל תִּמְחוֹל וְתִסְלַח לַעֲוֹנֵינוּ:

שְׁמַע קוֹלֵנוּ יְיָ אֱלֹהֵינוּ. חוּס וְרַחֵם עָלֵינוּ. וְקַבֵּל
בְּרַחֲמִים וּבְרָצוֹן אֶת־תְּפִלָּתֵנוּ.

Choir

We are Thy people, Thou art our King.

We are Thy children, Thou art our Father.

We are Thy possession, Thou art our Portion.

We are Thy flock, Thou art our Shepherd.

We are Thy vineyard, Thou art our Keeper.

We are Thy beloved, Thou art our Friend.

Reader

Praised be Thou, O Lord, who forgivest transgressions; Ruler of the world, who sanctifiest (the Sabbath,) Israel and the Day of Atonement.

Choir: Amen.

Choir

כִּי אָנוּ עַמֶּךָ   וְאַתָּה מַלְכֵּנוּ:

אָנוּ בָנֶיךָ   וְאַתָּה אָבִינוּ:

אָנוּ נַחֲלָתֶךָ   וְאַתָּה גוֹרָלֵנוּ:

אָנוּ צֹאנֶךָ   וְאַתָּה רוֹעֵנוּ:

אָנוּ כַרְמֶךָ   וְאַתָּה נוֹטְרֵנוּ:

אָנוּ רַעְיָתֶךָ   וְאַתָּה דוֹדֵנוּ:

Reader

בָּרוּךְ אַתָּה יְיָ מֶלֶךְ מוֹחֵל וְסוֹלֵחַ לַעֲוֹנוֹתֵינוּ
מֶלֶךְ עַל־כָּל־הָאָרֶץ מְקַדֵּשׁ (הַשַּׁבָּת וְ) יִשְׂרָאֵל וְיוֹם
הַכִּפּוּרִים:

Choir: Amen.

Reader

Look with favor, O Lord, upon us, and may our service ever be acceptable unto Thee. Praised be Thou, O God, whom alone we serve in reverence.

Congregation and Reader

We gratefully acknowledge, O Lord our God, that Thou art our Creator and Preserver, the Rock of our life and the Shield of our help. We render thanks unto Thee for our lives which are in Thy hand, for our souls which are ever in Thy keeping, for Thy wondrous providence and for Thy continuous goodness, which Thou bestowest upon us day by day. Truly, Thy mercies never fail and Thy lovingkindness never ceases. Therefore do we forever put our trust in Thee.

Reader

Our God and God of our fathers, may Thy blessing rest upon us, according to the gracious promise of Thy word:

Reader and Choir

May the Lord bless thee and keep thee.

Amen.

May the Lord let His countenance shine upon thee and be gracious unto thee.

Amen.

May the Lord lift up His countenance upon thee and give thee peace.

Amen.

Reader

רְצֵה יְיָ אֱלֹהֵינוּ בְּעַמְּךָ יִשְׂרָאֵל. וּתְפִלָּתָם
בְּאַהֲבָה תְקַבֵּל. וּתְהִי לְרָצוֹן תָּמִיד עֲבֹדַת יִשְׂרָאֵל
עַמֶּךָ: בָּרוּךְ אַתָּה יְיָ שְׁאוֹתְךָ לְבַדְּךָ בְּיִרְאָה נַעֲבוֹד:

Reader and Congregation

מוֹדִים אֲנַחְנוּ לָךְ. שָׁאַתָּה הוּא יְיָ אֱלֹהֵינוּ וֵאלֹהֵי
אֲבוֹתֵינוּ לְעוֹלָם וָעֶד. צוּר חַיֵּינוּ מָגֵן יִשְׁעֵנוּ אַתָּה
הוּא לְדוֹר וָדוֹר. נוֹדֶה לְךָ וּנְסַפֵּר תְּהִלָּתֶךָ. עַל-
חַיֵּינוּ הַמְּסוּרִים בְּיָדֶךָ. וְעַל-נִשְׁמוֹתֵינוּ הַפְּקוּדוֹת
לָךְ. וְעַל-נִסֶּיךָ שֶׁבְּכָל-יוֹם עִמָּנוּ. וְעַל-נִפְלְאוֹתֶיךָ
וְטוֹבוֹתֶיךָ שֶׁבְּכָל-עֵת. עֶרֶב וָבֹקֶר וְצָהֳרָיִם. הַטּוֹב
כִּי-לֹא כָלוּ רַחֲמֶיךָ. וְהַמְרַחֵם כִּי לֹא-תַמּוּ חֲסָדֶיךָ.
מֵעוֹלָם קִוִּינוּ לָךְ:

Reader

אֱלֹהֵינוּ וֵאלֹהֵי אֲבוֹתֵינוּ. בָּרְכֵנוּ בַּבְּרָכָה
הַמְשֻׁלֶּשֶׁת הַכְּתוּבָה בַּתּוֹרָה:

Reader and Choir

יְבָרֶכְךָ יְיָ וְיִשְׁמְרֶךָ:

יָאֵר יְיָ פָּנָיו אֵלֶיךָ וִיחֻנֶּךָּ:

יִשָּׂא יְיָ פָּנָיו אֵלֶיךָ וְיָשֵׂם לְךָ שָׁלוֹם:

Choir: Amen.

Reader

שִׂים שָׁלוֹם

Grant us peace, Thy most precious gift, O Thou eternal source of peace, and enable Israel to be its messenger unto the peoples of the earth. Bless our country that it may ever be a stronghold of peace, and its advocate in the council of nations. May contentment reign within its borders, health and happiness within its homes. Strengthen the bonds of friendship and fellowship among all the inhabitants of our land. Plant virtue in every soul, and may the love of Thy name hallow every home and every heart. Praised be Thou, O Lord, Giver of peace.

Choir: Amen.

Silent Devotion

אֱלֹהַי נְצוֹר

O God, keep my tongue from evil and my lips from speaking guile. Be my support when grief silences my voice, and my comfort when woe bends my spirit. Plant humility in my soul, and strengthen my heart with perfect faith in Thee. Help me to be strong in trial and temptation and to be patient and forgiving when others wrong me. Guide me by the light of Thy counsel, that I may ever find strength in Thee, my Rock and my Redeemer. Amen.

Choir

May the words of my mouth and the meditations of my heart be acceptable in Thy sight, O Lord, my Rock and my Redeemer.

READING OF SCRIPTURE
Reader
(Micah iv, 1–4)

In the end of days it shall come to pass that the mountain of the Lord's house shall be established as the top of the mountains, and it shall be exalted above the hills; and peoples shall flow unto it. And many nations shall go and say, Come ye, and let us go up to the mountain of the Lord, to the house of the God of Jacob; and He will teach us of His ways, and we will walk in His paths. For out of Zion shall go forth the law, and the word of the Lord from Jerusalem.

Choir

Lift up your heads, O ye gates, and be ye lifted up, ye everlasting doors, that the King of glory may come in. Who is the King of glory? The Lord of hosts; He is the King of glory.

שְׂאוּ שְׁעָרִים רָאשֵׁיכֶם.
וּשְׂאוּ פִּתְחֵי עוֹלָם. וְיָבֹא
מֶלֶךְ הַכָּבוֹד: מִי הוּא זֶה
מֶלֶךְ הַכָּבוֹד. יְיָ צְבָאוֹת.
הוּא מֶלֶךְ הַכָּבוֹד סֶלָה:

(Congregation rises)

Reader and Choir

The Lord, the Lord God is merciful and gracious, long-suffering and abundant in goodness and ever true; keeping mercy for thousands, forgiving iniquity, transgression and sin.

יְהֹוָה יְהֹוָה אֵל רַחוּם
וְחַנּוּן אֶרֶךְ אַפַּיִם וְרַב־
חֶסֶד וֶאֱמֶת. נוֹצֵר חֶסֶד
לָאֲלָפִים. נֹשֵׂא עָוֹן וָפֶשַׁע
וְחַטָּאָה:

PRAYER BY MINISTER

Reader, then Congregation

Our Father, our King, we have sinned before Thee.

Our Father, our King, inscribe us for blessing in the book of life.

Our Father, our King, grant us a year of happiness.

Our Father, our King, bestow upon us an abundance of Thy blessings.

Our Father, our King, have mercy upon us and upon our children.

Our Father, our King, keep far from our country, pestilence, war and famine.

Our Father, our King, cause every oppressor and reviler of men to vanish from our midst.

Our Father, our King, cause us to return unto Thee in perfect repentance.

Our Father, our King, forgive and pardon all our iniquities.

Our Father, our King, may this hour reveal to us Thy mercy and Thy favor.

Our Father, our King, be merciful and answer us; though we plead no merit, deal with us according to Thy lovingkindness and help us.

Choir: Amen.

Reader, then Congregation

אָבִינוּ מַלְכֵּנוּ. חָטָאנוּ לְפָנֶיךָ:

אָבִינוּ מַלְכֵּנוּ. כָּתְבֵנוּ בְּסֵפֶר חַיִּים טוֹבִים:

אָבִינוּ מַלְכֵּנוּ. חַדֵּשׁ עָלֵינוּ שָׁנָה טוֹבָה:

אָבִינוּ מַלְכֵּנוּ. כָּתְבֵנוּ בְּסֵפֶר פַּרְנָסָה וְכַלְכָּלָה:

אָבִינוּ מַלְכֵּנוּ. חֲמוֹל עָלֵינוּ וְעַל־עוֹלָלֵינוּ וְטַפֵּנוּ:

אָבִינוּ מַלְכֵּנוּ. כַּלֵּה דֶּבֶר וְחֶרֶב וְרָעָב מֵעָלֵינוּ:

אָבִינוּ מַלְכֵּנוּ. סְתוֹם פִּיּוֹת מַשְׂטִינֵנוּ וּמְקַטְרִיגֵנוּ:

אָבִינוּ מַלְכֵּנוּ. הַחֲזִירֵנוּ בִּתְשׁוּבָה שְׁלֵמָה לְפָנֶיךָ:

אָבִינוּ מַלְכֵּנוּ. סְלַח וּמְחַל לְכָל־עֲוֹנוֹתֵינוּ:

אָבִינוּ מַלְכֵּנוּ. תְּהִי הַשָּׁעָה הַזֹּאת שְׁעַת רַחֲמִים וְעֵת רָצוֹן מִלְּפָנֶיךָ:

אָבִינוּ מַלְכֵּנוּ. חָנֵּנוּ וַעֲנֵנוּ כִּי אֵין בָּנוּ מַעֲשִׂים עֲשֵׂה עִמָּנוּ צְדָקָה וָחֶסֶד וְהוֹשִׁיעֵנוּ:

Choir: Amen.

TAKING THE SCROLL FROM THE ARK

Reader

Let us declare the greatness of our God and render honor unto the Torah.

הָבוּ גֹדֶל לֵאלֹהֵינוּ
וּתְנוּ כָבוֹד לַתּוֹרָה.

Congregation and Choir

Praised be He who in His holiness has given the Torah unto Israel.

בָּרוּךְ שֶׁנָּתַן תּוֹרָה
לְעַמּוֹ יִשְׂרָאֵל בִּקְדֻשָּׁתוֹ:

Reader

O house of Jacob, let us walk in the light of the Lord.

בֵּית יַעֲקֹב לְכוּ וְנֵלְכָה
בְּאוֹר יְהֹוָה:

Congregation and Reader, then Choir

Hear, O Israel: The Lord, our God, the Lord is One.

שְׁמַע יִשְׂרָאֵל יְהֹוָה
אֱלֹהֵינוּ יְהֹוָה אֶחָד:

(Congregation is seated)

Choir

Thine, O Lord, is the greatness, and the power, the glory, and the vic-

לְךָ יְיָ הַגְּדֻלָּה וְהַגְּבוּרָה.
וְהַתִּפְאֶרֶת וְהַנֵּצַח וְהַהוֹד

tory, and the majesty; for all that is in the heaven and in the earth is Thine; Thine is the kingdom, O Lord, and Thou art exalted as head above all.

כְּיֹל בַּשָּׁמַיִם וּבָאָרֶץ. לְךָ יְיָ הַמַּמְלָכָה וְהַמִּתְנַשֵּׂא לְכֹל לְרֹאשׁ:

(Before reading from the Torah)

Reader

Praise ye the Lord to whom all praise is due.

בָּרְכוּ אֶת־יְיָ הַמְבֹרָךְ:

Praised be the Lord to whom all praise is due forever and ever.

בָּרוּךְ יְיָ הַמְבֹרָךְ לְעוֹלָם וָעֶד:

Praised be Thou, O Lord our God, Ruler of the world, who hast called us from among all peoples and hast given us Thy law. Praised be Thou, O Lord, Giver of the Law.

בָּרוּךְ אַתָּה יְיָ אֱלֹהֵינוּ מֶלֶךְ הָעוֹלָם. אֲשֶׁר בָּחַר־ בָּנוּ מִכָּל־הָעַמִּים וְנָתַן־לָנוּ אֶת־תּוֹרָתוֹ. בָּרוּךְ אַתָּה יְיָ נוֹתֵן הַתּוֹרָה:

(Deut. xxix, 9–14; xxx, 11–20)

Ye are standing this day all of you before the Lord your God: your heads, your tribes, your elders, and your officers, even all the men of Israel, your little ones, your wives, and thy stranger that is in the midst of thy camp, from the hewer of thy wood unto the drawer of thy water; that thou shouldest enter into the covenant of the Lord thy God—and into His oath —which the Lord thy God maketh with thee this day; that He may establish thee this day unto Himself for a people, and that He may be unto thee a God, as He spoke unto thee, and as He swore unto thy fathers, to Abraham, to Isaac, and to Jacob. Neither with you only do I make this covenant and this oath; but with him that standeth here with us this day before the Lord our God, and also with him that is not here with us this day.

For this commandment which I command thee this day, it is not too hard for thee, neither is it far off. It is not in heaven, that thou shouldest say: 'Who shall go up for us to heaven, and bring it unto us, and make us to hear it, that we may do it?' Neither is it beyond the sea, that thou shouldest say: 'Who shall go over the sea for us, and bring it unto us, and make us to hear it, that we may do it?' But the word is very nigh unto thee, in thy mouth, and in thy heart, that thou mayest do it.

(דברים כ״ט ל׳)

אַתֶּם נִצָּבִים הַיּוֹם כֻּלְּכֶם לִפְנֵי יְהֹוָה אֱלֹהֵיכֶם
רָאשֵׁיכֶם שִׁבְטֵיכֶם זִקְנֵיכֶם וְשֹׁטְרֵיכֶם כֹּל אִישׁ
יִשְׂרָאֵל: טַפְּכֶם נְשֵׁיכֶם וְגֵרְךָ אֲשֶׁר בְּקֶרֶב מַחֲנֶיךָ
מֵחֹטֵב עֵצֶיךָ עַד שֹׁאֵב מֵימֶיךָ: לְעָבְרְךָ בִּבְרִית
יְהֹוָה אֱלֹהֶיךָ וּבְאָלָתוֹ אֲשֶׁר יְהֹוָה אֱלֹהֶיךָ כֹּרֵת
עִמְּךָ הַיּוֹם: לְמַעַן הָקִים אֹתְךָ הַיּוֹם לוֹ לְעָם וְהוּא
יִהְיֶה־לְּךָ לֵאלֹהִים כַּאֲשֶׁר דִּבֶּר־לָךְ וְכַאֲשֶׁר נִשְׁבַּע
לַאֲבֹתֶיךָ לְאַבְרָהָם לְיִצְחָק וּלְיַעֲקֹב: וְלֹא אִתְּכֶם
לְבַדְּכֶם אָנֹכִי כֹּרֵת אֶת־הַבְּרִית הַזֹּאת וְאֶת־הָאָלָה
הַזֹּאת: כִּי אֶת־אֲשֶׁר יֶשְׁנוֹ פֹּה עִמָּנוּ עֹמֵד הַיּוֹם לִפְנֵי
יְהֹוָה אֱלֹהֵינוּ וְאֵת אֲשֶׁר אֵינֶנּוּ פֹּה עִמָּנוּ הַיּוֹם: כִּי
הַמִּצְוָה הַזֹּאת אֲשֶׁר אָנֹכִי מְצַוְּךָ הַיּוֹם לֹא־נִפְלֵאת
הִוא מִמְּךָ וְלֹא־רְחֹקָה הִוא: לֹא בַשָּׁמַיִם הִוא לֵאמֹר
מִי יַעֲלֶה־לָּנוּ הַשָּׁמַיְמָה וְיִקָּחֶהָ־לָּנוּ וְיַשְׁמִעֵנוּ אֹתָהּ
וְנַעֲשֶׂנָּה: וְלֹא־מֵעֵבֶר לַיָּם הִוא לֵאמֹר מִי יַעֲבָר־לָנוּ
אֶל־עֵבֶר הַיָּם וְיִקָּחֶהָ־לָּנוּ וְיַשְׁמִעֵנוּ אֹתָהּ וְנַעֲשֶׂנָּה: כִּי־
קָרוֹב אֵלֶיךָ הַדָּבָר מְאֹד בְּפִיךָ וּבִלְבָבְךָ לַעֲשֹׂתוֹ:

See, I have set before thee this day life and good, and death and evil, in that I command thee this day to love the Lord thy God, to walk in His ways, and to keep His commandments and His statutes and His ordinances; then thou shalt live and multiply, and the Lord thy God shall bless thee in the land whither thou goest in to possess it. But if thy heart turn away, and thou wilt not hear, but shalt be drawn away, and worship other gods, and serve them; I declare unto you this day, that ye shall surely perish; ye shall not prolong your days upon the land, whither thou passest over the Jordan to go in to possess it. I call heaven and earth to witness against you this day, that I have set before thee life and death, the blessing and the curse; therefore choose life, that thou mayest live, thou and thy seed; to love the Lord thy God, to hearken to His voice, and to cleave unto Him; for that is thy life, and the length of thy days; that thou mayest dwell in the land which the Lord swore unto the fathers, to Abraham, to Isaac, and to Jacob, to give them.

(After reading from the Torah)

Praised be Thou, O Lord our God, Ruler of the world, who hast given us the law of truth and hast implanted within us everlasting life. Praised be Thou, O Lord, Giver of the Law.

רְאֵה נָתַתִּי לְפָנֶיךָ הַיּוֹם אֶת־הַחַיִּים וְאֶת־הַטּוֹב וְאֶת־
הַמָּוֶת וְאֶת־הָרָע: אֲשֶׁר אָנֹכִי מְצַוְּךָ הַיּוֹם לְאַהֲבָה
אֶת־יְהֹוָה אֱלֹהֶיךָ לָלֶכֶת בִּדְרָכָיו וְלִשְׁמֹר מִצְוֺתָיו
וְחֻקֹּתָיו וּמִשְׁפָּטָיו וְחָיִיתָ וְרָבִיתָ וּבֵרַכְךָ יְהֹוָה אֱלֹהֶיךָ
בָּאָרֶץ אֲשֶׁר אַתָּה בָא שָׁמָּה לְרִשְׁתָּהּ: וְאִם יִפְנֶה
לְבָבְךָ וְלֹא תִשְׁמָע וְנִדַּחְתָּ וְהִשְׁתַּחֲוִיתָ לֵאלֹהִים
אֲחֵרִים וַעֲבַדְתָּם: הִגַּדְתִּי לָכֶם הַיּוֹם כִּי־אָבֹד
תֹּאבֵדוּן לֹא תַאֲרִיכֻן יָמִים עַל־הָאֲדָמָה אֲשֶׁר אַתָּה
עֹבֵר אֶת־הַיַּרְדֵּן לָבוֹא שָׁמָּה לְרִשְׁתָּהּ: הַעִדֹתִי בָכֶם
הַיּוֹם אֶת־הַשָּׁמַיִם וְאֶת־הָאָרֶץ הַחַיִּים וְהַמָּוֶת נָתַתִּי
לְפָנֶיךָ הַבְּרָכָה וְהַקְּלָלָה וּבָחַרְתָּ בַּחַיִּים לְמַעַן
תִּחְיֶה אַתָּה וְזַרְעֶךָ: לְאַהֲבָה אֶת־יְהֹוָה אֱלֹהֶיךָ
לִשְׁמֹעַ בְּקֹלוֹ וּלְדָבְקָה בוֹ כִּי הוּא חַיֶּיךָ וְאֹרֶךְ יָמֶיךָ
לָשֶׁבֶת עַל הָאֲדָמָה אֲשֶׁר נִשְׁבַּע יְהֹוָה לַאֲבֹתֶיךָ
לְאַבְרָהָם לְיִצְחָק וּלְיַעֲקֹב לָתֵת לָהֶם:

(After reading from the Torah)

בָּרוּךְ אַתָּה יְיָ אֱלֹהֵינוּ מֶלֶךְ הָעוֹלָם. אֲשֶׁר נָתַן
לָנוּ תּוֹרַת אֱמֶת וְחַיֵּי עוֹלָם נָטַע בְּתוֹכֵנוּ. בָּרוּךְ
אַתָּה יְיָ נוֹתֵן הַתּוֹרָה:

(Before reading the Haftarah)

בָּרוּךְ אַתָּה יְיָ אֱלֹהֵינוּ מֶלֶךְ הָעוֹלָם אֲשֶׁר בָּחַר
בִּנְבִיאִים טוֹבִים וְרָצָה בְדִבְרֵיהֶם הַנֶּאֱמָרִים בֶּאֱמֶת.
בָּרוּךְ אַתָּה יְיָ הַבּוֹחֵר בַּתּוֹרָה וּבְמשֶׁה עַבְדּוֹ
וּבְיִשְׂרָאֵל עַמּוֹ וּבִנְבִיאֵי הָאֱמֶת וָצֶדֶק:

Praised be the Lord our God, for the law of truth
and righteousness which He has revealed unto Israel,
for the words of the prophets filled with His spirit and
for the teachings of the sages whom He raised up
aforetime and in these days.

Reading of Haftarah
(Isaiah lvii, 14,–lviii, 14)

Cast ye up, cast ye up, clear the way, take up the
stumbling block out of the way of My people. For
thus saith the High and Lofty One that inhabiteth
eternity, whose name is Holy: I dwell in the high and
holy place, with him also that is of a contrite and
humble spirit, to restore the spirit of the humble, and
to revive the heart of the contrite ones. For I will not
contend forever, neither will I be always wroth; for the
spirit would fail before Me, yea, the souls which I have
made. For the iniquity of his covetousness was I
wroth and smote him, I hid Me and was wroth; and
he went on frowardly in the way of his heart. I have
seen his ways, and will heal him; I will lead him also,
and requite with comforts him and his mourners.
Peace, peace, to him that is far off and to him that is
near, saith the Lord that createth the fruit of the lips;
and I will heal him. But the wicked are like the trou-

bled sea; for it cannot rest, and its waters cast up mire and dirt. There is no peace, saith my God concerning the wicked.

Cry aloud, spare not, lift up thy voice like a horn, and declare unto My people their transgression, and to the house of Jacob their sins. Yet they seek Me daily, and delight to know My ways; as a nation that did righteousness, and forsook not the ordinance of their God; they ask of Me righteous ordinances, they delight to draw near unto God. Wherefore have we fasted, and Thou seest not? Wherefore have we afflicted our soul, and Thou takest no knowledge? Behold, in the day of your fast ye pursue your business, and exact all your labors. Behold, ye fast for strife and contention, and to smite with the fist of wickedness; ye fast not this day so as to make your voice to be heard on high. Is such the fast that I have chosen? The day for a man to afflict his soul? Is it to bow down his head as a bulrush, and to spread sackcloth and ashes under him? Wilt thou call this a fast, and an acceptable day to the Lord? Is not this the fast that I have chosen? To loose the fetters of wickedness, to undo the bands of the yoke, and to let the oppressed go free, and that ye break every yoke? Is it not to deal thy bread to the hungry, and that thou bring the poor that are cast out to thy house? When thou seest the naked, that thou cover him, and that thou hide not thyself from thine own flesh? Then shall thy light break forth as the morning, and thy healing shall spring forth speedily; and thy righteousness shall go before thee, the glory of the Lord shall be thy rear-guard. Then shalt thou call, and the Lord will answer; thou shalt cry, and He will

say: Here I am. If thou take away from the midst of
thee the yoke, the putting forth of the finger, and
speaking wickedness; and if thou draw out thy soul to
the hungry, and satisfy the afflicted soul; then shall thy
light rise in darkness, and thy gloom be as the noonday; and the Lord will guide thee continually, and
satisfy thy soul in drought, and make strong thy bones;
and thou shalt be like a watered garden, and like a
spring of water, whose waters fail not. And they that
shall be of thee shall build the old waste places, thou
shalt raise up the foundations of many generations; and
thou shalt be called: The rebuilder of the ruins, the
restorer of paths to dwell in.

(After reading the Haftarah)

For the Torah, for the privilege of worship, for the
prophets, and for this Day of Atonement, given us for
sanctification and rest, for honor and for glory, let us
thank and bless the Lord our God.

בָּרוּךְ אַתָּה יְיָ אֱלֹהֵינוּ מֶלֶךְ הָעוֹלָם צוּר כָּל־
הָעוֹלָמִים צַדִּיק בְּכָל־הַדּוֹרוֹת הָאֵל הַנֶּאֱמָן הָאוֹמֵר
וְעוֹשֶׂה הַמְדַבֵּר וּמְקַיֵּם שֶׁכָּל־דְּבָרָיו אֱמֶת וָצֶדֶק:

עַל־הַתּוֹרָה וְעַל־הָעֲבוֹדָה וְעַל־הַנְּבִיאִים וְעַל־
יוֹם (הַשַּׁבָּת וְ) יוֹם הַכִּפּוּרִים הַזֶּה שֶׁנָּתַתָּ לָנוּ יְיָ
אֱלֹהֵינוּ אֲנַחְנוּ מוֹדִים לָךְ וּמְבָרְכִים אוֹתָךְ. יִתְבָּרַךְ
שִׁמְךָ בְּפִי כָּל־חַי תָּמִיד לְעוֹלָם וָעֶד . בָּרוּךְ אַתָּה
יְיָ מְקַדֵּשׁ (הַשַּׁבָּת וְ) יִשְׂרָאֵל. וְיוֹם הַכִּפּוּרִים:

PRAYER

Thou, who art the source of all blessings, be with this congregation and with all its members, their families and their households; prosper them in their various callings and occupations, help them in their needs, and guide them in their difficulties. Hear Thou the prayers of all who worship here this morning, comfort the sorrowing and cheer the silent sufferers. Bless those who guide and who serve this congregation, and those who contribute to its strength. Reward with the joy of goodness the charitable and the merciful who aid the poor, care for the sick, teach the ignorant, and extend a helping hand to those who have lost their way in the world.

Fervently we invoke Thy blessing upon our country and our nation. Guard them, O God, from calamity and injury; suffer not their adversaries to triumph over them, but let the glories of a just, righteous and God-fearing people increase from age to age. Enlighten with Thy wisdom and sustain with Thy power those whom the people have set in authority, the President, his counselors, and advisers, the judges, law-givers and executives, and all who are entrusted with our safety and with the guardianship of our rights and our liberties. May peace and good-will obtain among all the inhabitants of our land; may religion spread its blessings among us and exalt our nation in righteousness. Amen.

RETURNING THE SCROLL TO THE ARK

(Congregation rises)

Reader

O magnify the Lord with me and let us exalt His name together.

גַּדְּלוּ לַיָי אִתִּי. וּנְרוֹמְמָה שְׁמוֹ יַחְדָּו:

Choir

His glory is in the earth and in the heavens. He is the strength of all His servants, the praise of them that truly love Him, the hope of Israel, the people He brought nigh to Himself. Hallelujah.

הוֹדוֹ עַל־אֶרֶץ וְשָׁמָיִם: וַיָּרֶם קֶרֶן לְעַמּוֹ תְּהִלָּה לְכָל־חֲסִידָיו לִבְנֵי יִשְׂרָאֵל עַם קְרֹבוֹ הַלְלוּיָה:

Reader

The law of the Lord is perfect, restoring the soul; the testimony of the Lord is sure, making wise the simple. The precepts of the Lord are right, rejoicing the heart; the judgments of the

תּוֹרַת יְיָ תְּמִימָה. מְשִׁיבַת נָפֶשׁ. עֵדוּת יְיָ נֶאֱמָנָה. מַחְכִּימַת פֶּתִי: פִּקּוּדֵי יְיָ יְשָׁרִים. מְשַׂמְּחֵי לֵב. מִשְׁפְּטֵי יְיָ אֱמֶת.

Lord are true; they are righteous altogether. Behold, a good doctrine has been given unto you; forsake it not.

צָדְקוּ יַחְדָּו: כִּי לֶקַח טוֹב נָתַתִּי לָכֶם תּוֹרָתִי אַל־תַּעֲזֹבוּ:

(Congregation is seated)

Choir

It is a tree of life to them that lay hold of it, and the supporters thereof are happy. Its ways are ways of pleasantness, and all its paths are peace.

עֵץ־חַיִּים הִיא לַמַּחֲזִיקִים בָּהּ וְתוֹמְכֶיהָ מְאֻשָּׁר: דְּרָכֶיהָ דַרְכֵי־נֹעַם וְכָל־נְתִיבוֹתֶיהָ שָׁלוֹם:

Turn us again unto Thee, O Lord, and we shall be restored; renew our days as of old.

הֲשִׁיבֵנוּ יְהֹוָה אֵלֶיךָ וְנָשׁוּבָה חַדֵּשׁ יָמֵינוּ כְּקֶדֶם:

SERMON

HYMN

Afternoon Service for the Day of Atonement

Choir

O would that I might be a servant unto Thee,
Thou God of all adored!
Then, though by friends outcast,
Thy hand would hold me fast,
And draw me near to Thee, my King and Lord.
Spirit and flesh are Thine,
O Heavenly Shepherd mine;
My hopes, my thoughts, my fears, Thou seest all,
Thou measurest my path, my steps dost know
When Thou upholdest, who can make me fall?
When Thou restrainest, who can bid me go?
O would that I might be
A servant unto Thee,
Thou God by all adored.
Then, though by friends outcast,
Thy hand would hold me fast,
And draw me near to Thee, my King and Lord.

Yehuda Halevi (11th–12th Cent.)

Choir

מִי־יִתְּנֵנִי עֶבֶד אֱלֹהַּ עֹשֵׂנִי

וִירַחֲקֵנִי כָּל־דּוֹד וְהוּא יַקְרִיבֵנִי

יִצְרִי וְרֵעִי נַפְשִׁי וְגֵוִי קָנִיתָ

בֶּנְתָּ לְרֵעִי וּמַחְשְׁבוֹתַי רָאִיתָ

אָרְחִי וְרִבְעִי וְכָל־דְּרָכַי זֵרִיתָ

אִם תַּעְזְרֵנִי מִי זֶה אֲשֶׁר יַכְשִׁילֵנִי

אוֹ תַעְצְרֵנִי מִי בִלְתְּךָ יַתִּירֵנִי

מִי־יִתְּנֵנִי עֶבֶד אֱלֹהַּ עֹשֵׂנִי

וִירַחֲקֵנִי כָּל־דּוֹד וְהוּא יַקְרִיבֵנִי׃

Reader

אלהים אלי אתה

Almighty, Thou art my God! I will invoke Thee in the assembly of Thy chosen; I will proclaim Thy truth and Thy greatness. Hear me on this solemn day, when I call upon Thee in the midst of Thy congregation.

Congregation

Open my lips, that they may speak Thy praise.

Reader

My deepest secrets are known to Thee, O God, and my body and my soul tremble in Thy presence. Hear me on this solemn day, when the erring yearn for Thy guidance.

Congregation

Guide my heart, that it may be whole with Thee and Thy law.

Reader

Guard my thoughts, O God, lest they lead me astray; guard my lips, that they may not ensnare me. Hear me on this solemn day, when the contemplation of Thy mercies assuages the painful memory of sin.

Congregation

Thy children long for Thy mercy.

Reader

Thou art my hope, my immovable rock, my stronghold, O God. Strengthen and sustain me, for without Thee I am all too weak. Hear me on this solemn day, on which Thou hast promised to purify the sinner and efface his guilt.

Congregation

Create in me a clean heart, O God, and renew a steadfast spirit within me.

Reader

Out of the depths I cry to Thee, O God, who art enthroned on high, yet art near unto the lowly. Hear me on this solemn day, when the contrite take refuge in Thy sanctuary.

Congregation

Let him who is wise repent for God will graciously pardon.

Reader

My thoughts yearn and aspire to approach Thee, O God, as I humble myself before Thee, lest there be in me sinful pride and presumption. Hear me on this solemn day, on which all delusions vanish.

Congregation

O purify me from guilt and cleanse my heart from wrong.

Reader

Most gracious God, adored by the heavenly hosts, remember and give heed to my longings and petitions which soar falteringly upward unto Thee. Hear me on this solemn day, on which I offer my supplications in the midst of Thy faithful children.

Congregation

Let all living creatures praise and glorify Thy name, O God.

Reader

O God, I stand before Thee, knowing all my weaknesses and overwhelmed by Thy greatness and majesty. But Thou wouldst have me to pray to Thee and offer homage to Thine exalted Name according to the measure of my knowledge. Thou knowest best what is for my good. If I recite my wants, it is not to remind Thee of them, but only that I may better understand how great is my dependence upon Thee. If, then, I ask Thee for the things that are not for my well-being, it is because I am ignorant; Thy choice is better than mine and I submit myself to Thine unalterable decrees and Thy supreme direction. Amen.

(Bachya ibn Pakudah, 11th Century)

Reader

(Isaiah xxv–xxvi)

O Lord, Thou art my God; I will exalt Thee, I will praise Thy name; for Thou hast done wonderful things; even counsels of old, in faithfulness and truth. Thou hast been a stronghold to the poor, a stronghold to the needy in his distress, a refuge from the storm, a shadow from the heat. The mind stayed on Thee Thou keepest in perfect peace, because it trusteth in Thee. Trust ye in the Lord forever, for the Lord is God, an everlasting rock. The way of the just is straight; Thou, Most Upright, makest plain the path of the just. For when Thy judgments are in the earth, the inhabitants of the world learn righteousness. The work of righteousness shall be peace; and the effect of righteousness quietness and confidence forever. And My people shall abide in a peaceable habitation, and in secure dwellings, and in quiet resting places. They shall see the glory of the Lord, the excellence of our God.

Responsive Reading

(Psalm lxxxvi)

Reader

Incline Thine ear, O Lord, and answer me; for I am poor and needy.

Congregation

Be gracious unto me, O Lord; for unto Thee do I cry all the day.

Let the soul of Thy servant rejoice; for unto Thee, O Lord, do I lift up my soul.

For Thou, Lord, art good, and ready to pardon and plenteous in mercy unto all them that call upon Thee.

Give ear, O Lord, unto my prayer; and attend unto the voice of my supplications.

In the day of my trouble I call upon Thee; and Thou wilt answer me.

There is none like unto Thee among the mighty, O Lord; and there are no works like Thine.

All the nations whom Thou hast made shall come and prostrate themselves before Thee, O Lord;

For Thou art great, and doest wondrous things; Thou art God alone.

Teach me O Lord, Thy way, that I may walk in Thy truth; make my heart whole in the fear of Thy name.

I will thank Thee, O Lord my God, with my whole heart; I will glorify Thy name for evermore.

For great is Thy mercy towards me; Thou hast delivered my soul from the lowest depths.

Thou, O Lord God, art full of compassion and gracious, slow to anger, and plenteous in mercy and truth.

O turn unto me, and be gracious unto me; give Thy strength unto Thy servant, and save the son of Thy handmaid.

Choir

Work in my behalf a sign for good; because Thou, Lord, hast helped me, and comforted me.

Meditation

In the height and depth of His glory
  Where mighty He sits on the throne,
He unveils His radiant story
  To all who revere Him alone.
His promises never are broken,
  His greatness all measure exceeds;
Then exalt Him who gives you for token
  His marvelous deeds.

He marshals the planets unbounded,
    He numbers the infinite years;
The seat of His empire is founded
    More deep than the nethermost spheres;
He looks on the lands from His splendor;
    They tremble and quiver like reeds;
Then exalt ye in lowly surrender
    His marvelous deeds.

The worlds He upholds in their flying,
    His feet on the footstool of earth;
His word hath established undying
    Whatever His word brought to birth.
The ruler of hosts is His title;
    Then exalt Him in worshipful creeds,
Declaring in solemn recital
    His marvelous deeds.

But of man—ah! the tale is another,
    His counsels are evil and vain;
He dwells with deceit as a brother,
    And the worm is the close of his reign.
Not so God!—In light He is clad as a raiment:
    His greatness no eulogy needs;
Yet exalt, 'tis your only repayment,
    His marvelous deeds.

(Meshullam b. Kalonymous, 11th Century)

Reader

Let us affirm the majesty and holiness of this day, for it is one of awe and dread. On this day, O God, Thy dominion is exalted and the throne of Thy mercy established. Verily, Thou art the supreme Judge, and Thy judgments are righteous altogether. Before Thee all our deeds are known and recorded. Man forgets but Thou rememberest all.

As the shepherd seeketh out his flock, counting his sheep as they pass under his staff, so dost Thou cause every living soul to pass before Thee, appointing the measure of every creature's life, and decreeing its destiny.

On these days of awe, our hearts awaken to the truth that in Thy providence Thou givest life and ordainest death. Thine omniscient judgment decides the fortunes and disasters of nations and of men, their joys and their griefs, and their length of days.

But in Thy grace, Thou hast taught us that penitence, prayer and charity avert the stern decree. For Thou desirest not that the sinner shall perish in his sin but that he shall turn from his evil way and live. Till the day of his death Thou waitest for him, that in penitence he may come unto Thee. Thou hast fashioned man and knowest the inclinations of his heart. Man is but flesh and blood, his origin dust, his end dust. He wears out his life for his daily bread, he is like the grass that withereth, the flower that fadeth; like a shadow that moveth on, like a cloud that passeth by, like a mote of dust driven by the wind, a dream that is forgotten. But Thou art the Eternal King, the ever-living God.

Reader

וּנְתַנֶּה תֹּקֶף קְדֻשַּׁת הַיּוֹם. כִּי הוּא נוֹרָא וְאָיוֹם.
וּבוֹ תִנָּשֵׂא מַלְכוּתֶךָ. וְיִכּוֹן בְּחֶסֶד כִּסְאֶךָ. וְתֵשֵׁב
עָלָיו בֶּאֱמֶת: אֱמֶת כִּי אַתָּה הוּא דַיָּן וּמוֹכִיחַ
וְיוֹדֵעַ וָעֵד. וְכוֹתֵב וְחוֹתֵם וְסוֹפֵר וּמוֹנֶה. וְתִזְכּוֹר
כָּל־הַנִּשְׁכָּחוֹת. וְכָל־בָּאֵי עוֹלָם תַּעֲבִיר לְפָנֶיךָ
כִּבְנֵי מָרוֹן. כְּבַקָּרַת רוֹעֶה עֶדְרוֹ. מַעֲבִיר צֹאנוֹ
תַּחַת שִׁבְטוֹ. כֵּן תַּעֲבִיר וְתִסְפּוֹר וְתִמְנֶה וְתִפְקוֹד
נֶפֶשׁ כָּל־חָי. וְתַחְתּוֹךְ קִצְבָה לְכָל־בְּרִיָּה. וְתִכְתּוֹב
אֵת גְּזַר דִּינָם:

Reader and Choir

כַּמָּה יַעַבְרוּן.   וְכַמָּה יִבָּרֵאוּן:

מִי יִחְיֶה וּמִי יָמוּת.   מִי בְקִצּוֹ וּמִי לֹא בְקִצּוֹ.

מִי בָאֵשׁ וּמִי בַמָּיִם.   מִי בַחֶרֶב וּמִי בָרָעָב.

מִי בָרַעַשׁ וּמִי בַמַּגֵּפָה.   מִי יָנוּחַ וּמִי יָנוּעַ.

מִי יִשָּׁקֵט וּמִי יִטָּרֵף.   מִי יִשָּׁלֵו וּמִי יִתְיַסָּר.

מִי יֵרוֹם וּמִי יִשָּׁפֵל.   מִי יֵעָשֵׁר וּמִי יֵעָנִי:

וּתְשׁוּבָה וּתְפִלָּה וּצְדָקָה מַעֲבִירִין אֶת רֹעַ הַגְּזֵרָה:

Reader

כִּי לֹא תַחְפּוֹץ בְּמוֹת הַמֵּת. כִּי אִם בְּשׁוּבוֹ
מִדַּרְכּוֹ וְחָיָה. וְעַד יוֹם מוֹתוֹ תְּחַכֶּה לוֹ. אִם יָשׁוּב

Choir

I hope in God
I pray to Him;
I ask that He grant
An answer to Prayer;
That in this assembly
I may sing of His strength
And joyously praise
His wondrous deeds.

Let man prepare his heart
God will in love respond;
O Lord, open Thou my lips
That my mouth may speak Thy praise.
May the words of my mouth
And the thoughts of my heart
Be acceptable to Thee
My Strength and my Redeemer.

מִיָּד תְּקַבְּלוּ: אֱמֶת כִּי אַתָּה הוּא יוֹצְרָם. וְאַתָּה
יוֹדֵעַ יִצְרָם. כִּי הֵם בָּשָׂר וָדָם: אָדָם יְסוֹדוֹ מֵעָפָר
וְסוֹפוֹ לֶעָפָר. בְּנַפְשׁוֹ יָבִיא לַחְמוֹ. מָשׁוּל כְּחָצִיר
יָבֵשׁ. וּכְצֵל עוֹבֵר. וְכַחֲלוֹם יָעוּף:
וְאַתָּה הוּא מֶלֶךְ אֵל חַי וְקַיָּם:

Choir

אוֹחִילָה לָאֵל, אֲחַלֶּה פָנָיו, אֶשְׁאֲלָה מִמֶּנּוּ מַעֲנֵה
לָשׁוֹן:
אֲשֶׁר בִּקְהַל עָם, אָשִׁירָה עֻזּוֹ, אַבִּיעָה רְנָנוֹת בְּעַד
מִפְעָלָיו:
לְאָדָם מַעַרְכֵי לֵב. וּמֵיְיָ מַעֲנֵה לָשׁוֹן:
אֲדֹנָי שְׂפָתַי תִּפְתָּח וּפִי יַגִּיד תְּהִלָּתֶךָ:
יִהְיוּ לְרָצוֹן אִמְרֵי פִי וְהֶגְיוֹן לִבִּי לְפָנֶיךָ יְיָ צוּרִי
וְגוֹאֲלִי:

(Congregation rises)

(Before the open Ark)

Reader

Let us adore the ever-living God, and render praise unto Him who spread out the heavens and established the earth, whose glory is revealed in the heavens above and whose greatness is manifest throughout the world. He is our God; there is none else.

Reader and Congregation, then Choir

We bow the head in reverence and worship the King of kings, the Holy One, praised be He.

Reader

Know ye this day, and take ye to heart that the Eternal, He is God; in the heavens above and on the earth beneath, there is none else.

(Congregation is seated)

(Congregation rises)
(Before the open Ark)

Reader

עָלֵינוּ לְשַׁבֵּחַ לַאֲדוֹן הַכֹּל. לָתֵת גְּדֻלָּה לְיוֹצֵר
בְּרֵאשִׁית. שֶׁהוּא נוֹטֶה שָׁמַיִם וְיוֹסֵד אָרֶץ. וּמוֹשַׁב
יְקָרוֹ בַּשָּׁמַיִם מִמַּעַל. וּשְׁכִינַת עֻזּוֹ בְּגָבְהֵי מְרוֹמִים.
הוּא אֱלֹהֵינוּ אֵין עוֹד:

Reader and Congregation, then Choir

וַאֲנַחְנוּ כֹּרְעִים וּמִשְׁתַּחֲוִים וּמוֹדִים לִפְנֵי מֶלֶךְ
מַלְכֵי הַמְּלָכִים. הַקָּדוֹשׁ בָּרוּךְ הוּא:

Reader

אֱמֶת מַלְכֵּנוּ אֶפֶס זוּלָתוֹ. כַּכָּתוּב בְּתוֹרָתוֹ.
וְיָדַעְתָּ הַיּוֹם וַהֲשֵׁבֹתָ אֶל־לְבָבֶךָ. כִּי יְיָ הוּא
הָאֱלֹהִים בַּשָּׁמַיִם מִמַּעַל וְעַל־הָאָרֶץ מִתָּחַת אֵין
עוֹד:

(Congregation is seated)

Reader

Our God and God of our fathers, we stand before Thee on this day, as the community of Israel. We feel Thy nearness to us yet we are deeply conscious of our disloyalty to Thee. We realize, alas, how remiss we have been as a community in upholding Thy name and sanctifying it before men. We confess that we have often failed to rise to the responsibility of glorifying Thee by our conduct and of vindicating by our lives the precious belief that we are Thy people.

We have gloried in proclaiming Thy unity before men. And yet, how often have we desecrated Thy name by showing our indifference to faith, to the duty of worship, and to the knowledge and the love of Thee which are the supreme bliss of life.

We have declared to the world that we were sent by Thee to teach justice and lovingkindness, brotherhood and peace. And yet, even in our own household, prejudices, class enmities, and the envious conflicts for the prizes of worldly gain, have not ceased. They have not been overcome by the belief that Thou art our Father, that Thou hast created us all, and that therefore we should not deal treacherously one man against his brother. Preaching peace to the world, we have not established it, even in the midst of Israel.

We have, by Thy grace, taught the world the sanctity of a weekly day of rest, and that the Sabbath is the sign of the tie that binds us to Thee. And yet, we have denied our teaching by refusing to hallow the week of toil with hours of rest and worship. Thus we are discrediting ourselves, as ministers of the Lord, as a kingdom of priests and as a holy people, called by Thee to give light to the world.

We confess also before Thee, that what should have been the most powerful challenge to our soul, calling forth the best in us, of humility, of duty, of self-sacrifice, was often turned by our erring minds into an excuse for our sins. We know only too well that what should have made us most scrupulous in self-searching, helped us rather to self-indulgence and self-justification. We have proclaimed to the world, even as law-giver and prophet taught, that we were Thine own treasure, a chosen people, Thy servant, upon whom Thou didst put Thy spirit. But we have not always lived so as to show ourselves worthy of this high and holy charge. Alas, we have contemned our holy heritage and made it minister to our own pride. Our sacred obligations we have turned into an oblation of incense to our own vanity.

Also the world's injustice, and the persecution of Israel, have forced upon us the task of self-defense to such a degree as not to leave us strength enough to examine our own lives with impartial search for the truth. We have not made our sufferings a discipline for our souls. We have found excuse for own sin in the iniquity of the persecutor. We have lacked the moral power, which our heroic forefathers had, even in the face of unjust hate, to point to our own breasts and say: we, too, have sinned, have committed iniquity, have transgressed.

Our God and Father, who are we, that we should seek to fathom the mystery of Thy benign Providence?

With awe and humility, we ask Thy forgiveness for our sin, in that we were unfaithful to the high purposes entrusted to Israel. Give us, we pray Thee, strength and courage, that we may bravely endure, and that we may sanctify Thee before men. Help us to turn the struggle and the suffering and the sacrifice, demanded of Israel, into means of sanctification for our daily lives, and put to nought the counsel of those that devise evil against us.

O Lord, hasten the day when all evil shall be destroyed and wickedness shall be no more. Quicken us to work with the righteous of all nations and creeds, to bring about Thy kingdom upon earth, so that hatred among men shall cease, that the walls of prejudice and pride, separating peoples, shall crumble and fall, and war be destroyed forever.

Turn our hearts to Thee, O God and Father, that we may serve Thee in sincerity and in truth. And serving Thee, may our example help to lead many to Thee. O Thou who hast founded the world on love, may this Atonement Day, by Thy grace, become a spiritual power to unite us with our fellowmen, in reconciliation, in forgiveness and in love. Praised be Thy name, O Holy One of Israel, who hast sanctified us for Thy service and hast consecrated us as a messenger of glad tidings to mankind. Amen.

Choir

They shall not hurt nor destroy in all My holy mountain; for the earth shall be full of the knowledge of the Lord, as the waters cover the sea.

Reader

Thou art our God and there is none else. Thou hast fashioned man in Thine image, Thou hast ordained the way of life in which he may walk so that he might become holy as Thou art holy. Thou didst make an everlasting covenant with Israel and didst appoint him to be the messenger of Thy truth and to bring the assurance of Thine all-sustaining love to the peoples of the earth.

On this most sacred of days, we call to mind the loving care with which Thou didst lead our fathers. When spiritual darkness covered the earth, Thy light illumined the dwellings of Israel. On Zion's height rose Thy sanctuary. To Thine altar our fathers brought the offerings of joy and gratitude, the sacrifice of contrition and repentance, of fervent devotion and steadfast purpose. From Thy courts flowed forth the stream of spiritual life whose waters have refreshed and quickened the souls of man. Zion fell, the Temple sank into ruins. Centuries have rolled by; generations have come and gone; kingdoms have risen and fallen. And today, wherever we dwell, we still look back with reverence to that sacred spot, remembering that from Zion went forth the law and the word of God from Jerusalem.

We have passed through many trials and endured countless ills. Yet the same faith which sustained our fathers, still lives within us. We are warmed by the same fervor, cheered by the same hope, guided by the same hand. And on this holy day, the faithful of Israel appear before Thee with contrite heart and repentant spirit as did our fathers of old. Notwithstanding the changes of time and despite oppression and persecution, we have sought to remain faithful to the trust which they have bequeathed unto us. Thy providence has preserved and sustained us in our struggles against superstition and error. May then the memory of the past impress us with the duty to remain faithful to our heritage and to be mindful of our obligations.

We recall the solemn ceremonies of this day in the ancient Temple, when the High Priest, arrayed in the garments of his holy office, entered the sanctuary and pleaded that God pardon the sins of the people. He prayed first for himself and his household that, freed of his sins, he might approach God as worthy spokesman for the people. Though guardian of the sanctuary, and set apart for its holy service, he felt himself to be as human as others and as prone to sin, for there is no man so righteous that doeth good and sinneth not. Like unto the High Priest, may Israel's teachers today bear themselves humbly and be watchful of their responsibility. May their lives in the sight of God testify to the truths which they proclaim unto men. Grant them wisdom and strength, O God, to expound Thy word with earnestness and courage, and thus awaken in the hearts of Thy people zeal for Thy cause and confidence in Thee. May these memories of the service of the High Priest on this day prompt us, of the House of Israel, to purify ourselves of error and iniquity so that our lives may be worthy of the name we bear and every

Jewish home may become a sanctuary consecrated by Thy presence and dedicated unto righteousness. Humbled by the sense of our weakness and our guilt, we ask Thee, O God of our fathers, to help us cleanse our hearts from the sins which have stained them. In the words of the ancient High Priest, we pray:

Congregation and Reader, then Choir

O Lord, pardon the sins, transgressions and iniquities which I have committed before Thee, I and my household, as it is said: On this day atonement shall be made for you to cleanse you; from all your sins shall ye be clean before the Lord.

אָנָּא יְיָ. כַּפֶּר־נָא.
לַחֲטָאִים. וְלַעֲוֹנוֹת.
וְלַפְּשָׁעִים. שֶׁחָטָאתִי.
וְשֶׁעָוִיתִי. וְשֶׁפָּשַׁעְתִּי
לְפָנֶיךָ. אֲנִי וּבֵיתִי:
כַּכָּתוּב. כִּי בַיּוֹם הַזֶּה
יְכַפֵּר עֲלֵיכֶם לְטַהֵר
אֶתְכֶם מִכֹּל חַטֹּאתֵיכֶם.
לִפְנֵי יְיָ תִּטְהָרוּ:

Reader

After the High Priest had made atonement for himself and his household, he entered the holy of holies. There he prayed for the whole congregation of Israel and made expiation for their sins.

Like unto the congregation of old, may all Israel be reunited with Thee this day. May the erring again

seek Thee in newness of heart; may those who have
strayed from the faith of the fathers return to their
heritage; may they who have grown cold and indiffer-
ent be filled with fervor, so that the house of Israel may
again become one congregation, bound together in the
worship of Thee and in devotion to Thy service. Then
shall we, Thy people, purified and re-consecrated, have
become worthy to stand in Thy presence and receive
again Thine ancient assurance: Yet now hear, O Jacob,
My servant, and Israel whom I have chosen. Thus
saith the Lord that made thee: Fear not, O Jacob, My
servant, and thou, Jeshurun, whom I have chosen.
For I will pour water upon the thirsty land, and streams
upon the dry ground; I will pour My spirit upon thy
seed, and My blessing upon thine offspring; and they
shall spring up among the grass, as willows by the
water-courses. One shall say: I am the Lord's; and
another shall call himself by the name of Jacob; and
another shall subscribe with his hand unto the Lord,
and shall surname himself by the name of Israel.

And so we pray again in the words of the High
Priest:

Congregation and Reader, then Choir

O Lord, pardon the אָנָּא יְיָ. כַּפֶּר־נָא.
sins, transgressions and לַחֲטָאִים. וְלָעֲוֹנוֹת.
iniquities which Thy וְלַפְּשָׁעִים. שֶׁחָטָאוּ.
people, the house of Is- וְשֶׁעָווּ. וְשֶׁפָּשְׁעוּ. לְפָנֶיךָ

rael have committed, as it is said: On this day atonement shall be made for you to cleanse you; from all your sins shall ye be clean before the Lord.

עַמְּךָ בֵּית יִשְׂרָאֵל:
כַּכָּתוּב. כִּי בַיּוֹם הַזֶּה
יְכַפֵּר עֲלֵיכֶם לְטַהֵר
אֶתְכֶם מִכֹּל חַטֹּאתֵיכֶם.
לִפְנֵי יְיָ תִּטְהָרוּ:

Reader

When the priests and the people who stood in the court heard the High Priest pronounce Thine ineffable name, they prostrated themselves before Thee in reverence and praised Thy name and the glory of Thine everlasting kingdom. In the same words we render homage to Thee today:

Congregation and Reader, then Choir

Praised be His name, whose glorious kingdom is forever and ever.

בָּרוּךְ שֵׁם כְּבוֹד
מַלְכוּתוֹ לְעוֹלָם וָעֶד:

Reader

Throughout the world, O Lord our God, Thy people stand this day before Thee to beseech Thy mercy and Thy pardon. The prophetic spirit lives in Israel as of yore; he is still Thy servant and Thy witness unto the peoples of the earth. Confidently we await the blessed day when Thou who didst reveal Thyself to our fathers shalt be acknowledged as God by all mankind. Not for ourselves alone, but for all whom Thou hast created in Thine image, do we implore Thy favor. Let the glad tidings of reconciliation and peace come to all Thy children and fill their hearts with holy joy.

When Solomon dedicated the Temple, he prayed: Moreover concerning the stranger that is not of Thy people Israel, when he shall come out of a far country for Thy name's sake—for they shall hear of Thy great name, and of Thy mighty hand, and of Thine outstretched arm—when he shall come and pray towards this house, hear Thou in heaven, Thy dwelling-place, and do according to all that the stranger asketh of Thee; that all the peoples of the earth may know Thy name, to fear Thee, as doth Thy people Israel and that they may know that Thy name is called upon this house which I have builded.

In this spirit we too pray for all men. Grant that wherever a heart sighs in anguish under the burden of guilt, wherever a soul yearns to return to Thee, it may feel the effect of Thy pardoning love and mercy. Let superstition, falsehood and malice vanish everywhere. Send forth Thy light and Thy truth to those who grope in darkness, and the knowledge of Thee to those who follow after strange gods; and may Thy house be called the house of prayer for all peoples. Hasten the time when the mountain of Thy house shall be established as the top of the mountains and shall be exalted above the hills and peoples shall flow unto it; when they shall beat their swords into plowshares and their spears into pruning-hooks; when nation shall not lift up sword against nation, neither shall they learn war any more; but they shall sit every man under his vine and under his fig-tree, and none shall make them afraid.

Then shall Thy kingdom be established on earth, and upon all the nations shall rest Thy spirit, the spirit of wisdom and understanding, the spirit of counsel and might, the spirit of knowledge and fear of Thee. Then as one great family shall all Thy children exclaim:

Congregation and Reader, then Choir

The Lord will reign forever, thy God, O Zion, from generation to generation. Hallelujah.

יִמְלֹךְ יְיָ לְעוֹלָם אֱלֹהַיִךְ צִיּוֹן לְדוֹר וָדוֹר הַלְלוּיָהּ:

Reader

On this day our fathers everywhere recalled with deep sorrow the solemn rites of atonement in the Temple at Jerusalem and lamented the glory which had departed from Zion's hill. In strains, both sad and rapturous, they gave voice to the sense of desolation with which these stirring memories filled their hearts. Happy the eyes, they chanted, that saw the high-priest in his sacred vestment, the snow-white robe of purity and honor, ministering at Thine altar. Happy the eyes that beheld the chief of the sons of Aaron as he stood with hands uplifted for blessing like the proud cedar of Lebanon. He appeared like the morning star which rises out of the dark night, like the sun which casts its splendor upon earth and sky. Happy the ears that heard the thousand-voiced song of the Levites, accompanied by the trumpet, the harp, and the flute, echoing the praises of the Most High in sweet and soul-stirring melodies.

But Thou, O Lord, dost not require of us sacrificial altars; priestly pomp pleases Thee not. Thou hast taught us through Thy prophets what is good and what Thou dost require of us: to do justly, to love mercy and to walk humbly with Thee; to plead the cause of the widow and the orphan; to protect the stranger, to feed the hungry and to clothe the naked; to break the bonds of wickedness and to free the oppressed. By such offerings of the spirit can we serve Thee most truly and bear witness to Thine eternal truth, and glorify Thy holy name throughout the world.

Choir

My soul thirsteth for God, for the living God!
When shall I come up and appear before God?
My tears have been my meat day and night, while they
　　continually say to me, where is thy God?
When I remember these things, I pour out my soul
　　within me. Why art thou cast down, O my
　　soul, and why art thou disquieted in me?
Hope Thou in God, for I shall yet praise Him, who is
　　the health of my countenance and my God.

Reader

We, therefore, give thanks and praise to Thee, our Guardian and Redeemer. Thou hast preserved and guided us through the centuries of hatred and persecution, that the love of Thy name and Thy law, rooted deep in the soul of Israel, might quicken every heart and draw it nigh unto Thee. As custodian and teacher of Thy truth, Israel, the light of the nations, lives on and keeps aglow the pure faith in Thee.

Not backward do we turn our eyes, O Lord, but forward to the promised and certain future. Wherever a sanctuary is dedicated to Thy service, Thou dwellest; and wherever Thy name is worshiped, Thou revealest Thyself anew. And though we cherish and revere the place where stood the cradle of our people, the land where Israel grew up like a tender plant, and the knowledge of Thee rose like the morning-dawn, our longings and aspirations reach out toward a still higher goal. The morning-dawn shall yet brighten into a radiant noonday; the tender sprout shall yet become a heaven-aspiring tree beneath which all the families of the earth will find shelter. This is the gracious promise proclaimed by Thy prophets; and with faith unshaken and heart undismayed, we shall labor and wait for its fulfilment. Then will the sanctuary be reared which shall be illumined by the sevenfold brightness of the sun of truth, that first arose on Sinai's mount. Then shall Thy law be established in the hearts of men, and all Thy children unite in peace and love to serve Thee, their Father and their God. Amen.

Silent Prayer

Guardian of Israel! As we recall the priestly service which our forefathers rendered through the centuries, we raise our hearts in humble thankfulness unto Thee. We are grateful for the lofty ideals revealed to us by Thy messengers, for the manifestation of the truths whereby men live, and for the faith which Thou didst kindle within us. We thank Thee, O God, for the steadfastness with which the passing generations of our people have clung to our heritage, for the ties of understanding and devotion which made us into one people, for the courage with which the lowly and the humble as well as the learned and the great have kept their heads erect and have borne the trials and the persecutions of the stormy centuries. And we thank Thee, O God, for their unflagging hope in a better and brighter future, and for their undying determination to struggle for the triumph of reason, justice and love among men.

May we, too, be strong in our loyalty to Thee so that we may never shame our people nor profane Thy name. When our burdens grow heavy, give us strength to bear them. Let the fire of sacrificial service burn continually upon the altar of our hearts, and let zeal for brotherhood and peace flame within our souls. Amen.

HYMN

All the world shall come to serve Thee,
And bless Thy glorious name,
And Thy righteousness triumphant
The islands shall acclaim.
Yea, the peoples shall go seeking,
Who knew Thee not before,
And the ends of earth shall praise Thee,
And tell Thy greatness o'er.

They shall build for Thee their altar,
Their idols over-thrown,
And their graven gods shall shame them
As they turn to Thee alone.
They shall worship Thee at sunrise
And feel Thy kingdom's might
And impart Thy understanding,
To those astray in night.

With coming of Thy kingdom
The hills will shout with song,
And the islands laugh exultant,
That they to God belong.
And through all Thy congregations,
So loud Thy praise shall ring,
That the utmost peoples, hearing,
Shall hail Thee crowned King.

Responsive Reading

(Psalm li)

Reader

Be gracious unto me, O God, according to Thy mercy;
according to the multitude of Thy compassions
blot out my transgressions.

Congregation

*Wash me thoroughly from mine iniquity, and cleanse
me from my sin.*

For I know my transgressions; and my sin is ever before me.

*Against Thee, Thee only, have I sinned, and done
that which is evil in Thy sight;*

That Thou mayest be justified when Thou speakest,
and be in the right when Thou judgest.

*Hide Thy face from my sins, and blot out all mine
iniquities.*

Create in me a clean heart, O God, and renew a steadfast spirit within me.

*Cast me not away from Thy presence; and take not
Thy holy spirit from me.*

Then I will teach transgressors Thy ways; and sinners
shall return unto Thee.

*O Lord, open Thou my lips; and my mouth shall
declare Thy praise.*

For Thou delightest not in sacrifice, else would I give
   it; Thou hast no pleasure in burnt-offerings.

Choir

The sacrifices of God are a broken spirit; a broken and
   contrite heart, O God, Thou wilt not despise.

Responsive Reading

Reader

O Lord, who art long-suffering and benign, Thou hast
taught us the way of repentance.

Congregation

Thine abundant mercy remember this day unto the
descendants of Thy beloved.

Turn unto us in Thine infinite compassion; for Thou
art the dispenser of mercy.

With prayer and supplication we appear before Thee;
in humility we crave Thy forgiveness.

Protect us under the shadow of Thy grace; remove
our transgressions and our sins.

Accept our prayers as on the day when Thou didst
reveal Thy glory unto Thy servant Moses.

The Lord passed by before him and said:

The Lord, the Lord God, merciful and gracious,
long-suffering, and abundant in goodness and
truth;

Keeping mercy unto the thousandth generation, forgiving iniquity and transgression and sin.

Yea, Thou wilt forgive our sins and iniquities, and
make us again Thy heritage.

Responsive Reading

אֵל אֶרֶךְ אַפַּיִם אַתָּה. וּבַעַל הָרַחֲמִים נִקְרֵאתָ. וְדֶרֶךְ תְּשׁוּבָה הוֹרֵיתָ:

גְּדֻלַּת רַחֲמֶיךָ וַחֲסָדֶיךָ. תִּזְכּוֹר הַיּוֹם לְזֶרַע יְדִידֶיךָ:

תֵּפֶן אֵלֵינוּ בְּרַחֲמִים. כִּי אַתָּה הוּא בַּעַל הָרַחֲמִים:

בְּתַחֲנוּן וּבִתְפִלָּה פָּנֶיךָ נְקַדֵּם. כְּהוֹדַעְתָּ לֶעָנָו מִקֶּדֶם:

וּבְצֵל כְּנָפֶיךָ נֶחֱסֶה וְנִתְלוֹנָן. כְּיוֹם וַיֵּרֶד יְיָ בֶּעָנָן:

תַּעֲבוֹר עַל פֶּשַׁע וְתִמְחֶה אָשָׁם. כְּיוֹם וַיִּתְיַצֵּב עִמּוֹ שָׁם:

תַּאֲזִין שַׁוְעָתֵנוּ וְתַקְשִׁיב מֶנּוּ מַאֲמָר. כְּיוֹם וַיִּקְרָא בְשֵׁם יְיָ. וְשָׁם נֶאֱמַר:

וַיַּעֲבֹר יְיָ עַל פָּנָיו וַיִּקְרָא:

יְיָ יְיָ אֵל רַחוּם וְחַנּוּן. אֶרֶךְ אַפַּיִם וְרַב חֶסֶד וֶאֱמֶת: נֹצֵר חֶסֶד לָאֲלָפִים. נֹשֵׂא עָוֹן וָפֶשַׁע וְחַטָּאָה. וְסָלַחְתָּ לַעֲוֹנֵנוּ וּלְחַטָּאתֵנוּ וּנְחַלְתָּנוּ:

Reader and Choir

Thy way, O God, is patience and compassion, alike to the wicked and the good; this is Thy glory.

Instil Thy healing balm into the sorrowing heart; have pity on those who are but dust and ashes.

Cast away our sins and be gracious to Thy handiwork. We have none to plead for us; deal with us according to Thy righteousness.

Responsive Reading

Reader

O my King who workest salvation, keepest mercy unto thousands, and forgivest transgressions, pardon my sins and in Thine abundant mercy be gracious unto me.

Congregation

O Lord, unto Thee I cry all this day.

Reader

This day heal our wounds and forgive our backslidings. We come unto Thee in penitence; accept us graciously.

Congregation

Let us forsake the evil way, and return unto the Lord this day.

Reader and Choir

דַרְכְּךָ אֱלֹהֵינוּ לְהַאֲרִיךְ אַפֶּךָ. לָרָעִים וְלַטוֹבִים.
וְהִיא תְהִלָּתֶךָ:
תַּעֲלֶה אֲרוּכָה. לְעָלֶה נִדָּף. תְּנַחֵם עַל עָפָר וָאֵפֶר:
תַּשְׁלִיךְ חַטֹּאֵינוּ. וְתָחוֹן בְּמַעֲשֶׂיךָ. תֵּרָא כִּי אֵין אִישׁ.
עֲשֵׂה עִמָּנוּ צְדָקָה:

Responsive Reading

Reader

מַלְכִּי מִקֶּדֶם פּוֹעֵל יְשׁוּעוֹת בְּקֶרֶב הֲמוֹנִי. נֹצֵר
חֶסֶד לָאֲלָפִים וְנֹשֵׂא פְּשָׁעַי וַעֲוֹנִי. כַּסֵּה חָטָאֵי
וּבְרַחֲמֶיךָ הָרַבִּים חָנֵּנִי יְיָ:

Congregation

כִּי אֵלֶיךָ אֶקְרָא כָּל־הַיּוֹם:

Reader

הַיּוֹם רְפָא מְשׁוּבוֹתֵינוּ. כִּי אָתָאנוּ לְךָ וְהִנֶּנּוּ.
שַׁבְנוּ אֵלֶיךָ אֱלֹהֵינוּ. וּבְחַסְדְּךָ חָנֵּנוּ. דֶּרֶךְ רֶשַׁע
עֲזַבְנוּ וְהִנֵּה אֵינֶנּוּ.

Congregation

פֹּה עִמָּנוּ הַיּוֹם:

Reader

This day reveal unto us Thy power, O Lord; requite us not according to our sins; turn unto us in Thine infinite love and have compassion upon us.

Congregation

Like as a father pitieth his children, so have pity upon us this day.

Reader

This day blot out our misdeeds and inscribe us in the book of life; for Thou hast graciously promised forgiveness and pardon.

Congregation

Be nigh unto us, for on Thee do we call this day.

Reader

This day we lift up our hearts unto Thee, and proclaim Thy might. With song and praise we approach Thee and magnify Thy name.

Congregation

We confess and forsake our sins; pardon us this day.

Reader

This day Thy people knock at Thy door; unto Thee

Reader

הַיּוֹם יִגְדַּל נָא כֹּחַ יְיָ וְכַעֲוֹנוֹתֵינוּ אַל תִּגְמוֹל.
כְּרַחֵם אָב עַל־בָּנִים רַחֵם עָלֵינוּ וַחֲמוֹל. רַחֲמֶיךָ
וַחֲסָדֶיךָ פְּנֵה אֵלֵינוּ כִּתְמוֹל שִׁלְשׁוֹם.

Congregation

גַּם תְּמוֹל גַּם־הַיּוֹם:

Reader

הַיּוֹם רִשְׁעֵנוּ תָסִיר וּבְסֵפֶר הַחַיִּים אוֹתָנוּ תָחוֹק.
בְּיוֹם קָרְאֵנוּ אֵלֶיךָ קָרֵב אַל תַּעֲמוֹד מֵרָחוֹק.
סְלִיחָה וְכַפָּרָה שַׂמְתּוֹ לַחוֹק.

Congregation

וּלְמִשְׁפָּט לְיִשְׂרָאֵל עַד־הַיּוֹם:

Reader

הַיּוֹם כַּפָּיו יִפְרוֹשׂ אֵלֶיךָ וּגְבוּרוֹתֶיךָ יְמַלֵּל.
בְּצֶדֶק יֶחֱזֶה פָנֶיךָ וּבְשִׁירוֹ אוֹתְךָ יְהַלֵּל. עֲוֹנוֹ מוֹדֶה
וְעוֹזֵב יְבַקֵּשׁ מְחִילָה וְיִתְפַּלֵּל:

Congregation

בַּעֲדוֹ תָמִיד כָּל־הַיּוֹם:

Reader

הַיּוֹם סָמוּךְ עַם אֲשֶׁר דְּלָתֶיךָ דוֹפְקִים. וְתִיקָר

is their longing and upon Thee do they lean. Stretch forth Thy hand and receive them; make them glad with Thine assurance.

Choir

Ye who cleave unto the Lord your God, are living, all of you, this day.

Silent Devotion

O God, who is like unto Thee?

Thou art majestic and glorious, creator of heaven and earth. O God, who is like unto Thee?

Thou revealest secret things; Thou declarest righteousness. O God, who is like unto Thee?

Thou art clothed with majesty and there is none besides Thee. O God, who is like unto Thee?

Thou art mindful of the covenant and art gracious to the remnant of Israel. O God, who is like unto Thee?

Thou art pure of eye, Thou dwellest in the heavens. O God, who is like unto Thee?

Thou art above iniquity and art robed in righteousness. O God, who is like unto Thee?

Thou art King of kings; Thou art awe-inspiring and exalted. O God, who is like unto Thee?

Thou upholdest the falling and answerest the prayer of the oppressed. O God, who is like unto Thee?

Thou redeemest the burdened and savest with great power. O God, who is like unto Thee?

נָא נַפְשָׁם כִּי עָלֶיךָ מִתְרַפְּקִים. פְּרוֹשׂ יָדְךָ לָהֶם
וְקַבְּלֵם וּבְשָׂרֵם:

Choir

וְאַתֶּם הַדְּבֵקִים בַּיְיָ אֱלֹהֵיכֶם חַיִּים כֻּלְּכֶם הַיּוֹם:

Silent Devotion

אַדִּיר וְנָאוֹר בּוֹרֵא דוֹק וָחֶלֶד.	מִי אֵל כָּמוֹךָ:
גּוֹלֶה עֲמוּקוֹת דּוֹבֵר צְדָקוֹת.	מִי אֵל כָּמוֹךָ:
הָדוּר בִּלְבוּשׁוֹ וְאֵין זוּלָתוֹ.	מִי אֵל כָּמוֹךָ:
זוֹכֵר הַבְּרִית חוֹנֵן שְׁאֵרִית.	מִי אֵל כָּמוֹךָ:
טָהוֹר עֵינַיִם יוֹשֵׁב שָׁמַיִם.	מִי אֵל כָּמוֹךָ:
כּוֹבֵשׁ עֲוֹנוֹת לוֹבֵשׁ צְדָקוֹת.	מִי אֵל כָּמוֹךָ:
מֶלֶךְ מְלָכִים נוֹרָא וְנִשְׂגָּב.	מִי אֵל כָּמוֹךָ:
סוֹמֵךְ נוֹפְלִים עוֹנֶה עֲשׁוּקִים.	מִי אֵל כָּמוֹךָ:
פּוֹדֶה וּמַצִּיל צָעֶה בְּרָב כֹּחַ.	מִי אֵל כָּמוֹךָ:

Thou art nigh unto those who call upon Thee, Thou
art merciful and gracious. O God, who is like
unto Thee?

Thou inhabitest the heights; Thou art the stay of the
upright. O God, who is like unto Thee?

Reader

O God, who is like unto Thee, that pardonest iniquity and passest by the transgression of the remnant
of Thy heritage? Thou retainest not Thine anger forever, because Thou delightest in mercy. Thou wilt
again have compassion on us. Thou wilt subdue our
iniquities; yea, Thou wilt cast all our sins into the
depths of the sea. Thou wilt show faithfulness to
Jacob, mercy to Abraham, as Thou hast sworn unto
our fathers from the days of old.

קָרוֹב לְקוֹרְאָיו רַחוּם וְחַנּוּן.　מִי אֵל כָּמְוֹךָ:

שׁוֹכֵן שְׁחָקִים תּוֹמֵךְ תְּמִימִים.　מִי אֵל כָּמְוֹךָ:

Reader

מִי אֵל כָּמְוֹךָ נֹשֵׂא עָוֹן וְעֹבֵר עַל פֶּשַׁע לִשְׁאֵרִית

נַחֲלָתוֹ. לֹא הֶחֱזִיק לָעַד אַפּוֹ. כִּי חָפֵץ חֶסֶד הוּא:

יָשׁוּב יְרַחֲמֵנוּ. יִכְבֹּשׁ עֲוֹנֹתֵינוּ. וְתַשְׁלִיךְ בִּמְצֻלוֹת

יָם כָּל־חַטֹּאתָם: תִּתֵּן אֱמֶת לְיַעֲקֹב. חֶסֶד לְאַבְרָהָם.

אֲשֶׁר נִשְׁבַּעְתָּ לַאֲבוֹתֵינוּ מִימֵי קֶדֶם:

Reader and Choir

אָמֵן: הַיוֹם תְּאַמְּצֵנוּ.

אָמֵן: הַיוֹם תְּבָרְכֵנוּ.

אָמֵן: הַיוֹם תְּגַדְּלֵנוּ.

אָמֵן: הַיוֹם תִּדְרְשֵׁנוּ לְטוֹבָה.

אָמֵן: הַיוֹם תִּשְׁמַע שַׁוְעָתֵנוּ.

אָמֵן: הַיוֹם תִּתְמְכֵנוּ בִּימִין צִדְקֶךָ.

Reader and Choir

This day, strengthen us!

> Choir: Amen.

This day, bless us!

> Choir: Amen.

This day, exalt us!

> Choir: Amen.

This day, show us Thy favor!

> Choir: Amen.

This day, hear our supplication!

> Choir: Amen.

This day, support us with the right hand of Thy righteousness!

> Choir: Amen.

READING OF SCRIPTURE

Reader
(Isaiah lx)

Arise, shine, for thy light is come and the glory of
the Lord is risen upon thee. For, behold, darkness
shall cover the earth, and gross darkness the peoples;
but upon thee the Lord will arise, and His glory shall be
seen upon thee. And nations shall walk at thy light,
and kings at the brightness of thy rising. Violence
shall no more be heard in thy land, desolation within
thy borders; but thou shalt call thy walls Salvation, and
thy gates Praise. Thy people also shall be all righteous,
the branch of My planting, the work of My hands,
wherein I glory.

Choir

There is none like unto Thee, O Lord, and there are no works like Thine. Thy kingdom is a kingdom for all ages, and Thy dominion endureth throughout all generations. Thou art King eternal. Thou hast reigned and shalt reign forevermore. The Lord will give strength unto His people, the Lord will bless His people with peace.

אֵין כָּמוֹךָ בָאֱלֹהִים יְיָ
וְאֵין כְּמַעֲשֶׂיךָ: מַלְכוּתְךָ
מַלְכוּת כָּל־עוֹלָמִים
וּמֶמְשַׁלְתְּךָ בְּכָל־דּוֹר
וָדֹר: יְיָ מֶלֶךְ. יְיָ מָלָךְ.
יְיָ יִמְלֹךְ לְעוֹלָם וָעֶד: יְיָ
עֹז לְעַמּוֹ יִתֵּן. יְיָ יְבָרֵךְ
אֶת־עַמּוֹ בַשָּׁלוֹם:

Reader

Let us declare the greatness of our God and render honor unto the Torah. Praised be He who in His holiness has given the Torah unto Israel.

Congregation and Reader

Hear, O Israel: The Lord our God, the Lord is One.

Choir

Thine, O Lord, is the greatness, and the power, the glory, and the victory, and the majesty; for all that is in the heaven and in the earth is Thine; Thine is the kingdom, O Lord, and Thou art exalted as head above all.

(Before reading from the Torah)

Reader

Praise ye the Lord to whom all praise is due.

Praised be the Lord to whom all praise is due forever and ever.

Praised be Thou, O Lord our God, Ruler of the world, who hast chosen us from among all peoples and hast given us Thy law. Praised be Thou, O Lord, Giver of the Law.

Reader

(From Leviticus xix)

And the Lord spoke unto Moses, saying: Speak unto all the congregation of the children of Israel, and say unto them:

TAKING THE SCROLL FROM THE ARK
(Congregation rises)

Reader

הָבוּ גְדֶל לֵאלֹהֵינוּ וּתְנוּ כָבוֹד לַתּוֹרָה.
בָּרוּךְ שֶׁנָּתַן תּוֹרָה לְעַמּוֹ יִשְׂרָאֵל בִּקְדֻשָּׁתוֹ:

Reader and Congregation

שְׁמַע יִשְׂרָאֵל יְהוָֹה אֱלֹהֵינוּ יְהוָֹה אֶחָד:

Choir

לְךָ יְיָ הַגְּדֻלָּה וְהַגְּבוּרָה. וְהַתִּפְאֶרֶת וְהַנֵּצַח
וְהַהוֹד כִּי כֹל בַּשָּׁמַיִם וּבָאָרֶץ. לְךָ יְיָ הַמַּמְלָכָה.
וְהַמִּתְנַשֵּׂא לְכֹל לְרֹאשׁ:

(Before reading from the Torah)

Reader

בָּרְכוּ אֶת־יְיָ הַמְבֹרָךְ:
בָּרוּךְ יְיָ הַמְבֹרָךְ לְעוֹלָם וָעֶד:
בָּרוּךְ אַתָּה יְיָ אֱלֹהֵינוּ מֶלֶךְ הָעוֹלָם. אֲשֶׁר בָּחַר
בָּנוּ מִכָּל־הָעַמִּים וְנָתַן־לָנוּ אֶת־תּוֹרָתוֹ. בָּרוּךְ אַתָּה
יְיָ נוֹתֵן הַתּוֹרָה:

(ויקרא יֵ״ט)

וַיְדַבֵּר יְהוָֹה אֶל־מֹשֶׁה לֵּאמֹר: דַּבֵּר אֶל־כָּל־

Ye shall be holy: for I the Lord your God am holy.
Ye shall fear every man his mother, and his father, and
ye shall keep My sabbaths: I am the Lord your God.
And when ye reap the harvest of your land, thou shalt
not wholly reap the corners of thy field, neither shalt
thou gather the gleaning of thy harvest. And thou
shalt not glean thy vineyard, neither shalt thou gather
the fallen fruit of thy vineyard; thou shalt leave them
for the poor and for the stranger: I am the Lord your
God. Ye shall not steal; neither shall ye deal falsely,
nor lie one to another. And ye shall not swear by my
name falsely, so that thou profane the name of thy
God: I am the Lord. Thou shalt not oppress thy
neighbor, nor rob him: the wages of a hired servant
shall not abide with thee all night until the morning.
Thou shalt not curse the deaf, nor put a stumbling-
block before the blind, but thou shalt fear thy God:
I am the Lord. Ye shall do no unrighteousness in judgment: thou shalt not respect the person of the poor,
nor favor the person of the mighty, but in righteousness
shalt thou judge thy neighbor. Thou shalt not go up
and down as a talebearer among thy people; neither
shalt thou stand idly by the blood of thy neighbor: I
am the Lord. Thou shalt not hate thy brother in thy
heart: thou shalt surely rebuke thy neighbor, and not
bear sin because of him. Thou shalt not take vengeance, nor bear any grudge against the children of thy
people, but thou shalt love thy neighbor as thyself: I
am the Lord.

And if a stranger sojourn with thee in your land, ye

עֲדַת בְּנֵי־יִשְׂרָאֵל וְאָמַרְתָּ אֲלֵהֶם קְדֹשִׁים תִּהְיוּ כִּי־
קָדוֹשׁ אֲנִי יְהֹוָה אֱלֹהֵיכֶם: אִישׁ אִמּוֹ וְאָבִיו תִּירָאוּ
וְאֶת־שַׁבְּתֹתַי תִּשְׁמֹרוּ אֲנִי יְהֹוָה אֱלֹהֵיכֶם: וּבְקֻצְרְכֶם
אֶת־קְצִיר אַרְצְכֶם לֹא תְכַלֶּה פְּאַת שָׂדְךָ לִקְצֹר
וְלֶקֶט קְצִירְךָ לֹא תְלַקֵּט: וְכַרְמְךָ לֹא תְעוֹלֵל
וּפֶרֶט כַּרְמְךָ לֹא תְלַקֵּט לֶעָנִי וְלַגֵּר תַּעֲזֹב אֹתָם
אֲנִי יְהֹוָה אֱלֹהֵיכֶם: לֹא תִּגְנֹבוּ וְלֹא־תְכַחֲשׁוּ וְלֹא־
תְשַׁקְּרוּ אִישׁ בַּעֲמִיתוֹ: וְלֹא־תִשָּׁבְעוּ בִשְׁמִי לַשָּׁקֶר
וְחִלַּלְתָּ אֶת־שֵׁם אֱלֹהֶיךָ אֲנִי יְהֹוָה: לֹא־תַעֲשֹׁק אֶת־
רֵעֲךָ וְלֹא תִגְזֹל לֹא־תָלִין פְּעֻלַּת שָׂכִיר אִתְּךָ עַד־
בֹּקֶר: לֹא־תְקַלֵּל חֵרֵשׁ וְלִפְנֵי עִוֵּר לֹא תִתֵּן מִכְשֹׁל
וְיָרֵאתָ מֵאֱלֹהֶיךָ אֲנִי יְהֹוָה: לֹא־תַעֲשֹׂוּ עָוֶל בַּמִּשְׁפָּט
לֹא־תִשָּׂא פְנֵי־דָל וְלֹא תֶהְדַּר פְּנֵי גָדוֹל בְּצֶדֶק
תִּשְׁפֹּט עֲמִיתֶךָ: לֹא־תֵלֵךְ רָכִיל בְּעַמֶּיךָ לֹא תַעֲמֹד
עַל־דַּם רֵעֶךָ אֲנִי יְהֹוָה: לֹא־תִשְׂנָא אֶת־אָחִיךָ
בִּלְבָבֶךָ הוֹכֵחַ תּוֹכִיחַ אֶת־עֲמִיתֶךָ וְלֹא־תִשָּׂא עָלָיו
חֵטְא: לֹא־תִקֹּם וְלֹא־תִטֹּר אֶת־בְּנֵי עַמֶּךָ וְאָהַבְתָּ
לְרֵעֲךָ כָּמוֹךָ אֲנִי יְהֹוָה: וְכִי־יָגוּר אִתְּךָ גֵּר בְּאַרְצְכֶם

shall not do him wrong. The stranger that sojourneth with you shall be unto you as the home-born among you, and thou shalt love him as thyself; for ye were strangers in the land of Egypt: I am the Lord your God. Ye shall do no unrighteousness in judgment, in meteyard, in weight, or in measure. Just balances, just weights, a just ephah, and a just hin, shall ye have: I am the Lord your God, who brought you out of the land of Egypt. And ye shall observe all My statutes, and all Mine ordinances, and do them: I am the Lord.

(After reading from the Torah)

Praised be Thou, O Lord our God, Ruler of the world, who hast given us the law of truth and hast implanted within us everlasting life. Praised be Thou, O Lord, Giver of the Law.

לֹא תוֹנוּ אֹתוֹ: כְּאֶזְרָח מִכֶּם יִהְיֶה לָכֶם הַגֵּר הַגָּר
אִתְּכֶם וְאָהַבְתָּ לוֹ כָּמוֹךָ כִּי־גֵרִים הֱיִיתֶם בְּאֶרֶץ
מִצְרָיִם אֲנִי יְהֹוָה אֱלֹהֵיכֶם: לֹא־תַעֲשׂוּ עָוֶל בַּמִּשְׁפָּט
בַּמִּדָּה בַּמִּשְׁקָל וּבַמְּשׂוּרָה: מֹאזְנֵי צֶדֶק אַבְנֵי־צֶדֶק
אֵיפַת צֶדֶק וְהִין צֶדֶק יִהְיֶה לָכֶם אֲנִי יְהֹוָה
אֱלֹהֵיכֶם אֲשֶׁר־הוֹצֵאתִי אֶתְכֶם מֵאֶרֶץ מִצְרָיִם:
וּשְׁמַרְתֶּם אֶת־כָּל־חֻקֹּתַי וְאֶת־כָּל־מִשְׁפָּטַי וַעֲשִׂיתֶם
אֹתָם אֲנִי יְהֹוָה:

(After reading from the Torah)

בָּרוּךְ אַתָּה יְיָ אֱלֹהֵינוּ מֶלֶךְ הָעוֹלָם. אֲשֶׁר נָתַן
לָנוּ תּוֹרַת אֱמֶת וְחַיֵּי עוֹלָם נָטַע בְּתוֹכֵנוּ. בָּרוּךְ
אַתָּה יְיָ נוֹתֵן הַתּוֹרָה:

(Before reading the Haftarah)

Praised be the Lord our God, for the law of truth and righteousness revealed in Israel, for the words of the prophets filled with His spirit and for the teachings of the sages whom He raised up aforetime and in these days.

(Jonah iii–iv)

And the word of the Lord came unto Jonah, saying: Arise, go unto Nineveh, that great city, and make unto it the proclamation that I bid thee. So Jonah arose, and went unto Nineveh, according to the word of the Lord. Now Nineveh was an exceeding great city, of three days' journey. And Jonah began to enter into the city a day's journey, and he proclaimed, and said: Yet forty days, and Nineveh shall be overthrown.

And the people of Nineveh believed God; and they proclaimed a fast, and put on sackcloth, from the greatest of them even to the least of them. And the tidings reached the king of Nineveh, and he arose from his throne, and laid his robe from him, and covered him with sackcloth, and sat in ashes. And he caused it to be proclaimed and published through Nineveh by the decree of the king and his nobles, saying: Let neither man nor beast, herd nor flock, taste any thing; let them not feed, nor drink water; but let them be covered with sackcloth, both man and beast, and let them cry mightily unto God; yea, let them turn every one from his evil way, and from the violence that is in their hands. Who knoweth whether God will not turn and repent, and turn away from His fierce anger, that we perish not?

And God saw their works, that they turned from their evil way; and God repented of the evil, which He said He would do unto them; and He did it not. But it displeased Jonah exceedingly, and he was angry. And he prayed unto the Lord, and said: I pray Thee, O Lord, was not this my saying, when I was yet in mine own country? Therefore I fled beforehand unto Tarshish; for I knew that Thou art a gracious God, and compassionate, long-suffering, and abundant in mercy, and repentest Thee of the evil. Therefore now, O Lord, take, I beseech Thee, my life from me; for it is better for me to die than to live. And the Lord said: Art thou greatly angry?

Then Jonah went out of the city, and sat on the east side of the city, and there made him a booth, and sat under it in the shadow, till he might see what would become of the city. And the Lord God prepared a gourd, and made it to come up over Jonah, that it might be a shadow over his head, to deliver him from his evil. So Jonah was exceeding glad because of the gourd. But God prepared a worm when the morning rose the next day, and it smote the gourd, that it withered. And it came to pass, when the sun arose, that God prepared a vehement east wind; and the sun beat upon the head of Jonah, that he fainted, and requested for himself that he might die, and said: It is better for me to die than to live. And God said to Jonah: Art thou greatly angry for the gourd? And he said: I am greatly angry even unto death. And the Lord said: Thou hast had pity on the gourd, for which thou hast not labored, neither madest it grow, which came up in a night, and perished in a night; and should not I have pity on Nineveh, that great city, wherein are more than sixscore thousand persons that cannot discern between their right hand and their left hand, and also much cattle?

Reader

This Day of Atonement is given to us to reconcile us with God, to restore peace with our fellowmen and with ourselves, wherever discontent and selfishness have marred the harmony of our lives. It reminds us that all we are and all we have come from God. To Him we owe life and health, success and happiness. He has given us dominion over the works of His hands, so that, as faithful stewards, we may dispense wisely for the good of all His creatures. Rich and poor, strong and weak, wise and simple, He has bound us together by ties of sympathy and fellowship, so that we may form one loving brotherhood, one united family in the presence of our heavenly Father.

The knowledge of this truth was ever fostered in Israel by the Sabbath. It was ordained as a day of redemption from servitude, so that on that day the laborer might be free as his master. Likewise the Sabbatical year brought release to every one in Israel who bore the yoke of slavery or of debt. But most solemnly did the Day of Atonement affirm God's law of justice and human brotherhood, when, in each jubilee year, the Shofar proclaimed liberty throughout the land unto all the inhabitants thereof. Then was each man to return to his home and his patrimony, and families and friends were to be reunited in concord and good will. Thereby the truth was made known, that God is the Lord of all the earth, the creator and owner of the land, and all that is thereon. For the heaven and the earth are His, and we are but day-laborers and sojourners before Him.

Therefore, on this Sabbath of Sabbaths, God would have us make reparation for every wrong done to our fellowmen in the eager struggle for existence. And those who have been bruised and beaten down in life's battle, He would have restored to their birthright of freedom and independence. In His all-wise providence, God has appointed this Day of Atonement to reconcile each human being to his destiny, and to restore peace and tranquillity to every heart and home.

Choir

For He satisfieth the longing heart and filleth the hungry with good. Oh, that men would praise the Lord for His goodness and for His kindness to the children of men.

Reader

O Lord, the earth is Thine and the fulness thereof. Out of the vast abundance of Thy storehouse, Thou wouldst satisfy the wants of every living creature. But, often man's greed thwarts Thy benign purposes and countless numbers of Thy children go hungry and naked. If many know only of scarcity and want, it is not because the earth, Thy handiwork, has ceased to yield, but because men reserve for themselves the blessings that should be enjoyed by the entire human family. Hence great plenty and abject poverty, limitless power and utter weakness, exist side by side. We are thankful that good and wise men are troubled by the manner in which the earth's increase is shared; that they are unwilling to accept these inequalities as justified and permanent and are seeking a way to enable all men to share more securely and abundantly of Thy beneficence.

We, of the household of Israel, have been taught that the wrongs done to our fellowmen can be righted only if we think of all men as Thy children. When we are conscious of Thee as our common Father, we grow sensitive to the indignities and injustices visited upon our fellowmen. We realize that whatever does not serve to make our neighbor contented and trustful cannot receive Thy blessing and the sanction of Thy law. No law emanating from Thy will can be invoked to justify any conditions that deny men opportunities and cause them sorrow and suffering.

May we never be misled into believing that the ills of society are the law of nature, which cannot be changed by men. Let us confess that such thinking arises not from human helplessness but from our unwillingness to make the needful sacrifices to right wrongs and share blessings.

Our forefathers have always been deeply concerned about the hardships of those that toil. Our prophets and sages have warned us that wealth and the possession of power tend to make men callous to the needs and struggles of others. On the very threshold of our history, we were admonished not to forget the injustices we suffered when we were in Egypt as strangers and slaves. But we, in the pride of possession, often forget the true nature and source of human wealth, unmindful of the fact that no one, however strong or wise, can control the destinies of his own life singlehanded. Fair dealing between man and man enriches the whole world. But when one takes advantage of the other, then disappointment, strife and hatred ensue.

On this day of self-examination, teach us, O God, to search our ways and make acknowledgment that we ourselves have not been sufficiently mindful of the interests and rights of our neighbors. Let us confess humbly that often, in seeking to hold what we have, we give but little thought to the effect of our pursuits upon the lives of our fellowmen.

In this solemn hour we pray Thee that we may stand by the side of the men of vision; and may we in our daily pursuits, through generous sympathy and personal sacrifice, help to build the better world.

Silent Prayer
(For the Congregation)

My God, as I look into the recesses of my heart on this day of days, I am reminded of the many sacred obligations which have been placed upon me as a member of a congregation in Israel. I recall with joy how I was solemnly and hopefully confirmed in the faith of my fathers; how parents and teachers and friends impressed upon me the beauty of holiness and the many obligations which lay upon me. I remember how, with fervent heart and soul, I pledged myself to discharge my duties towards Thee and my fellowmen. Now that I have reached maturity of mind and heart, may I not be heedless of my faith nor negligent of my duties. Inspire my heart and soul that I may grow from strength to strength in the observance of those institutions and statutes which Thou hast ordained for our good and for the good of our fellowmen. Grant me firmness of purpose and loyalty of heart that I may never shirk in the face of opportunity nor fail in the hour of testing. May I stand ever ready to assume my share of the duties to the congregation and the community of which I am a part. May I ever uphold the hands of those who are giving of themselves to serve Thee and their fellows so that they may be encouraged in the arduous tasks to which they have given themselves. May I understand life as an ever increasing opportunity for service to prove the strength and the beauty of the world which Thou hast imparted to us. May my life be in the ranks of those who would sacrifice, if need be, to sanctify Thy name before mankind. Grant, I pray Thee, that my portion be with those whose daily lives demonstrate the sincerity of their professions. Towards the poor and the needy, towards the bearers of burdens and the sad heart, towards those who lead and those who follow, towards those who have vision and understanding, towards my fellow Jew and my fellowmen, may I so deport myself as to merit their approval and Thy blessings of love and strength. Through prayer and through service, may I go to each day's work with better heart and purer mind and so rise nearer to Thee and the ideal of a true Jew. May my work and deeds reflect honor upon those I serve and give glory to Thy holy name. Amen.

Reader

The Almighty takes no delight in the proud and arrogant, whose arm crushes the feeble, and who call their strength their god. His help goes forth to the weak, and their supplications are answered from on high. He champions the cause of the oppressed and requites evil-doers for their unrighteousness. Affliction of the body and fasting alone cannot cleanse the soul of sin and relieve the conscience of its weight of guilt. But these are the true means of atonement: Let justice well up as waters, and righteousness as a mighty stream. Show compassion every man to his brother; oppress not the stranger, the fatherless, and the widow, and let none of you devise evil in his heart against his neighbor. Speak ye every man the truth with his neighbor; execute the judgment of truth and peace in your gates. Do justly, love mercy and walk humbly with thy God.

O God, grant that we may hearken to the solemn admonition of this Sabbath of Sabbaths in true contrition of heart and humbleness of spirit. Help us to fulfil our obligation to the needy and distressed. Incline our hearts to compassion, that we may aid the poor, the homeless and the suffering; help us to be as a father to the needy, eyes to the blind, and feet to the lame. Imbue us with an understanding of our responsibility to our brethren of the house of Israel and to the institutions which minister to their needs. Teach us to be generous in our support of all good works. Bless all who labor unselfishly for the welfare and happiness of their fellowmen, and show Thy favor and Thy grace to all who serve Thee in truth and faithfulness. On this Day of Repentance, we return to Thee with chastened heart; receive us with favor, O God, our Father and our King, our Redeemer and our Savior. Amen.

RETURNING THE SCROLL TO THE ARK

(Congregation rises)

Reader

O magnify the Lord with me and let us exalt His name together.

גַּדְּלוּ לַיָי אִתִּי. וּנְרוֹמְמָה שְׁמוֹ יַחְדָּו:

Choir

His glory is in the earth and in the heavens. He is the strength of all His servants, the praise of them that truly love Him, the hope of Israel, the people He brought nigh to Himself. Hallelujah.

הוֹדוֹ עַל־אֶרֶץ וְשָׁמָיִם: וַיָּרֶם קֶרֶן לְעַמּוֹ תְּהִלָּה לְכָל־חֲסִידָיו לִבְנֵי יִשְׂרָאֵל עַם קְרֹבוֹ הַלְלוּיָהּ:

Reader

The law of the Lord is perfect, restoring the soul; the testimony of the Lord is sure, making wise the simple. The precepts of the Lord are right, rejoicing the heart; the judgments of the Lord are true; they are righteous altogether. Behold, a good doctrine has been given unto you; forsake it not.

תּוֹרַת יְיָ תְּמִימָה. מְשִׁיבַת נָפֶשׁ. עֵדוּת יְיָ נֶאֱמָנָה. מַחְכִּימַת פֶּתִי: פִּקּוּדֵי יְיָ יְשָׁרִים. מְשַׂמְּחֵי־לֵב. מִשְׁפְּטֵי יְיָ אֱמֶת. צָדְקוּ יַחְדָּו: כִּי לֶקַח טוֹב נָתַתִּי לָכֶם תּוֹרָתִי אַל־תַּעֲזֹבוּ:

(Congregation is seated)

Choir

It is a tree of life to them that hold fast to it, and its supporters are happy. Its ways are ways of pleasantness, and all its paths are peace.

עֵץ חַיִּים הִיא לַמַּחֲזִיקִים בָּהּ וְתוֹמְכֶיהָ מְאֻשָּׁר: דְּרָכֶיהָ דַרְכֵי־נֹעַם וְכָל־נְתִיבוֹתֶיהָ שָׁלוֹם:

Turn us again unto Thee, O Lord, and we shall be restored; renew our days as of old.

הֲשִׁיבֵנוּ יְהֹוָה אֵלֶיךָ וְנָשׁוּבָה חַדֵּשׁ יָמֵינוּ כְּקֶדֶם:

SERMON

Memorial Service for Atonement Day

Choir

O Lord! what is man that Thou takest knowledge of him; or the son of man, that thou makest account of him! Man is like unto vanity; his days are as a shadow that passeth away. In the morning he flourisheth, and groweth up; in the evening he is cut down, and withereth. Thou turnest man to contrition, and sayest: Return, ye children of men! O that they were wise, that they would consider their latter end! For when man dieth, he shall carry nothing away; his glory shall not descend after him. Mark

יְיָ מָה־אָדָם וַתֵּדָעֵהוּ.
בֶּן־אֱנוֹשׁ וַתְּחַשְּׁבֵהוּ: אָדָם
לַהֶבֶל דָּמָה. יָמָיו כְּצֵל
עוֹבֵר · בַּבֹּקֶר יָצִיץ
וְחָלָף. לָעֶרֶב יְמוֹלֵל
וְיָבֵשׁ: תָּשֵׁב אֱנוֹשׁ עַד־
דַּכָּא. וַתֹּאמֶר שׁוּבוּ בְנֵי
אָדָם: לוּ חָכְמוּ יַשְׂכִּילוּ
זֹאת יָבִינוּ לְאַחֲרִיתָם: כִּי
לֹא בְמוֹתוֹ יִקַּח הַכֹּל.
לֹא־יֵרֵד אַחֲרָיו כְּבוֹדוֹ:

306

the perfect man, and be-
hold the upright; for the
end of that man is peace.
The Lord redeemeth the
soul of His servants; and
none of them that trust
in Him shall be desolate.

שְׁמָר־תָּם וּרְאֵה יָשָׁר . כִּי־
אַחֲרִית לְאִישׁ שָׁלוֹם:
פֹּדֶה יְיָ נֶפֶשׁ עֲבָדָיו . וְלֹא
יֶאְשְׁמוּ כָּל־הַחֹסִים בּוֹ:

Responsive Reading

Reader

Lord, Thou hast been our dwelling-place in all generations. Before the mountains were brought
forth, or ever Thou hadst formed the earth and
the world.

Congregation

Even from everlasting to everlasting, Thou art God.

Thou turnest man to contrition; and sayest: Return ye
children of men.

*For a thousand years in Thy sight are but as yester-
day when it is past, and as a watch in the night.*

Thou carriest them away as with a flood; they are as a
sleep;

In the morning they are like grass which groweth up.

In the morning it flourisheth, and groweth up; in the
evening it is cut down and withereth.

*The days of our years are threescore years and ten,
or even by reason of strength fourscore years;*

Yet is their pride but travail and vanity; for it is speedily gone, and we fly away.

So teach us to number our days, that we may get us a heart of wisdom.

What man is he that liveth and shall not see death, that shall deliver his soul from the power of the grave?

Seeing his days are determined; the number of his months is with Thee.

Lord, make me to know mine end, and the measure of my days what it is; let me know how short-lived I am.

The Lord redeemeth the soul of His servants, and none of them that take refuge in Him shall be desolate.

Thou makest me to know the path of life; in Thy presence is fulness of joy, in Thy right hand bliss forevermore.

How precious is Thy lovingkindness, O God.

And the children of men take refuge in the shadow of Thy wings.

For with Thee is the fountain of life; in Thy light do we see light.

Reader

O Lord, God of the spirits of all flesh, who givest life and takest it away, Thou hast appointed this Day of Atonement that we might sanctify our lives on earth and attain unto life eternal.

In this solemn hour when we consider the swift flight of the years, our thoughts turn to those whom Thou hast taken from our midst. O Heavenly Father, may the lofty message and the tender memories of this service strengthen and purify us that we may meet every task and every test with firm and courageous faith. On this Sabbath of the soul, we seek the strength which comes from the contemplation of Thine abiding love. For man is feeble and perishable; his best laid plans are subject to disappointment and failure. Scarcely ushered into life, he begins his pilgrimage to the sepulchre. Through trial and suffering he hastens to the darkness of the grave. Thousands moisten their morsel of bread with tears and with the sweat of ceaseless toil, till their fondest hopes vanish in death. Evil passions burn in the human breast and beguile to pleasure and to sinfulness. But the delight ends with the enjoyment. Sin consumes the marrow of life; indulgence dwarfs the best impulses of the soul. Success and disappointment, pleasure and pain, mark the pathway of our earthly pilgrimage. Human life is a continual struggle against forces without and weakness within. Man prevails, only to succumb; he fails, only to renew the combat the next moment.

Reader, then Choir

Oh, what is man, the child of dust? What is man, O Lord?

Reader

The eye is never satisfied with seeing; endless are the desires of the heart. No mortal has ever had enough of riches, honor and wisdom, when death ended his career. Man devises new schemes on the grave of a thousand disappointed hopes. Discontent abides in the palace and in the hut, rankling alike in the breast of prince and pauper. Death finally terminates the combat, and grief and joy, success and failure, all are ended. Like a child falling asleep over his toys, man loosens his grasp on earthly possessions only when death overtakes him. The master and the servant, the rich and the poor, the strong and the feeble, the wise and the simple, all are equal in death; the grave levels all distinctions and makes the whole world kin.

Reader, then Choir

Oh, what is man, the child of dust? What is man, O Lord?

Reader

We are strangers before Thee, O God, and sojourners as were our fathers; our days on earth vanish like shadows. But the speedy flight of life, and the gloom of the grave should not dismay us, but should teach us wisdom. It should prompt us to put our trust in Thee, who wilt not suffer Thy children to see destruction.

For only the dust returns to the dust; the spirit which Thou hast breathed into us, returns to Thee, its ever-living source. Into us Thou has infused a portion of Thy divinity; within us we sense our own weakness and Thy mighty strength. Human achievements are transitory and human strivings vain; but Thy word endureth forever, and Thy purposes are fulfilled. When we become servants of Thy Law, witnesses of Thy truth, champions of Thy kingdom, then indeed do we endow our fleeting days with abiding value.

O that we might die the death of the righteous and our end be like theirs. Suffer us not to pass away in our sins, O Judge of life and death. Teach us so to number our days, that we may get us a heart of wisdom. Grant us strength and understanding, that we may not delay to remove from our midst all that is displeasing in Thy sight, and thus become reconciled to Thee.

Congregation and Reader
(Psalm xxiii)

The Lord is my shepherd; I shall not want. He maketh me to lie down in green pastures; He leadeth me beside the still waters. He restoreth my soul; He guideth me in straight paths for His name's sake. Yea, though I walk through the valley of the shadow of death, I will fear no evil, for Thou art with me; Thy rod and Thy staff, they comfort me. Thou preparest a table before me in the presence of mine enemies; Thou hast anointed my head with oil; my cup runneth over. Surely goodness and mercy shall follow me all the days of my life; and I shall dwell in the house of the Lord forever.

Meditation

O soul, with storms beset,
Thy griefs and cares forget!
Why dread earth's transient woe,
When soon thy body in the grave unseen
Shall be laid low,
And all will be forgotten then, as though
It had not been?
Wherefore, my soul, be still!
Adore God's holy will,
Face death's supreme decree.

Thus mayst thou save thyself, and win high aid
To profit thee,
For, like a bird, unto thy nest away,
Thou wilt take flight.
Why for a land lament
In which a lifetime spent
Is as a hurried breath?

Where splendor turns to gloom, and honors show
A faded wreath,
Where health and healing soon must sink beneath
The fatal blow.
What seemeth good and fair
Is often falsehood there.
Gold melts like shifting sands,

Thy hoarded riches pass to other men,
      And strangers' hands.

And what will all thy treasured wealth and lands
      Avail thee then?
      Life is a vine, whose crown
      The reaper Death cuts down.
      His ever-watchful eyes
Mark every step, until night's shadows fall,
      And swiftly flies
The passing day, and ah! how distant lies
      The goal of all.

      Therefore, rebellious soul,
      Thy base desires control;
      With scantly given bread
Content thyself, nor let thy memory stray
      To splendors fled.

With sorrow's load, at every step implore
      His succor bless'd.
      Before God's mercy-seat
      His pardoning love entreat.
      Make pure thy thoughts from sin,
And bring a contrite heart as sacrifice
      His grace to win.

Reader

O God, who art Master of life and death, we know how limited is our wisdom, how short our vision. One by one the children of men, passing along the road of life, disappear from our view. We know that each of us must walk the same path to the doorway of the grave. We strain our eyes to see what lies beyond the gate, but all is darkness to our mortal sight. Yet even the darkness of death is not too dark for Thee, O God, but the night shineth as the day, the darkness is even as the light. Thou hast created us in Thine image and hast made us share in Thine enduring righteousness. Thou hast put eternity into our hearts, hast implanted within us a vision of life everlasting. This hope we cherish in humility and faith, trusting in Thine endless goodness and Thy wondrous love. Into Thy gracious hands we commit the spirits of our dear ones who are gone from this earth, assured that Thou keepest faith with Thy children in death as in life. Sustain us, O God, that we may meet, with calm serenity, the dark mysteries that lie ahead, knowing that when we walk through the valley of the shadow of death, Thou art with us. Thou art our loving Father, in Thee we put our trust; Thou art the light of our life, our hope in eternity.

Choir

Why art thou cast down, my soul?
Why disquieted in me?
Feelest not the Father nigh,
Caring tenderly for all?
Lives for thee no God on high,
Loving while His judgments fall?
        Look above!
        God is Love!
Comfort take, O soul, in God,
        To the skies
        Turn thine eyes;
Every tear on earth that flows,
God, the world's great Ruler, knows.

Responsive Reading

Reader

Let us call to remembrance the great and good, through
   whom the Lord hath wrought great glory.

Congregation

Those who were leaders of the people by their judgment, giving counsel by their understanding and
   foresight.

Wise and eloquent in their teachings, and through
   knowledge and might, fit helpers of the people.

All these were honored in their generation, and were
   the glory of their times.

There be some who have left a name behind them;
whose remembrance is as sweet honey in all
mouths.

*People will declare their wisdom and the congrega-
tion will tell of their goodness.*

And there be some who have no memorial; whose
names have vanished as though they had never
been.

*But the goodness of their lives has not been lost and
their work cannot be blotted out.*

אלה אזכרה

These things do I remember; through all the years
Ignorance like a monster hath devoured
Our martyrs as in one long day of blood.
Rulers have arisen through the endless years
Oppressive, savage in their witless power
Filled with a futile thought: To make an end
Of that which God hath cherished.

O Lord of life, our times are in Thy hands. One generation cometh into the world to be blessed with days
of peace and safety; another goeth through the valley
of the shadow enduring the cruelties of persecution and
war. Sorrowful and dangerous have been the times
which Thou, O God, hast assigned to us. We have
lived through years of tyranny and destruction and are
now schooled in sorrow and well acquainted with grief.
We have seen the just defeated, the innocent driven

into exile and the righteous brought to a martyrdom as merciless as any the ages had ever beheld.

At this hour of memorial, we recall with loving reverence all of Thy children who have perished through the cruelty of the oppressor. Not punished for any individual guilt, but without discrimination, the aged and the young, the learned and the simple were driven in multitudes along the road of pain and pitiless death. Their very presence on earth was begrudged them for they brought to the mind of man the recollection of Thy covenant of mercy and justice. For no sin of theirs did they perish but because they were a symbol of Thine eternal law. They have died, as did the martyrs of bygone days, for the sanctification of Thy Name on earth.

They lie at rest in nameless graves. Their resting-places in far-off forests and lonely fields are lost to the eyes of revering kin. Yet they shall not be forgotten. We take them into our hearts and give them place beside the cherished memories of our own beloved. They now are ours.

We pray to Thee, O Merciful Father, that Thy Law, to which these Thy children have borne witness in life and death, shed now a renewed light in the hearts of men, that all these martyrs, nameless to us but known to Thee, shall not have suffered in vain. May their memory be an enduring blessing to all Thy children.

Choir

I set the Lord before me at all times, since He is at my right hand, I

שִׁוִּיתִי יְיָ לְנֶגְדִּי תָמִיד.
כִּי מִימִינִי בַּל־אֶמּוֹט:

shall not be moved. Therefore, my heart is glad, and my spirit rejoiceth; yea, my flesh dwelleth in security. For Thou wilt not give me up to destruction: nor wilt Thou suffer Thy beloved to see corruption. Thou wilt show me the path of life; in Thy presence is fulness of joy; at Thy right hand are pleasures forevermore.

לָכֵן שָׂמַח לִבִּי וַיָּגֶל כְּבוֹדִי. אַף־בְּשָׂרִי יִשְׁכּוֹן לָבֶטַח: כִּי לֹא־תַעֲזֹב נַפְשִׁי לִשְׁאוֹל. לֹא־תִתֵּן חֲסִידְךָ לִרְאוֹת שָׁחַת: תּוֹדִיעֵנִי אֹרַח חַיִּים. שֹׂבַע שְׂמָחוֹת אֶת־פָּנֶיךָ. נְעִימוֹת בִּימִינְךָ נֶצַח:

Reader

Almighty God, we thank Thee for the gift of memory which unites generation to generation. This hour of memorial bids us be mindful of the supreme hour which will call us to the realm of eternal rest and gather us to our fathers, to all the unnumbered generations that have gone before us. We remember all our beloved who have already reached the goal whither we are tending. We think of the days when they were with us and we rejoiced in the blessing of their companionship and affection. They are near us even now, though many years have passed over their graves.

Grant, O Lord, that when the time of our departure comes, we may look back without sorrow upon the life we leave, and with trust in Thy mercy enter that life which Thou hast prepared for the righteous. Amen.

יזכר

Silent Devotion

IN MEMORY OF A FATHER

Thy memory, my dear father, fills my soul at this solemn hour. It revives in me thoughts of the love and friendliness which thou didst bestow upon me. The thought of thee inspires me to a life of virtue; and when my pilgrimage on earth is ended and I shall arrive at the throne of mercy, may I be worthy of thee in the sight of God and man. May our merciful Father reward thee for the faithfulness and kindness thou hast ever shown me; may He grant thee eternal peace. Amen.

IN MEMORY OF A MOTHER

I remember Thee in this solemn hour, my dear mother. I remember the days when thou didst dwell on earth, and thy tender love watched over me like a guardian angel. Thou hast gone from me, but the bond which unites our souls can never be severed; thine image lives within my heart. May the merciful Father reward thee for the faithfulness and kindness thou hast ever shown me; may He lift up the light of His countenance upon thee, and grant thee eternal peace! Amen.

IN MEMORY OF A HUSBAND

I remember thee in this solemn hour, thou dear companion of my life. I remember the happy days we lived together; I remember thy tender affection and self-denial while hand in hand we trod the path of our wedded life, when thy love and fidelity were my comfort and thy counsel and aid were my support. Though death has summoned thee from my side, thine image still lives in my heart; and continues to be an inspiration to me. May God have thee in His keeping and give thee bliss eternal! Amen.

IN MEMORY OF A WIFE

Thy memory, dear companion of my life, now fills my soul. It revives in me the thought of the love, fidelity and self-denial which sweetened the days of my life. I treasure it in my heart and strive to become worthy of thee. Though death has summoned thee from my side, thine image still lives within me and continues to be an inspiration to me. May God have thee in His keeping and give thee bliss eternal! Amen.

IN MEMORY OF A CHILD

I remember thee in this solemn hour, my beloved child. I remember the days, when I watched thy bodily and mental unfolding, and fostered beautiful hopes for thy future. God has taken thee from me, yet in my heart the fond remembrance of thee can never die. He has called thee into His presence, His paternal love is my solace, my staff and support. As a father pitieth his children, so may He look with compassion upon thee and grant thee eternal bliss. Amen.

IN MEMORY OF A BROTHER, A SISTER, OR A FRIEND

I remember thee in this solemn hour, my beloved brother (sister, friend). I remember the days when we lived together in happy companionship and thy loving friendship were my delight and support. Though thou hast gone from me, thine image abides with me. I think of thee with gratitude and bless thy memory for all the devotion thou didst show me. May God bless thee with everlasting joy, may He have thee in His keeping and grant thee eternal bliss. Amen.

Reader

O God, be near us in the sorrow of our hearts. Send comfort and consolation to all who are bowed down with grief and affliction. Let them see Thy help speedily. May their troubled spirits find solace in the beauty of holiness which fills this memorial hour. May Thy fatherly protection sustain them and may Thy peace abide with them.

We remember with sorrowing hearts those whom death has taken from our midst during the past year.
. . . .
We name in our hearts all our beloved and in recalling them, we sanctify Thy name.

(Congregation rises)

Reader

Extolled and hallowed be the name of God throughout the world which He has created according to His will. And may He speedily establish His kingdom of righteousness on earth. Amen.

Congregation

Praised be His glorious name unto all eternity.

Reader

Praised and glorified be the name of the Holy One, though He be above all the praises which we can utter. Our guide is He in life and our redeemer through all eternity.

Congregation

Our help cometh from Him, the creator of heaven and earth.

Reader

The departed whom we now remember have entered into the peace of life eternal. They still live on earth in the acts of goodness they performed and in the hearts of those who cherish their memory. May the beauty of their life abide among us as a loving benediction.

Congregation: Amen.

Reader

May the Father of peace send peace to all who mourn, and comfort all the bereaved among us.

Congregation: Amen.

(Congregation is seated)

(Congregation rises)

Reader

יִתְגַּדַּל וְיִתְקַדַּשׁ שְׁמֵהּ רַבָּא. בְּעָלְמָא דִּי־בְרָא
כִרְעוּתֵהּ. וְיַמְלִיךְ מַלְכוּתֵהּ. בְּחַיֵּיכוֹן וּבְיוֹמֵיכוֹן
וּבְחַיֵּי דְכָל־בֵּית יִשְׂרָאֵל. בַּעֲגָלָא וּבִזְמַן קָרִיב.
וְאִמְרוּ אָמֵן:

Congregation

יְהֵא שְׁמֵהּ רַבָּא מְבָרַךְ לְעָלַם וּלְעָלְמֵי עָלְמַיָּא:

Reader

יִתְבָּרַךְ וְיִשְׁתַּבַּח וְיִתְפָּאַר וְיִתְרוֹמַם וְיִתְנַשֵּׂא
וְיִתְהַדָּר וְיִתְעַלֶּה וְיִתְהַלָּל שְׁמֵהּ דְּקוּדְשָׁא. בְּרִיךְ
הוּא. לְעֵלָּא מִן כָּל־בִּרְכָתָא וְשִׁירָתָא. תֻּשְׁבְּחָתָא
וְנֶחָמָתָא. דַּאֲמִירָן בְּעָלְמָא. וְאִמְרוּ אָמֵן:

עַל יִשְׂרָאֵל וְעַל צַדִּיקַיָּא. וְעַל־כָּל־מַן דְּאִתְפְּטַר
מִן עָלְמָא הָדֵין כִּרְעוּתֵהּ דֶּאֱלָהָא. יְהֵא לְהוֹן
שְׁלָמָא רַבָּא וְחִנָּא וְחִסְדָּא מִן־קֳדָם מָרֵא שְׁמַיָּא
וְאַרְעָא. וְאִמְרוּ אָמֵן:

יְהֵא שְׁלָמָא רַבָּא מִן־שְׁמַיָּא וְחַיִּים. עָלֵינוּ וְעַל־
כָּל־יִשְׂרָאֵל. וְאִמְרוּ אָמֵן:

עֹשֶׂה שָׁלוֹם בִּמְרוֹמָיו. הוּא יַעֲשֶׂה שָׁלוֹם עָלֵינוּ
וְעַל־כָּל־יִשְׂרָאֵל. וְאִמְרוּ אָמֵן:

(Congregation is seated)

THE MOURNER'S KADDISH

Reader

Yis-gad-dal v'yis-kad-dash sh'meh rab-bo, b'ol-mo
di'v-ro kir'-u-seh v'yam-lich mal-chu-seh, b'cha-ye-chon
u-v'yo-me-chon u-v'cha-yeh d'chol bes yis-ro-el, ba-a-
go-lo u-viz-man ko-riv, v'im-ru O-men.

Congregation

Y'heh sh'meh rab-bo m'vo-rach, l'o-lam ul'ul'meh ol-
ma-yo:

Reader

Yis-bo-rach v'yish-tab-bach, v'yis-po-ar, v'yis-ro-mam,
v'yis-nas-seh, v'yis-had-dor, v'yis-al-leh, v'yis-hal-lol, sh'-
meh d'kud'-sho, b'rich hu. L'e-lo min kol bir-cho-so
v'shi-ro-so, tush-b'cho-so v'ne-cho-mo-so, da-a-mi-ron
b'ol-mo, v'im-ru: O-men.

Al yis-ro-el v'al tsa-de-ka-yo, v'al kol man d'isp'tar min
ol-mo ho-dain kir-ooseh de-e-lo-ho, y'hai l'hon shlo-mo
rab-bo v'chino v'chis-do min ko-dom mo-rai sh'ma-yo
v'ar-o, v'im-ru: O-men.

Y'heh sh'lo-mo rab-bo min sh'ma-yo v'cha-yim, o-le-
nu v'al kol yis-ro-el, v'imru: O-men.

O-seh sho-lom bim'-ro-mov, hu ya-a-seh sho-lom,
o-le-nu v'al kol yis-ro-el, v'imru: O-men.

Concluding Service for the Day of Atonement

Choir

The sun goes down, the shadows rise,
The day of God is near its close;
The glowing orb now homeward flies,
A gentle breeze foretells repose.
Lord, crown our work before the night:
In the eve let there be light.

While still in clouds the sun delays,
Let us soar up, soar up to heaven;
That love may shed its peaceful rays,
New hope unto our souls be given.
O may the parting hour be bright:
In the eve let there be light.

And when our sun of life retreats,
When evening shadows 'round us hover,
Our restless heart no longer beats,
And grave-ward sinks our earthly cover,
We shall behold a glorious sight:
In the eve there shall be light.

Responsive Reading

(Psalm ciii)

Reader

Bless the Lord, O my soul; and all that is within me, bless His holy name.

Congregation

Bless the Lord, O my soul, and forget not all His benefits;

Who forgiveth all thine iniquities; who healeth all thy diseases;

Who redeemeth thy life from destruction; who encompasseth thee with lovingkindness and tender mercies;

Who satisfieth thine old age with good things; so that thy youth is renewed like the eagle.

The Lord executeth righteousness and acts of justice for all that are oppressed.

The Lord is full of compassion and gracious, slow to anger, and plenteous in mercy.

He hath not dealt with us after our sins, nor requited us according to our iniquities.

For as the heaven is high above the earth, so great is His mercy toward them that fear Him.

As far as the east is from the west, so far hath He removed our transgressions from us.

As a father hath compassion upon his children, so hath
the Lord compassion upon them that fear Him.

For He knoweth our frame, He remembereth that
we are dust.

As for man, his days are as grass; as a flower of the field,
so he flourisheth.

For the wind passeth over it, and it is gone; and the
place thereof knoweth it no more.

But the mercy of the Lord is from everlasting to everlasting upon them that fear Him;

And His righteousness unto children's children; to
such as keep His covenant, and to those that
remember His precepts to do them.

The Lord hath established His throne in the heavens,
and His kingdom ruleth over all.

Bless the Lord, ye messengers of His, ye mighty in
strength, that fulfil His word, hearkening unto
the voice of His word.

Bless the Lord, all ye His hosts; ye ministers of His,
that do His pleasure.

Choir

Bless the Lord, all ye, His works, in all places of His
dominion. Bless the Lord, O my soul!

Reader

Praised be Thou, O Lord, God of our fathers, God of Abraham, Isaac and Jacob, great, mighty, and exalted. Thou bestowest lovingkindness upon all Thy children. Thou rememberest the devotion of the fathers. In Thy love, Thou bringest redemption to their descendants for the sake of Thy name. Thou art our King and Helper, our Savior and Protector.

Remember us unto life, O King, who delightest in life and seal us in the book of life, for Thy sake, O God of life. Thou, O King, art our helper, savior and protector. Praised be Thou, O Lord, Shield of Abraham.

Eternal is Thy power, O Lord, Thou art mighty to save. In lovingkindness Thou sustainest the living; in the multitude of Thy mercies, Thou preservest all. Thou upholdest the falling and healest the sick; freest the captives and keepest faith with Thy children in death as in life. Who is like unto Thee, Almighty God, Author of life and death, Source of salvation?

Who is like unto Thee, Father of mercies, who rememberest Thy children unto life eternal? Praised be Thou, O Lord, who hast implanted within us immortal life.

Reader

בָּרוּךְ אַתָּה יְיָ אֱלֹהֵינוּ וֵאלֹהֵי אֲבוֹתֵינוּ. אֱלֹהֵי
אַבְרָהָם אֱלֹהֵי יִצְחָק וֵאלֹהֵי יַעֲקֹב. הָאֵל הַגָּדוֹל
הַגִּבּוֹר וְהַנּוֹרָא. אֵל עֶלְיוֹן. גּוֹמֵל חֲסָדִים טוֹבִים.
וְקֹנֵה הַכֹּל וְזוֹכֵר חַסְדֵי אָבוֹת. וּמֵבִיא גְאֻלָּה לִבְנֵי
בְנֵיהֶם לְמַעַן שְׁמוֹ בְּאַהֲבָה:

זָכְרֵנוּ לַחַיִּים. מֶלֶךְ חָפֵץ בַּחַיִּים. וְחָתְמֵנוּ בְּסֵפֶר
הַחַיִּים. לְמַעַנְךָ אֱלֹהִים חַיִּים: מֶלֶךְ עוֹזֵר וּמוֹשִׁיעַ
וּמָגֵן. בָּרוּךְ אַתָּה יְיָ מָגֵן אַבְרָהָם:

אַתָּה גִבּוֹר לְעוֹלָם אֲדֹנָי. רַב לְהוֹשִׁיעַ. מְכַלְכֵּל
חַיִּים בְּחֶסֶד. מְחַיֶּה הַכֹּל בְּרַחֲמִים רַבִּים. סוֹמֵךְ
נוֹפְלִים וְרוֹפֵא חוֹלִים וּמַתִּיר אֲסוּרִים וּמְקַיֵּם
אֱמוּנָתוֹ לִישֵׁנֵי עָפָר. מִי כָמוֹךָ בַּעַל גְּבוּרוֹת. וּמִי
דוֹמֶה־לָּךְ. מֶלֶךְ מֵמִית וּמְחַיֶּה. וּמַצְמִיחַ יְשׁוּעָה:
מִי כָמוֹךָ אַב הָרַחֲמִים. זוֹכֵר יְצוּרָיו לַחַיִּים
בְּרַחֲמִים: בָּרוּךְ אַתָּה יְיָ נֹטֵעַ בְּתוֹכֵנוּ חַיֵּי עוֹלָם:

SANCTIFICATION

(Congregation rises)

Reader

We sanctify Thy name on earth, as the heavens declare Thy glory; and in the words of the prophet we say:

Congregation and Choir

Holy, holy, holy is the Lord of hosts; the whole earth is full of His glory.

Reader

God our Strength, God our Lord, how excellent is Thy name in all the earth.

Congregation and Choir

Praised be the glory of God in all the world.

Reader

Our God is One; He is our Father, He is our King, He is our Helper and in His mercy He will answer our prayers in the sight of all the living.

Congregation and Choir

The Lord will reign forever, thy God, O Zion, from generation to generation.   Hallelujah.

(Congregation is seated)

SANCTIFICATION

(Congregation rises)

נְקַדֵּשׁ אֶת־שִׁמְךָ בָּעוֹלָם. כְּשֵׁם שֶׁמַּקְדִּישִׁים אוֹתוֹ
בִּשְׁמֵי מָרוֹם. כַּכָּתוּב עַל־יַד נְבִיאֶךָ. וְקָרָא זֶה אֶל־
זֶה וְאָמַר:

Choir and Congregation

קָדוֹשׁ קָדוֹשׁ קָדוֹשׁ יְיָ צְבָאוֹת. מְלֹא כָל־הָאָרֶץ
כְּבוֹדוֹ:

Reader

אַדִּיר אַדִּירֵנוּ יְיָ אֲדוֹנֵנוּ מָה־אַדִּיר שִׁמְךָ בְּכָל־
הָאָרֶץ:

Choir and Congregation

בָּרוּךְ כְּבוֹד יְיָ מִמְּקוֹמוֹ:

Reader

אֶחָד הוּא אֱלֹהֵינוּ. הוּא אָבִינוּ. הוּא מַלְכֵּנוּ.
הוּא מוֹשִׁיעֵנוּ: וְהוּא יַשְׁמִיעֵנוּ בְּרַחֲמָיו לְעֵינֵי כָּל־חָי:

Choir and Congregation

יִמְלֹךְ יְיָ לְעוֹלָם אֱלֹהַיִךְ צִיּוֹן לְדוֹר וָדוֹר
הַלְלוּיָהּ:

(Congregation is seated)

Reader and Congregation

Reader

The Lord is King, the Lord did reign, the Lord will reign forever.

Ere yet the sky and earth were formed, the Lord was King.

Before the lights in heaven shone, the Lord did reign.

Though like a garment earth decay, and heaven all as smoke dissolve,

Congregation

The Lord will reign forever.

Reader

Ere yet the earth's expanse was spread, the Lord was King.

And when He formed its creatures all, the Lord did reign.

Though earth from out its orbit reel, and tremble to its lowest depths.

Congregation

The Lord will reign forever.

Responsive Reading

Reader
O God whose deeds are mighty, grant pardon for our sins, as the closing hour draws nigh.

Congregation
O Lord, we stand in awe before Thy deeds.

Reader and Congregation

Reader

יְיָ מֶלֶךְ. יְיָ מָלָךְ. יְיָ יִמְלוֹךְ לְעוֹלָם וָעֶד:

בְּטֶרֶם שְׁחָקִים וַאֲרָקִים נִמְתָחוּ.   יְיָ מָלָךְ:

וְעַד־לֹא מְאוֹרוֹת זָרָחוּ.   יְיָ מָלָךְ:

וְהָאָרֶץ כְּבֶגֶד תִּבְלֶה. וְהַשָּׁמַיִם כְּעָשָׁן נִמְלָחוּ.

Congregation

יְיָ יִמְלוֹךְ לְעוֹלָם וָעֶד:

Reader

וְעַד־לֹא עָשָׂה אֶרֶץ וְחוּצוֹת.   יְיָ מָלָךְ:

וּבַהֲכִינוֹ יְצוּרִים עֲלֵי אֲרָצוֹת.   יְיָ מָלָךְ:

יַרְגִּיז אֶרֶץ מִמְּקוֹמָהּ. וַתְּכַס עַמּוּדֶיהָ פַּלָּצוּת.

Congregation

יְיָ יִמְלוֹךְ לְעוֹלָם וָעֶד:

Responsive Reading

אֵל נוֹרָא עֲלִילָה. הַמְצֵא לָנוּ מְחִילָה. בִּשְׁעַת
הַנְּעִילָה:

אֵל נוֹרָא עֲלִילָה:

We who are few in number, lift our eyes in worship, and trembling we approach Thee as the closing hour draws nigh.

O Lord, we stand in awe before Thy deeds.

We pour out our hearts before Thee; blot out our transgressions, grant our sins forgiveness as the closing hour draws nigh.

O Lord, we stand in awe before Thy deeds.

Give us Thy protection; deliver us from danger; grant us joy and honor as the closing hour draws nigh.

O Lord, we stand in awe before Thy deeds.

All their sins forgiving, show favor to Thy chosen as the closing hour draws nigh.

O Lord, we stand in awe before Thy deeds.

O God whose deeds are mighty, grant pardon for our sins as the closing hour draws nigh.

O Lord, we stand in awe before Thy deeds.

מָתַי מִסְפָּר קְרוּאִים. לְךָ עַיִן נוֹשְׂאִים. וּמְסַלְּדִים
בְּחִילָה. בִּשְׁעַת הַנְּעִילָה:

אֵל נוֹרָא עֲלִילָה:

שׁוֹפְכִים לְךָ נַפְשָׁם. מְחֵה־נָא פִּשְׁעָם. וְהַמְצִיאֵם
מְחִילָה. בִּשְׁעַת הַנְּעִילָה:

אֵל נוֹרָא עֲלִילָה:

הֱיֵה לָהֶם לְסִתְרָה. וְחַלְּצֵם מִמְּאֵרָה. וְזָכְרֵם לְהוֹד
וּלְגִילָה. בִּשְׁעַת הַנְּעִילָה:

אֵל נוֹרָא עֲלִילָה:

מְחַה כָעָב פְּשָׁעִים. וַעֲשֵׂה חֶסֶד עִם מְקוֹרָאִים
סְגֻלָּה. בִּשְׁעַת הַנְּעִילָה:

אֵל נוֹרָא עֲלִילָה:

אֵל נוֹרָא עֲלִילָה. הַמְצֵא לָנוּ מְחִילָה. בִּשְׁעַת
הַנְּעִילָה:

אֵל נוֹרָא עֲלִילָה:

Responsive Reading

The day of rest is ending, still we stand before Thee;
O turn to us and hearken, O Thou enthroned
on high.

Listen to our song, hearken to our prayer.

The sighing of Thy worshipers ascends unto Thy
throne; grant the prayer of those who proclaim
Thee One.

*Hearken to the prayer of those who come before
Thee.*

Israel is saved forever by Thee, O Lord of Hosts; send
Thou Thy help this day, O Thou who dwellest
on high.

Abundantly Thou pardonest, Master of mercies.

Let us find protection in the shadow of Thy wings.
With kindliness Thou searchest the erring heart
to heal it. Arise, O Lord our God, manifest Thy
might.

Lord, hearken to our cry.

Sound Thy word of pardon from Thy hidden Presence,
send Thy saving power, unto Thy lowly people.
Give answer to our prayer with Thy wondrous
grace.

Lord, be Thou our Helper.

Responsive Reading

בְּמוֹצָאֵי מְנוּחָה. קִדַּמְנוּךָ תְּחִלָּה. הַט אָזְנְךָ
מִמָּרוֹם יוֹשֵׁב תְּהִלָּה.

לִשְׁמוֹעַ אֶל־הָרִנָּה וְאֶל־הַתְּפִלָּה:

אָנְקַת מְסַלְּדֶיךָ. תַּעַל לִפְנֵי כִסֵּא כְבוֹדֶךָ. מַלֵּא
מִשְׁאֲלוֹת עַם מְיַחֲדֶךָ.

שׁוֹמֵעַ תְּפִלַּת בָּאֵי עָדֶיךָ:

יִשְׂרָאֵל נוֹשַׁע בַּיָי תְּשׁוּעַת עוֹלָמִים. גַּם־הַיּוֹם
יִוָּשְׁעוּ מִפִּיךָ שׁוֹכֵן מְרוֹמִים.

כִּי אַתָּה רַב סְלִיחוֹת וּבְעַל הָרַחֲמִים:

יַחְבִּיאֵנוּ צֵל יָדוֹ תַּחַת כַּנְפֵי הַשְּׁכִינָה. חוֹן יָחוֹן
כִּי יִבְחוֹן לֵב עָקוֹב לְהָכִינָה. קוּמָה נָא אֱלֹהֵינוּ.
עֻזָּה עֻזִּי נָא:

יְיָ לְשַׁוְעָתֵנוּ הַאֲזִינָה:

יַשְׁמִיעֵנוּ סָלַחְתִּי יוֹשֵׁב בְּסֵתֶר עֶלְיוֹן. בִּימִין יֶשַׁע
לְהוֹשֵׁעַ עַם עָנִי וְאֶבְיוֹן. בְּשַׁוְּעֵנוּ אֵלֶיךָ נוֹרָאוֹת
בְּצֶדֶק תַּעֲנֵנוּ.

יְיָ הֱיֵה עוֹזֵר לָנוּ:

338 CONCLUDING SERVICE FOR ATONEMENT DAY

Entreating we approach Thee; from Thee cometh
   mercy. Shame us not, O Father, dismissing us
   unanswered.

*Forgive Thou us and grant us Thy mercy and salva-
   tion.*

We come to seek salvation; awe-inspiring art Thou, O
   Refuge in our trouble; graciously grant life anew;
   upon Thy Name we call.

*Forgive Thou us and grant us Thy mercy and Thy
   pardon.*

Reader

Thou puttest forth Thy hand unto those who go
astray, and Thy right hand is extended to take back in
love those who turn again unto Thee. Thou hast
taught us, O Lord, to acknowledge all our sins before
Thee, to the end that we may withhold our hands
from unrighteousness. Receive our sincere repentance.
Thou knowest, O Lord, that we are but dust and ashes;
therefore Thou dost abundantly pardon. For what
are we, what is our life, what our goodness, what our
power? What can we say in Thy presence? Are not
all the mighty men as naught before Thee and those of
great renown as though they had never been; the
wisest as if without knowledge, and men of understanding as if without discernment? Many of our works
are vain, and our days pass away like a shadow.

אֶתָאנוּ לְחַלּוֹת פָּנֶיךָ. כִּי חֶסֶד וֶאֱמֶת יְקַדְּמוּ
פָנֶיךָ: נָא אַל־תְּבִישֵׁנוּ. נָא אַל־תְּשִׁיבֵנוּ רֵיקָם
מִלְּפָנֶיךָ:

סְלַח לָנוּ. וּשְׁלַח לָנוּ יְשׁוּעָה וְרַחֲמִים מִמְּעוֹנֶיךָ:
אֶתָאנוּ לְבַקֵּשׁ מִמְּךָ כַּפָּרָה. אָיֹם וְנוֹרָא. מְשַׂגָּב
לְעִתּוֹת בַּצָּרָה. תְּחַיֵּינוּ וּתְחָנֵּנוּ. וּבְשִׁמְךָ נִקְרָא:

סְלַח לָנוּ. וּשְׁלַח לָנוּ סְלִיחָה וְרַחֲמִים מִמְּעוֹנֶיךָ:

Reader

אַתָּה נוֹתֵן יָד לְפוֹשְׁעִים וִימִינְךָ פְּשׁוּטָה לְקַבֵּל
שָׁבִים. וַתְּלַמְּדֵנוּ יְיָ אֱלֹהֵינוּ לְהִתְוַדּוֹת לְפָנֶיךָ עַל
כָּל עֲוֹנוֹתֵינוּ וּתְקַבְּלֵנוּ בִּתְשׁוּבָה שְׁלֵמָה לְפָנֶיךָ
לְמַעַן דְּבָרֶיךָ אֲשֶׁר אָמָרְתָּ. וְאַתָּה יוֹדֵעַ שֶׁאַחֲרִיתֵנוּ
רִמָּה וְתוֹלֵעָה לְפִיכָךְ הִרְבֵּיתָ סְלִיחָתֵנוּ. מָה אָנוּ
מֶה חַיֵּינוּ מֶה חַסְדֵּנוּ מַה צִּדְקֵנוּ מַה יִשְׁעֵנוּ מַה
כֹּחֵנוּ מַה גְּבוּרָתֵנוּ וּמַה נֹּאמַר לְפָנֶיךָ יְיָ אֱלֹהֵינוּ
וֵאלֹהֵי אֲבוֹתֵינוּ. הֲלֹא כָּל הַגִּבּוֹרִים כְּאַיִן לְפָנֶיךָ
וְאַנְשֵׁי הַשֵּׁם כְּלֹא הָיוּ וַחֲכָמִים כִּבְלִי מַדָּע וּנְבוֹנִים
כִּבְלִי הַשְׂכֵּל כִּי רוֹב מַעֲשֵׂיהֶם תֹּהוּ וִימֵי חַיֵּיהֶם
הֶבֶל לְפָנֶיךָ:

Thou hast distinguished man from the beginning and hast singled him out to stand before Thee. Yet who dare say unto Thee, what doest Thou? And though man be righteous, what does he give to Thee? In Thy love Thou hast given us this Day of Atonement for the remission and pardon of all our sins, that we may refrain from every form of exploitation and return to Thee to do Thy will with a perfect heart. Have pity upon us in Thy great mercy, for it is not Thy desire that mankind should be destroyed. As it is said, Seek ye the Lord while He may be found, call ye upon Him while He is near; let the wicked forsake his ways, and the unrighteous man his evil thoughts, and let him return unto the Lord, who will have mercy upon him, and to our God, who will abundantly pardon. Yea, Thou art merciful and gracious, long-suffering and of infinite patience and faithfulness; Thou acceptest with favor the repentance of the wicked and desirest not their death, as Thy prophet has spoken: Say to them, As I live, saith the Lord God, I have no pleasure in the

אַתָּה הִבְדַּלְתָּ אֱנוֹשׁ מֵרֹאשׁ. וַתַּכִּירֵהוּ לַעֲמוֹד
לְפָנֶיךָ. כִּי מִי יֹאמַר לְךָ מַה תִּפְעָל. וְאִם יִצְדַּק
מַה יִּתֶּן לָךְ: וַתִּתֶּן לָנוּ יְיָ אֱלֹהֵינוּ. בְּאַהֲבָה אֶת יוֹם
הַכִּפֻּרִים הַזֶּה. לִמְחִילָה וּסְלִיחָה עַל כָּל עֲוֹנוֹתֵינוּ.
לְמַעַן נֶחְדַּל מֵעֹשֶׁק יָדֵינוּ. וְנָשׁוּב אֵלֶיךָ לַעֲשׂוֹת חֻקֵּי
רְצוֹנְךָ בְּלֵבָב שָׁלֵם: וְאַתָּה בְּרַחֲמֶיךָ הָרַבִּים רַחֵם
עָלֵינוּ. כִּי לֹא תַחְפֹּץ בְּהַשְׁחָתַת עוֹלָם. שֶׁנֶּאֱמַר
דִּרְשׁוּ יְיָ בְּהִמָּצְאוֹ קְרָאֻהוּ בִּהְיוֹתוֹ קָרוֹב: וְנֶאֱמַר
יַעֲזֹב רָשָׁע דַּרְכּוֹ וְאִישׁ אָוֶן מַחְשְׁבֹתָיו. וְיָשֹׁב אֶל יְיָ
וִירַחֲמֵהוּ וְאֶל אֱלֹהֵינוּ כִּי יַרְבֶּה לִסְלוֹחַ: וְאַתָּה
אֱלוֹהַּ סְלִיחוֹת. חַנּוּן וְרַחוּם אֶרֶךְ אַפַּיִם וְרַב חֶסֶד
וֶאֱמֶת וּמַרְבֶּה לְהֵיטִיב. וְרוֹצֶה אַתָּה בִּתְשׁוּבַת
רְשָׁעִים וְאֵין אַתָּה חָפֵץ בְּמִיתָתָם. שֶׁנֶּאֱמַר אֱמֹר
אֲלֵיהֶם חַי אָנִי נְאֻם אֲדֹנָי יֱהֹוִה. אִם אֶחְפֹּץ בְּמוֹת

death of the wicked, but that the wicked turn from his way and live; turn ye, turn ye from your evil ways; for why will ye die, O house of Israel?   Have I any pleasure at all that the wicked should die? saith the Lord God; and not rather that he should return from his ways, and live?

Reader and Congregation

Our God and God of our fathers, pardon our transgressions on this Day of Atonement; remove our guilt, and blot out our iniquities, as Thou hast promised: I, even I, blot out thine iniquities for My sake, and thy sins will I remember no more.   I have made thy sins to vanish like a cloud, and thy transgressions, like a mist; return to Me for I have redeemed thee.   On this day shall ye be forgiven and cleansed from all your sins; before God ye shall be pure.

Praised be Thou, O Lord, who forgivest transgressions, King of the world, who sanctifiest Israel, and the Day of Atonement.

Choir: Amen

הָרָשָׁע. כִּי אִם בְּשׁוּב רָשָׁע מִדַּרְכּוֹ וְחָיָה: שׁוּבוּ
שׁוּבוּ מִדַּרְכֵיכֶם הָרָעִים. וְלָמָּה תָמוּתוּ בֵּית
יִשְׂרָאֵל: וְנֶאֱמַר. הֶחָפֹץ אֶחְפֹּץ מוֹת רָשָׁע. נְאֻם
אֲדֹנָי יֶהֱוִֹה. הֲלֹא בְּשׁוּבוֹ מִדְּרָכָיו וְחָיָה:

Congregation and Reader

אֱלֹהֵינוּ וֵאלֹהֵי אֲבוֹתֵינוּ. מְחַל לַעֲוֹנוֹתֵינוּ בְּיוֹם
הַכִּפֻּרִים הַזֶּה. מְחֵה וְהַעֲבֵר פְּשָׁעֵינוּ וְחַטֹּאתֵינוּ
מִנֶּגֶד עֵינֶיךָ. כָּאָמוּר. אָנֹכִי אָנֹכִי הוּא מֹחֶה פְשָׁעֶיךָ
לְמַעֲנִי וְחַטֹּאתֶיךָ לֹא אֶזְכֹּר: וְנֶאֱמַר. מָחִיתִי כָעָב
פְּשָׁעֶיךָ. וְכֶעָנָן חַטֹּאתֶיךָ. שׁוּבָה אֵלַי כִּי גְאַלְתִּיךָ:
וְנֶאֱמַר. כִּי בַיּוֹם הַזֶּה יְכַפֵּר עֲלֵיכֶם. לְטַהֵר אֶתְכֶם
מִכֹּל חַטֹּאתֵיכֶם. לִפְנֵי יְיָ תִּטְהָרוּ:

בָּרוּךְ אַתָּה יְיָ מֶלֶךְ מוֹחֵל וְסוֹלֵחַ לַעֲוֹנוֹתֵינוּ
מֶלֶךְ עַל־כָּל־הָאָרֶץ מְקַדֵּשׁ יִשְׂרָאֵל וְיוֹם הַכִּפּוּרִים:

Choir: Amen

Congregation and Reader, then Choir

Open unto us, O God, the gates of mercy, before the closing of the gates, ere the day is done. The day vanishes, the sun is setting; let us enter Thy gates.

פְּתַח לָנוּ שַׁעַר. בְּעֵת נְעִילַת שַׁעַר. כִּי פָנָה יוֹם: הַיּוֹם יִפְנֶה. הַשֶּׁמֶשׁ יָבֹא וְיִפְנֶה. נָבוֹאָה שְׁעָרֶיךָ:

Reader

The day is fading, the sun is setting; the silence and peace of night descend upon the earth. Vouchsafe rest, O God, unto our disquieted hearts; lift up the soul that is cast down. Turn, in Thine all-forgiving love, to Thy children who yearn for Thy mercy; turn, O Father, to all fainting hearts, to all heavy-laden souls. Let this hour bring us the assurance that Thou hast forgiven, that we have found favor in Thy sight. Consecrate our hearts unto Thee, and make them Thy living altars, whereon shall burn the holy flame of devotion to Thee.

From Thy house, O merciful Father, we are about to return to our homes, to seek shelter in the communion of our family life. Open unto us the gates of Thy love! Enter Thou with us into our home so that it may become Thy sanctuary, and Thy spirit may abide within its walls. Then will our habitation stand firm amidst the storms of life, a refuge from evil, a bulwark against temptation.

And still another dwelling Thou hast destined for us, O Source of life; an eternal abode to which we shall go after our brief day on earth has closed. Open unto us the gate of Thy grace; unlock for us the portals of eternal peace when the gates of our earthly home shall have closed behind us. Be Thou our guiding star on our homeward journey. Let Thy light shine in the night of our death as the dawn of a new morning, that from our grave may sprout not the barren thistle but the fragrant myrtle, a blessed memory redounding to Thine honor and glory.

This twilight hour reminds us also of the eventide when, according to Thy gracious promise, Thy light will arise over all the children of men, and Israel's spiritual descendants will be as numerous as the stars in heaven. Endow us, our Guardian, with strength and patience for our holy mission. Grant that all the children of Israel may recognize the goal of their changeful career, so that they may exemplify by their zeal and love for mankind the truth of Israel's message: One humanity on earth even as there is but one God in heaven.

Thou alone knowest when this work of reconciliation shall be fulfilled; when the day shall dawn on which the light of Thy truth shall illumine the whole earth. But that great day shall come, as surely as none of Thy words returns void, except it have accomplished that for which Thou didst send it. Then joy will thrill all hearts, and from one end of the earth to the other will echo the gladsome cry: Hear, O Israel, hear, all mankind: The Lord our God, the Lord is One! Then Thy house shall be called a house of prayer for all peoples, and all nations shall flow unto it. And in triumphant joy shall they cry out: Lift up your heads, O ye gates, and be ye lifted up, ye everlasting doors, that the King of glory may come in. Who is the King of glory? The Lord of hosts, He is the King of glory.

Choir

Lift up your heads, O ye gates, and be lifted up, ye everlasting doors, that the King of glory may come in.

Who is the King of glory? The Lord of hosts, He is the King of glory. Selah!

Reader
(Before the open Ark)

O Lord, whither shall I go from Thy spirit? Or whither shall I flee from Thy presence? If I ascend up into heaven, Thou art there; if I make my bed in the nether-world, behold, Thou art there. If I take the wings of the morning and dwell in the uttermost parts of the sea, even there would Thy hand lead me, and Thy right hand would hold me. And if I say: Surely the darkness shall envelop me and the light about me shall be night; even the darkness is not too dark for Thee, but the night shineth as the day, the darkness is even as the light. Wonderful are Thy works, and that my soul knoweth right well.

When I behold the heavens, the work of Thy hands, the countless hosts of stars which Thou hast set in the firmament; when I consider the wonders of the universe and endeavor to comprehend the excellence of Thy majesty, I am overwhelmed by Thy greatness and power. The myriads of worlds are but a breath of Thy spirit, the luminous orbs but beams of Thy light. What is man that Thou hast enabled him to perceive Thy truth, and to fathom the purposes of Thy creation? Yet upon the earth with all its abundance and beauty, with forests filled with song, with mountains reared like pillars, with roaring billows of the sea; with all the mysteries of the boundless depths and the immeasurable heights, Thou hast placed man to proclaim Thy grandeur and to voice the longing of all beings for Thee, O King of the Universe, Fountain of life? In man, the son of dust and the child of heaven, Thou hast blended the two worlds, perishable earth and immortal soul; finite matter, fettered to time and space, and infinite spirit, which endures through eternity. Thou hast made him to have dominion over all the works of Thy hands, Thou hast put all things under his feet. But Thou desirest that he subdue his pride and bow his head in reverence before Thee.

Yet when he should rise above earth's temptations and glorify Thee by a life of righteousness, passion leads him astray and rebellion fills his heart. Life loses its beauty and within him reigns the voice of self reproach: man, where art thou? How has thou fallen, son of the Most High!

But Thy mercy, O Lord, is without end. Thou desirest not the death of the sinner, but that he return to Thee and live. Wide open are the gates of Thy forgiveness to all who truly seek to be reconciled with Thee.

Trusting in Thy gracious promise, we have come before Thee, O Father, conscious of our guilt, and yearning for Thine altars of peace. Condemned by the judge within us, we reflected sorrowfully on a life misused and filled with regrets, on opportunities neglected and resolves come to naught.

O how beautiful are Thy dwellings, Lord of hosts! Better one day spent in Thy courts than a thousand elsewhere. Now at the fall of eve, light dawns within us; our hope and our trust revive. The shadow which darkened our spirit is vanished; and through the passing cloud there breaks, with the last rays of the setting sun, the radiance of Thy forgiving peace. We feel renewed in spirit, and strengthened in will. We know our destiny to be in Thy hand, and whatever it be, we are content. O God, what is man, that Thou art mindful of him, what the son of earth that Thou thinkest of him? Where shall mortal man find words to thank Thee worthily? The only praise we can offer Thee is to humble ourselves before Thee, to proclaim Thy holy name, and adore Thee:

(Congregation rises)

וַאֲנַחְנוּ כֹּרְעִים וּמִשְׁתַּחֲוִים וּמוֹדִים לִפְנֵי מֶלֶךְ
מַלְכֵי הַמְּלָכִים הַקָּדוֹשׁ בָּרוּךְ הוּא:

We bow the head in reverence, and worship the King of kings, the Holy One, praised be He.

שְׁמַע יִשְׂרָאֵל יְהֹוָה אֱלֹהֵינוּ יְהֹוָה אֶחָד:

Hear, O Israel: The Lord our God, the Lord is One.

בָּרוּךְ שֵׁם כְּבוֹד מַלְכוּתוֹ לְעוֹלָם וָעֶד:

Praised be His name whose glorious kingdom is forever and ever.

יְהֹוָה הוּא הָאֱלֹהִים:

The Lord, He is God.

(The Shofar is sounded)

BENEDICTION

Reader

And now, at the close of this day's service, we implore Thee, O Lord our God:

Let the year upon which we have entered be for us, for Israel, and for all mankind:

A year of blessing and of prosperity.

Choir: Amen.

A year of salvation and comfort.

Choir: Amen.

A year of peace and contentment, of joy and of spiritual welfare.

Choir: Amen.

A year of virtue and of fear of God.

Choir: Amen.

A year which finds the hearts of parents united with the hearts of the children.

Choir: Amen.

A year of Thy pardon and favor.

Choir

May the Lord bless thy going out and thy coming in from this time forth and forever. Amen.